# Funny
## Sports Stories

## John Scally

BLACKWATER PRESS

Editor

*Ciara McNee*

Design & Layout

*Paula Byrne*

Cover Illustration

*Bronagh O'Hanlon*

Cover Design

*Melanie Gradtke*

ISBN

1 84131 630 X

Produced in Ireland by
Blackwater Press
c/o Folens Publishers
Hibernian Industrial Estate
Greenhills Road
Tallaght
Dublin 24

# Acknowledgements

My thanks to Ollie Campbell, Brian Carthy, Paul Collins, PJ Cunningham, Dermot Earley, Seán Freyne, Jimmy Magee, Andrew O'Connor, Tony Ward, Charles J. Haughey, Brian Kerr, Archie O'Leary, Noel O'Reilly and Peter Woods for their support and encouragement. I am very grateful for the hospitality and kindness shown to me by Brian, Frank and Geraldine O'Driscoll. Martina Cleary is a pleasure to know, a model student, a wonderful doctor and a great supplier of funny sports stories. I am very grateful to the many players, past and present, who shared their personal anecdotes with me. Special thanks to Mick Quinn for his amazing treasure trove of stories and to the peerless Pat Spillane – simply for being Pat Spillane. Thanks to John O'Connor and all at Blackwater Press for their enthusiastic support of this book.

## Dedication

In friendship to the wonderful Ger Loughnane who never fails to make me laugh.

# Contents

# ınd Jimmy Magee

MY LOVE of sport nearly cost me my family.

They say confession is good for the soul. I hope so. For over twenty years, I have harboured a dark secret from my nearest and dearest. Many's the sleepless night I have turned and twisted in my bed as the pangs of guilt racked my troubled conscience. No amount of counting sheep could shake off the tidal waves of remorse that swept over me.

In my defence it wasn't really my fault. The real villain was Jimmy Magee. The great sports commentators share a magical capacity to raise and refresh the spirit and to heighten the quality of human perception. Jimmy Magee is one of them. His is a world of wonder, admiration and enchantment. He is the exception to Alexander Pope's rule, 'Words are like leaves and where they most abound much fruit of sense beneath is rarely found'.

It was FA Cup final day in 1979 and my only worry was whether Liam Brady would lead Arsenal to triumph over Manchester United. My family though were in a tizzy because my aunt Sheila was getting married two days later, after a twelve-year courtship. Nobody could accuse her of marrying in haste. The match had thankfully provided me with a pretext for missing the rehearsal. All I had to do was deposit the newly acquired three-tiered wedding cake into my uncle-in-law-to-be's car, for safe transportation to the hotel, while the rest of the family went to the church.

With five minutes to go, Arsenal were cruising with a 2–0 lead and Jimmy assured me that the cup was theirs. This was the moment to leave out the cake. It was starting to rain. The rain slid, tapping, through the branches, and swept in windy puffs across the fields. As I carefully placed the cake on the back seat of William's Capri I could hear Jimmy recklessly abandoning his normal calm, mellifluous tones for a state of near frenzy. I raced back inside to see that United had scored. Jimmy could scarcely contain his excitement. A minute later United equalised. Jimmy's voice pulsated with enthusiasm. Then with time almost up, Chippy Brady produced another piece of wizardry to sensationally set up the winning goal. By now Jimmy was in a state of near mystical rapture.

As the cup was presented, a feeling of panic descended on me. I raced outside. My worst fears were realised. I had left the car door open and our dog – imaginatively called Lassie – was licking the wedding cake.

Lassie was warm, brown and smooth-coated, with a cream arrow on her forehead and flecks of cream on her two front feet. She was a very knowing, friendly creature and I loved her with a passion. At that moment I could have killed her, especially as icing dripped off her whiskers like a snowman melting in a heatwave.

The damage to the cake was surprisingly small and a little surgery with a knife seemed to do the trick. Blood may be thicker than water, but it is also a great deal nastier. I decided that news of Lassie's appreciation for the wedding cake was best kept to myself. Whoever said silence is golden knew what they were talking about.

Such was my acute anxiety that overnight I was attacked by a virulent form of acne. My mother thought that was the reason that during the wedding I sought the shadows as resolutely as the Phantom of the Opera.

A look of adoration passed onto my aunt's face as she cut the cake, like the look of the mother of a child who has just won first prize. To my eyes the icing looked as buttery and soft as white custard. So acute was the sensation of panic across my chest, I felt I might explode.

Everyone agreed they had never tasted nicer wedding cake. Perhaps my failure to make it in the sporting world was punishment for my crime.

Appropriately enough my football career began in a graveyard. An under-12 club match in Knockcroghery marked my initiation to championship football. There was no dressing-room available at that time so we 'togged out' in a graveyard. It was so cold that I thought I had discovered God's frozen people. It was to prove a metaphor for my career. My opponent was not the quickest. The milk in our kitchen turns faster. Although I never let him get a touch of the ball, I was substituted at half-time. I never recovered from the injustice or the ignominy. Okay, so we were getting hammered but it wasn't my fault. It was obviously a political decision. What can a right full back do when he can't even get close to the ball more than three times?

My career only really took off when I joined the ranks of the armchair fans. Some time later I drifted into sports writing. Again things didn't really go to plan. One of my first books was reviewed in *The Irish Times*. It should have been one of the great moments of my life, but I was bemused to discover that I had a name change and that I was now 'Jean Scally'. I wrote a little note to the then books editor, John Banville, and informed him, 'Reports of my sex change have been greatly exaggerated'.

Bill Shankly famously said that, 'Football is not a matter of life and death. It's more important.' In professional sport today and increasingly at amateur levels, the desire to win is the dominant force. Sometimes it seems that we've taken the sport out of sporting activity. In a small way this book attempts to act as a corrective to that tendency. It strives simply to celebrate the fun that is attached to sport and to give people a laugh or two.

Many of the stories in this collection are strange but true. However, the veracity of some of the stories would not measure up to that expected in a court of law. These stories are based on real events. Only the facts have been changed! They should not be read by the easily offended or the politically correct.

*John Scally*
September 2003

# Chapter One
# Fever Pitch

THE CELEBRATED film director John Ford once observed, 'If the legend is more interesting than the truth tell the legend'. To no Irish sports figure does this adage apply more than George Best. He shrugs his shoulders nonchalantly when asked about these stories. 'There's generally a tiny grain of truth in them but then it's blown out of all proportion.'

Best is able to completely deny two apocryphal stories that are told about him. The first is that he once said of an Irish international 'he couldn't pass wind'. The second is that he spent months chasing a girl because he overheard two men describing her as having loose morals. In fact, what one – a dentist – had said was that she had loose molars!

## Rites of Passage

In 1961 two fifteen-year-olds, Eric McMordie and George Best, set sail from Belfast for Liverpool for a two-week trial period with Manchester United. When they got to Manchester, they asked a cab driver to take them to Old Trafford. They were stunned when he replied: 'Which Old Trafford?' They had no idea that Old Trafford was also a cricket ground. The trip to Manchester was a big cultural shock to Best, not least because it was the first time he ever wore long trousers!

## Simply the Best

Best made his debut for United's reserve team in 1962 against West Brom. His immediate opponent was Brom's regular full back, Graham Williams, a Welsh international who was rehabilitating from an injury. Williams was a hard man of the game with an imposing physical presence. A year later, Best made his full debut against West Brom and again his marker was Williams. United won 1–0 and Best earned good reviews for his performance. A few months later Best made his debut for Northern Ireland against

Wales, and again he faced Williams. The Irish won 3–2, with Best having two 'assists'. After the game Williams made a dash for Best in the players' lounge. The debutante was petrified as the Welshman grabbed him roughly by the face and looked him deep in the eye, before taking the wind out of Best's sails by saying: 'So that's what your face looks like. I've played against you three times now, and all I've seen of you so far is your arse!'

Inevitably given his skill Best was a persistent target of the hard men of the game, but such was his speed that he seldom gave them the chance. A recurring feature of United matches were the attempts by Best's opponents to psyche him out as he took the field. An example of this trend was former Irish international Terry Mancini – who had a reputation as a 'robust' tackler. His comment to the United star before their duel began was, 'Don't look so worried, George. I'm in humane mood today. I've put iodine on my studs.'

Best's importance to the United side is revealed in the story of a staff member at Old Trafford who was informed by colleague:

'I have terrible news for you.'

'What?'

'I'm afraid your wife is having an affair.'

'Is that all? I thought you were going to tell me that George Best was injured.'

### The Lawman

During the 1960s, Best was one of the players at United who felt that they deserved a pay increase. They decided to delegate Denis Law to negotiate with the manager on their behalf. Law went to speak to Matt Busby, man to man, while his colleagues waited with bated breath. They expected a protracted mediation but Law returned within minutes. To their disappointment he reported that the news was bad; Busby had pleaded poverty and that he was lucky to get £5 out of him. The only consolation his fellow players could find was that it was better than nothing. At the end of the week, the players found that not only had their pay not increased, it had actually decreased. Mustering all the indignation they could manage, the players complained bitterly to their manager. Busby calmly replied: 'Take it up with Denis. When he came to me looking for money, I let him know how tight we are for money just now and persuaded him to accept a wage cut of £5 a man to help the club out.'

Best had some memorable verbal exchanges with Law. One of the most famous came when the 'Lawman' was complaining about the people from the Inland Revenue:

'I've had a final demand from the tax people. Eight hundred and fifty frigging quid. But I wrote them a letter.'

**Best**: Saying what?

**Law**: Saying I couldn't remember borrowing it from them!

### The Fab Five

A hero for his role in rescuing people after the Munich crash, Harry Gregg later showed great bravery in the 1966 European Cup quarter-final when United defeated Benefica 5–1 in the away leg. George Best had one of his finest games ever for United, scoring two goals. After the game, the Portuguese fans started shouting 'El Beatle' at him because his hairstyle was so similar to the Fab Fours'. One fan though charged at Best waving a butcher's knife. Gregg rushed to his team-mate's defence and wrestled the knife from the fan. The police were quickly on hand, and after interrogating the fan they discovered that all he wanted was a lock of Best's hair!

### Stormin' Norman

Any United player who showed promise of flair was invariably compared to Best. Among the great pretenders was Norman Whiteside who famously said, 'All George Best and I have in common is that we were born in the same area, discovered by the same scout and played for the same club and country'.

### A Shared Passion

Best's attraction for the opposite sex was brilliantly illustrated on a trip to hospital, following an injury during a match. A nurse brought him to a cubicle and told him to take off his clothes and that she would examine him in a minute. As he turned around to take off his clothes, Best asked where he should leave them. The nurse replied, 'On top of mine'. She had returned totally naked. As Best says himself, 'If I had been born ugly you would never have heard of Pelé'.

Best was also noted for his womanising. A United fan once said of him, 'If I come back in the next life, I want to come back as George Best's fingertips'.

Best was going out with a former Miss World, who often complained that she had a headache when Best asked her to spend the night with him. One evening, he wined and dined her before they went out to a club.

'Thanks for a beautiful evening,' she said when he had driven her home.

'Ah, but the night's not over,' he said, pouring her a glass of champagne. As she sipped the drink, he pushed two white tablets towards her.

'Aren't these Disprins?' she asked.

'Indeed they are,' he replied.

'But I haven't got a headache.'

'Good,' he said. 'Then let's go to bed.'

### The Demon Drink

Best is always able to joke at his capacity for self-destruction. In 2002, he was critically ill and needed major surgery that necessitated him receiving a lot of blood. In a subsequent media interview, Best was asked how much blood he had required. He quipped, 'I was on the operation table for ten hours and I needed forty pints. Taking in forty pints in that time was just twenty minutes short of my all-time record!'

Best's battle with alcohol addiction, culminating in the debacle on the Terry Wogan show, was not the stuff of good public relations. Hence one journalist's claim: 'George Best, a legend in his own stupor.' His wild friends though, Oliver Reed and Alex Higgins, rang him up and said, 'We don't know what all the fuss is about, George. You looked fine to us!'

At the height of his fame Best was prevented from getting into his car by a policeman who said, 'I'm sorry, sir. I can't let you drive. You're drunk.'

'I'm not drunk.'

'Well, if you're not drunk you should be on stage because your act is fantastic.'

## O'Shay, O'Shay, O'Shay

Shay Brennan was Manchester United's full back in the 1968 European Cup–winning side. Brennan was at the heart of a memorable exchange with his colleague Bill Foulkes.

**Brennan:** How's the mouth?

**Foulkes** *(with four stitches in his mouth)*: She's at home with the kids.

Brennan was also involved in a famous incident with Irish rugby legend, Moss Keane. As part of the 1982 Triple Crown–winning side, Keane went down to Greystones to play in a match to mark Greystones' jubilee season. Brennan was also down for the game. In Greystones, they are well used to visits by big names in the rugby world, but they are not accustomed to famous soccer personalities like Brennan. Mossie was with Brennan in the bar, having a few drinks. He was a little cheesed off that Brennan was getting all the attention, with everyone asking Brennan questions and nobody passing any remarks on him. Eventually Mossie threw in a question: 'Who played soccer for Scotland and cricket for England?' There was total silence. Everyone in the bar was a sports fan and they were all scratching their heads trying to figure out this riddle. Finally they were all forced to concede defeat. Moss walked out as soon as he provided the answer: 'Denis Law and Ian Botham!'

## Chinese Takeaway

Northern Ireland are not as famous for their generous application of the parentage laws as their southern counterparts. In 1980 Everton manager Gordon Lee rang up Billy Bingham to recommend one of his midfielders, Eamon O'Keefe, for the Irish squad. Lee was shocked to discover that he did not qualify because he was not Irish. He indignantly asked. 'Well, what business has anyone got naming him Eamon O'Keefe if he isn't Irish?' Bingham replied, 'Probably the same business they have naming you Lee when you're not Chinese!'

## Literary Centre Circles

Canadian-born Jimmy Nicholl moved with his family to Belfast in 1957. He joined United as an apprentice straight from school in 1972 and turned professional two years later. Nicholl was capped seventy-three times for Northern Ireland, culminating in appearances at the World Cup finals in 1982 and 1986.

George Best tells a wonderful story about Jimmy Nicholl's involvement with the Northern Irish team. In 1978, the Northern Ireland squad were making their way from their hotel to Windsor Park for a fixture against Iceland. Their manager was Billy Bingham, a very erudite man. Throughout the bus journey, Bingham was enthralled by the book he was reading and oblivious to everything that was going on around him. Eventually some officials summoned him to the top of the bus. George rushed up to see what he was reading. Nicholl asked him the title of this book. '*The Diaries of James Joyce 1930 to 1935*,' George replied. A few minutes later Nicholl tapped Best on the shoulder and said: 'This Joyce must have been some kid to have kept a diary up to when he was a five-year-old child!'

## The Doc

Tommy Docherty became the Manchester United manager, having just guided Scotland through the qualifying rounds of the 1974 World Cup finals. In fairness, this was a major achievement as was evident from the old joke:

Q: What do you call a Scotsman at the knockout stages of a major football tournament?'

A: A referee.

In typical Doc style, he boasted that being United manager was the 'best job in football'. Moreover, he was prepared 'to walk from Scotland to Old Trafford for the job'. One wag was heard to mutter that was probably because the Scottish FA was too mean to give him the expenses. At United, the Doc's salary was £15,000 a year, twice as much as he earned for the Scottish job.

The Doc had a frosty relationship with George Best, but one day he saw Best down in the dumps. He wondered why, because Best left the club the previous evening with a beautiful blonde on his arm.

'What happened?' asked Docherty.

George replied, 'I took her to dinner, bought her chocolates and champagne and we went back to my place for the night.'

'Then why are you gloomy?'

'I spent a fortune,' said George, 'and the lads have just told me I could have got the same result with a couple of beers and a packet of crisps.'

Docherty was once told he was too impatient. His response was quicker than a bullet from a chamber: 'That's not true. I have patience. I just don't like to use it.'

## Off the Wall

Ron Atkinson became Manchester United manager, having made his name with West Bromich Albion. In the late 1970s, WBA were a high-flying team in the old First Division. They went on an end of season tour to China. At one stage, the players were offered the opportunity to visit the Great Wall of China. One player, who would have preferred to stay in his room playing cards, was asked his opinion on one of the wonders of the world. 'See one wall,' he replied, 'and you've seen them all.'

## Big Ron

In his book *United to Win*, Atkinson gives an amusing insight into how personality clashes between a player and a manager can end a player's career at a club. In his pre-United days, Atkinson had succeeded John Giles as manager of West Brom. One of the players he inherited was Irish international Paddy Mulligan, who had given great service to the club but who was then in the autumn of his career. Big Ron took an instant dislike to the Irish man's verbosity, and Mulligan found himself in the reserves. Atkinson's assistant, Colin Addison, suggested the manager should meet Mulligan in an effort to lift his spirits. When Paddy arrived in the office he took the initiative and said: 'Boss, I don't think you like me.'

True to form Atkinson did not mince his words and replied: 'Paddy, I can't stand you!'

Mulligan responded: 'Can I take it, then, that I'll be going at the end of the season?'

'You can bet money on it!' Atkinson countered.

After Mulligan left the office, Colin Addison commented: 'Thanks, Ron. I only brought him in so that you could give him a bit of a confidence boost.'

## You'll Never Walk Alone

One of the great managerial wits was Bill Shankly, the man who made Liverpool the force they were in the 1970s. In 1951, Third Division Carlisle United pulled off a shock 0–0 draw at mighty Arsenal in the FA Cup. When the aristocrats arrived at Brunton Park for the replay, the Carlisle boss, Bill Shankly, burst into his side's dressing-room to announce with a flourish: 'Boys, I've just seen them getting out of their coach. They should be in hospital; they're in a right state.' Arsenal won 4–1, but after the game Shankly told his team: 'Boys, you've just lost to the greatest side in England – but it took them two games.' It was a tactic he was to employ throughout his managerial career: make your players feel great, and if you have to criticise them, do so in private.

Shankly's dry wit was most evident in his comment to Alan Ball after he joined Everton: 'Congratulations on your move, son. You'll be playing near a great side.'

Shankly was once asked his opinion on the young Mick Channon. Shanks replied that he was a very good winger. The reporter pushed him further and asked: 'Is he as good a player as Stanley Matthews?'

'Oh, aye, he's as good a player as Stan – but you have to remember Stan is sixty-five now!'

Shanks' waspish wit was also evident in his comment on former Spurs forward Martin Chivers: 'The big boy is deceptive. He's slower than he looks.'

### More than Words

Shanks was replaced by Bob Paisley as Liverpool manager. Like Shankly, Paisley was a wonderful manager, but, unlike Shanks, he was not very articulate. Before his first match in charge, Paisley gave a passionate speech. Steve Highway said afterwards, 'I didn't understand a damned word he said but it sounded frightfully impressive'.

### Some Mother's Son

Liverpool signed Avi Cohen and made him the first Israeli international to play for the reds. Avi's mother was a devout member of the Jewish faith and was concerned that Avi would lose his faith in Liverpool. A few weeks after he arrived at the club, she rang her son and asked, 'Do you still wear your skull cap?

**Avi:** No one wears skull caps in Liverpool.

**Mrs Cohen:** Do you still go the synagogue on the Sabbath?

**Avi:** How can I? We have a match every Saturday.

**Mrs Cohen** *[attributed]*: Tell me, are you still circumcised?

## Nicknames

Nicknames are an important part of the football culture. During his playing days, Gary Megson, who managed West Brom to a place in the Premiership in 2002, was known as 'Suitcase' because he was never at one club for long. During his brief stay at Sheffield Wednesday, Megson played alongside Paul Hart. Hart had two nicknames, 'Fossil' and 'Horlicks'. He was known as 'Fossil' because of his lived-in looks and 'Horlicks' because most of his conversation had the same effect on people as the bedtime drink.

## Cloughie

Brian Clough didn't seem to visit the barber very often; he just did his job with no hairs or graces. During the late 1970s, Larry Lloyd was Forest's centre-half. Lloyd had won three England caps at Liverpool, but fell out of the international reckoning until he joined Forest. On Lloyd's recall to the heart of the English defence, England were thrashed 4–1 by Wales. Shortly afterwards in the Forest dressing-room, Lloyd was confronted by Clough, 'Larry, which England international got two caps on the same day?'

'I don't know, boss. Who was it?'

'You. Your fourth and your last!'

At Forest, Clough was the uncrowned king. When he managed Derby, Cloughie was not always treated with such reverence, despite his success with the club. One day he rang down to the dressing-room for a cup of tea. The apprentice who answered said simply, 'Bugger off', and slammed down the phone. Clough rang down again, asking: 'Do you know who I am?' The apprentice answered with another question: 'Do you know who I am?'

'No.'

'Well, bugger off again, then.'

## Moore to the Point

Bobby Moore captained England to the World Cup in 1966. Some time later, he brought his wife out to a restaurant for Sunday lunch. As they sat waiting to order, a young couple at a nearby table caught their attention. They had both chosen soup, but there seemed to be something wrong with the woman's helping, as she was toying with it. After examining the offending dish, her partner called the waiter over who looked into the bowl and then rushed off. A moment later he reappeared with a straw and the woman started drinking her soup with it. When the same waiter came to take their order shortly afterwards, Moore asked, 'Please excuse my vulgar curiosity, but why is that young lady drinking soup with a straw?'

'Well, sir, it's the best option when you've dropped your contact lens in there.'

A few minutes later a different waiter arrived with the Moores' soup. Bobby's wife noticed he had his thumb in one of the bowls and pointed this out to him.

'Don't worry, madame,' he replied calmly, 'the soup is not hot.'

Another time Moore attended a wedding of a friend, who was also a Leeds United official. His task was to escort worshippers to their seats before the service. As he returned to the sanctuary entrance to show the next party to their pews, he greeted two players and asked them where they would like to sit. Looking confused, the Leeds captain Billy Bremner smiled and answered, 'Non-smoking, please'.

The groom had turned up in the church obviously under the influence of drink. In fact, Moore had to hold him up. When the vicar saw this, he told the best man to take the groom outside and bring him back when he was sober.

'Sure, I had to make him drunk to get him here in the first place,' groaned Bobby.

All through the ceremony the groom was very nervous. When he went with his blushing bride into the vestry to sign the register, the vicar, wanting to change for the reception, said, 'Sign your names here and wait'. Moore was delegated to oversee proceedings. He burst out laughing when he saw what his friend had written: 'Michael Finn, 174 lbs.'

At one point Moore was invited to a big, public dinner and found himself seated between a famous bishop and a respected rabbi. He was determined to be witty, though everyone was engrossed in serious conversation. He interrupted the rabbi, 'I feel as if I were a leaf between the Old and the New Testaments,' he said. The rabbi turned to him and answered, 'That page, Mr Moore, is usually a blank.'

After his retirement Moore was in great demand as an after-dinner speaker. One of his favourite lines was to quote George Bernard Shaw, who was asked at a dinner to give his observations on sex. Shaw rose and said, 'Ladies and Gentlemen, it gives me great pleasure,' and resumed his seat.

Moore also featured in a number of commercials. One of them involved the slogan 'Keep it up'. The phrase, though, has taken on a new connotation in the world of celebrity endorsement, since Pelé became spokesman for Viagra.

## Hair-raising

One of Moore's team-mates on the 1966 World Cup–winning team was Bobby Charlton. Bobby once went to the gardening shop to buy fertiliser. As he was standing in line waiting to pay, a little boy asked him, 'What have you got in your trolley?'

'Fertiliser,' Bobby replied.

'What are you going to do with it?' the little boy asked.

'Put it on my strawberries,' Charlton answered.

'You ought to live with us,' the little boy advised him. 'We put sugar and cream on ours.'

Even in his playing days Bobby Charlton was follicly challenged. He tried to disguise his bald spots with a combover. Long after

Bobby's retirement, his wife was out with a group of friends for an evening meal. One noticed that Mrs Charlton was wearing a beautiful new locket and said, 'It's beautiful. I suppose you carry a momento of some sort in it.'

Mrs Charlton replied, 'Yes, it's a lock of Bobby's hair.'

'But Bobby is still alive.'

'I know, but his hair is gone.'

Bobby never had the closest relationship with George Best. Thus it is not a major surprise that Best famously poked fun at Bobby's lack of hair. He once remarked, 'I sent my son to Bobby Charlton's school of soccer skills. He came back bald.'

## Big Jack

Bobby is reputed to have asked his brother, Jack, for his help with his hair problem. 'My hair is starting to fall out, can you suggest anything to keep it in?' Jack was not very sympathetic, 'How about a cardboard box?'

Jack was noted for being tight with money. In his Leeds days, he borrowed a fiver off Peter Lorimer, who was a young apprentice at the time. Not only that, but he got Lorimer to babysit for him for an evening. When Big Jack and his wife returned from their night out, Lorimer asked Jack if he could have his money back. Jack replied, 'What do you mean? That fiver was for the rent of my couch for the evening.'

## Nobby

Nobby Stiles played on England's 1966 World Cup–winning side. Nobby's brother-in-law is John Giles. In Giles' final season with Manchester United, both he and Stiles were in and out of the United side. Matt Busby had a habit of asking Nobby how he was playing. Invariably Stiles would say 'okay' and then Busby would inform him that he was dropped.

Giles advised his brother-in-law that he was handling the manager all wrong. When he was asked how he was playing, he should always say he was playing brilliantly and that the team couldn't do without him. Stiles took this advice the next time the manager questioned him in that way. The only problem was that

Busby asked an unexpected supplementary question: 'Yes, but can you play better?'

'Yes,' was Nobby's instinctive reply.

'You're dropped for the next match,' was the Boss's riposte.

In other company, though, Stiles was well able to get in the last word himself. Once, as Peter Hauser was writhing in agony after a tackle from Stiles, Hauser roared, 'The pain is excruciating'. Stiles replied, 'Excruciating? You can't be that badly hurt if you can think of a word like that!'

Sir Alf Ramsey was giving his team talk before England played Portugal, when he turned to Nobby Stiles. Knowing that Nobby had a reputation for being a hard tackler, he said, 'They've only got one good player, and that's Eusebio. So, Nobby, I'd like you to take him out of the game.'

Nobby replied, 'What, for this game – or forever?'

## Marsh Mellow

One of the most skilful strikers in English football in the early 1970s was Rodney Marsh. As England struggled to qualify for the 1974 World Cup, the manager Sir Alf Ramsey was feeling under pressure. In the previous two matches, England had missed penalties. Ramsey was seeking a volunteer to take penalties before the match. Everybody declined his invitation. His face lit up when he turned to Marsh. 'Ah Rodney, surely you'd have the confidence to score a penalty tonight?'

'No problem, boss. It wouldn't cost me a thought. There's just a tiny problem, boss.'

'Oh, what's that Rodney?'

'You haven't picked me on the team.'

## Dire Straits

Football managers are not noted for their intelligence. After he was appointed manager of Queens Park Rangers for the second time, Gerry Francis was asked about the barren state of the club's coffers. With a classic 'Colemanball' he replied, 'It's not just money, there's financial problems as well.'

As a player at QPR, one of Francis's team-mates was Don Givens. In 1974 Givens was given a rather unusual task. His team-mate and fellow Irish international, Terry Mancini, was having such a run of scoring own goals that Givens was brought back to mark him every time QPR conceded a corner!

## Stan the Man

England and QPR striker Stan Bowles was as renowned for his gambling as for his mercurial talent. On the day of the Grand National, Stan had backed Red Rum. As he was back defending a corner during a home match on the day of the race, he heard the commentary of the race on a transistor radio in the crowd. He deliberately kept conceding corners for the next few minutes, so that he could continue to listen to the commentary. As soon as he heard the result he cleared the ball up field, and went on to play the game of his life.

Another time Stan was asked what he did after he lost a lot of money at the races. Bowles answered, 'I go home and play cards with my dog'.

'Good gracious. You must have a very clever dog.'

'Not really. Every time he gets a good hand he wags his tail.'

## A Tall Story

The last time QPR were in the Premiership, they were managed by Ray Wilkins. After QPR were relegated to Division One, they came up against Oxford United, who featured the 6 ft 7 in tall Kevin Francis. (It gives a whole new meaning to the Big League!) Afterwards Wilkins gave his opinion of Francis: 'To be fair he's got quite a good touch, but he's quite daunting. If I ever need my guttering fixed I'll give him a call.'

## Angry at Twelve Men

Different managers have different styles. Some favour a fire and brimstone approach. During his time with Birmingham City, former Shelbourne star striker, Eric Barber, was twelfth man for a league match, at a time when no substitutes were used during play. The twelfth man was only used if there was an injury or illness. Birmingham were slaughtered in the match but that indignity was as nothing compared to the humiliation each player was subjected to by their manager. He started off with the goalkeeper and went one by one to the other ten players – pointing out very emphatically and in great detail just how ineffectual each of them was. Eric was fervently thanking God that he had not been selected, because he would escape the tongue-lashing. He was wrong. After the manager had finished with the players, he turned to Barber and said, 'And as for you. You're not even good enough to play for this shower of useless no-hopers.'

## Gilesie

### *Rocking the Boat*

One manager not in that tradition is John Giles. During his tenure as Irish manager, Giles is credited with finally dragging the Republic of Ireland into the professional era. He was blessed with Irish diplomacy, namely, the ability to tell a man to go hell in such a way that he actually looks forward to the trip.

Ray Treacy has great respect for his former Irish boss but he regularly exploited Giles' one weakness. He couldn't say the words 'specific' or 'specifically'. Instead he said 'pacific' or 'pacifically'. When Giles gave his team talks he would always get it wrong and Treacy would start pretending to row a boat and start singing: 'Row, row, row the boat, gently down the stream.' It always made Giles red in the face and he would get really annoyed and bark at Ray to shut up.

### *A Bun Deal*

Politics does intrude into all facets of sport. In 1980 Giles resigned as Irish manager. A sixteen-man committee of the FAI was chosen to decide who would be the next Irish manager and were deliberating on the respective merits of Eoin Hand and Paddy Mulligan. Hand emerged victorious 9–7 in the vote. It could very easily have been a hung jury: one of the sixteen is reported to have said that the only reason he voted for Hand was that he thought Mulligan was the person who had thrown a bun at him on one of the foreign trips.

## Jeepers Keepers

Italia '90 made a national hero out of Packie Bonner. Packie had the prayers of the nation behind him. One woman took it to extremes. She lit a candle and put it over the place on the television set that Packie occupied. Then she changed it in the second half when Packie changed positions, to ensure that it would be burning over his head.

Packie's new status as one of the top goalies in the world did not come without a price. He attracted adulation from people of all ages – including nuns. Packie once had to go in for a hernia operation to the Bon Secours hospital, which is run by nuns. He had missed Mass on a Sunday and, because he was in such a holy place, he thought he would go to Mass during the week. Packie went down to 10 o'clock Mass; it was full of nuns, bar himself.

He was being extra holy that day. In most churches in Ireland, people leave as soon as the priest is finished but Packie decided he was going to stay as long as the nuns, in order to make a good impression. As the priest finished the Mass, a nun came up beside Packie and said, 'Excuse me, Mr Bonner, I wonder if you could sign my Bible for me'. Packie's sure she's still doing penance somewhere for that!

The Irish clergy also react to Irish victories over England. A famous example of their holy wit is a story set in Africa, where there was a river infested with crocodiles. On the other side of the river, there was a tribe which various missionaries wanted to convert. However, nobody was willing to take the risk of crossing the river. In 1993, along came a group of Irish priests who waded across the river without coming to any harm. Shortly after they revealed their secret. 'We wore T-shirts bearing the words "England – World Cup Champions 1994". And, sure, not even a crocodile was willing to swallow that!'

## Celtic Warriors

### *The Brady Bunch*

Liam Brady was not the most popular Celtic manager with the fans. However, Manchester City fans appear to hold him in higher esteem. When Alan Ball was appointed City manager, the terraces rang out with a parody of Oasis's hit single 'Wonderwall':

'Maybe, just maybe, we should have gone for Liam Brady, 'cos after all we've got Alan Ball.'

### Shocker

John Barnes' brief reign as Celtic manager was doomed to a sad end, when Celtic lost a 2000 cup tie 3–1 to First Division minnows Inverness Caledonian Thistle FC. It created a seismic shock in Scottish football. The *Sun* captured the moment brilliantly with its headline:

Super Caley Go Balistic, Celtic Are Atrocious.

Who said lightning doesn't strike twice? Three years later, and just four days after Martin O'Neill was a candidate for canonisation when his club beat Liverpool to qualify for the UEFA Cup semifinal, Inverness beat Celtic again in the fifth round of the Scottish Cup. In that moment O'Neill understood a statement Alex Ferguson had made the previous day, 'It's going to get very twitchy over the next few weeks; it's squeeze your bum time'.

After he 'parted company' with Celtic, John Barnes was asked about the role the media played in his demise. Barnes simply quoted Leo Tolstoy, 'All newspaper and journalistic activity is an intellectual brothel from which there is no retreat'.

Celtic fans are pretty good in the quip department themselves. When Andy Goram was goalkeeper for Rangers, it emerged in the media that he suffered from schizophrenia. At the next Old Firm clash the Celtic fans sang in unison, 'There's only two Andy Gorams'.

## A Bird's-Eye View

For many people in Ireland, the voice of Scottish soccer is Roddy Forysth, because of his authoritative reports on RTÉ radio. Roddy was in full flow of a report on a Rangers match, when he came to an abrupt halt. After a little expletive, Roddy explained the cause of his problem, 'A pigeon just s*** all over my notes and it's really big. It's on my coat as well.' Clearly the pigeon was a Celtic fan.

A young Celtic fan was decorating his room, so he wrote to Parkhead and asked for 'stickers, brochures, and penance'. A few days later, he received a package with the following note, 'We are sending you the brochure and stickers but would suggest that for "penance" you spend an hour a day with the Oxford Dictionary'.

## The Memory Man

Jimmy Magee's classic commentaries have provided Irish soccer with many hours of entertainment. One notable example is: 'Ardiles is stroking the ball as if it was part of his anatomy.' In my memory during an Ireland-Russia soccer match, when a Russian striker missed an open goal, Jimmy said, 'It's the salt-mines for him'.

In 1988, the morning after the night before when Ireland famously beat England 1–0 in the European Championships, Jimmy met two dishevelled-looking Irish fans very much the worse for wear. They called him over, 'You're the memory man, Jimmy, isn't that right?'

'Some people call me that,' Jimmy conceded.

'And there's no question about sport you don't know the answer to. Could you help us sort out the problem we're having? We've a serious question here and I wonder if you could help.'

'I'd be delighted if I can.'

'We were out on the tear last night and can't remember where we're staying. Is there any chance you might know the hotel we're supposed to be staying in?'

## Jungle Book

It was the jungle's soccer classic of the year, the annual grudge match between animals and the insects. By half-time, the elephants, zebras and cheetahs had proved too much for the grasshoppers, beetles and ants and were leading with an emphatic score of 63–0. However, when the match resumed, the animals noted a substitute player running onto the field with the insects. It was a shiny black centipede. From then on, the centipede became the star of the game peppering the goal from all angles. Indeed the animals failed to score another goal and the insects ran out winners, 63–64.

At the bar afterwards, the animals' captain, a teak-tough elephant, said to the insects' skipper, a gentle grasshopper, 'Great game, but you were damned lucky that centipede arrived at half-time'.

'You're so wrong,' said the grasshopper. 'He was here from the start of the game, but it took him until half-time to put his boots on!'

## Consuming Passions

Drink features prominently in the lore of Irish soccer. Cork City famously played Bayern Munich in a European tie. Cork's manager Noel O'Mahony was not too perturbed when asked if he was afraid of losing the away leg: 'We'd still be happy if we lose. It's on the same time as the beer festival.'

Irish internationals tend to be less au fait with food than with drink. Jason McAteer delights in telling the story of Mark Kennedy. Kennedy walked into a Pizza Hut one night. When the pizza was ready, he was asked: 'Sir, would you like your pizza cut into four or eight slices?'

'Please cut it into four,' Kennedy replied. 'I could never eat eight.'

## United We Stand

Alex Ferguson does not react well to defeat, which explains why it's always somebody else's fault when United lose. Fergie's most imaginative excuse was when United lost 3–1 to Southampton in 1996. The team's new grey strip, he claimed, meant that the players were unable to pick out their team-mates.

Soccer's two other contenders for the award for best excuse are David James and Kenny Dalglish. James earned the nickname 'Calamity James' during his Liverpool days, for a series of blunders which cost the Merseysiders dearly in 1997. His excuse was that he was fatigued because of the effects of the ten-hour sessions on his PlayStation. A new riddle was born:

Q: What's the difference between Jesus and David James?

A: Jesus saves.

The following year non-league Stevenage held mighty Newcastle to a 1–1 draw. Newcastle manager Dalglish's excuse was, 'Newcastle would have won but the balls were too bouncy'.

### Denis the Menace

At Denis Irwin's testimonial dinner, Jack Charlton brought the house down with his unconventional tribute to Denis. Jack said,

'Denis was the consummate professional; the best full back to play for Manchester United; the best full back to play for the Republic of Ireland; he was always our most consistent player; he never made mistakes; he never gave the ball away; he was always on time for training; always first on the bus after training; he never let you down nor never once caused a problem. What a boring, f****** b******?!'

## The French Connection

Another of Ferguson's better buys was Eric Cantona. When he first came to England, Cantona struggled with the culture change. It took him a few years to figure out the English class system. It can be surmised as follows: You are part of the upper class when you drive to work and your name is written in the reserved car park, part of the middle class when your name is written on your desk and part of the working class when your name is written on a badge on your shirt.

Cantona's biggest problem, seemingly, was understanding how the late Princess Diana married Prince Charles. He couldn't figure out why she married a bloke with big ears and who talks to plants. Somebody told him she thought she was getting married to Prince the singer!

Cantona's most infamous moment was when he assaulted a fan. When the furore was at its height, United were said to have provided Cantona with a driver to protect him from the pressure of the media. At one stage Cantona asked his driver, 'Tell me, Fred, does your wife give you a hard time now that you are driving for me?'

'Difficult to say, Mr Cantona,' the driver replied. 'Since I started driving for you, she's stopped talking to me altogether.'

There is no such thing as bad publicity. A few mornings after the assault, Cantona was woken up at an ungodly hour by a call from his agent. He was so excited that Eric found it difficult at first to understand what he was saying. Cantona had been offered a role in a forthcoming Hollywood blockbuster – the remake of Dracula. Eric decided to decline the offer. It was only a bit part.

Cantona was a lot more cerebral than most footballers. Once when he met Gazza, Cantona talked about philosophy. Eric had no difficulty proving to Gazza that he didn't exist. Asked what he thought about Gazza, Cantona is reputed to have said, 'There's nothing I'd change about him – apart from his face and body. He has the sort of face that once seen is never forgotten.'

One night Cantona and his wife went to the local school to see a production of *The Wizard of Oz*. During the show, he heard people whispering that it had started to snow heavily, and he decided to leave before the driving conditions became hazardous. As Cantona dashed out of the school, the headmaster looked at him quizzically.

'We're off to flee the blizzard!' he called back to him.

## The Dutch Wizard

Another famous continental import was Ruud Gullit. Gullit had great respect for Nottingham Forest player, Stuart Pearce, whose nickname was Psycho. In Psycho's case, it was not the winning but the taking someone apart that counted.

Gullit was a failure as Newcastle manager but a great success with women, unlike another Newcastle striker, Peter Beardsley. When he was young Beardsley used to play hide-and-seek but no one ever came to look for him.

Alan Shearer was not a womaniser either. In fact two directors of Newcastle were quoted in the *News of the World* calling their star player 'Mary Poppins' and 'boring'. The players bought Shearer the video of *Mary Poppins*.

## Salt and Lineker

Gary Lineker's best-known nickname is 'Big Ears', thanks to the constant ribbing he gets on *They Think It's All Over*. The star of Walker's crisps ads is also known as 'Junior Des' because of his admiration for Des Lynam. In the early days, Lineker struggled as Des's replacement as anchor for BBC's soccer coverage. His most notable gaffe came in a Montpellier–Manchester United match when he was describing the poor condition of the pitch and said, 'Most of the players will be wearing rubbers tonight'.

Although he was a phenomenal scorer, Lineker was not known for his eagerness for the physical side of the game. In a match against Wimbledon, he was marked by Vinnie Jones, who shadowed him for the whole match. Vinnie appeared to be very hungry, as he kept saying, 'I'm going to eat you'. Lineker barely touched the ball all night because Jones was virtually in his shorts. Lineker spent the match in terror, with his hands covering his reproductive organs, because of the memory of Vinnie's infamous contact with the most tender parts of England's prince of football, Paul Gascoigne. He spent so much time with his hands over his private parts that his Spurs team-mates rechristened him Holden McGroin!

## Keeping Up with the Jones

Tony Cascarino tells the story that, during his playing days, Vinnie volunteered to organise Chelsea's Christmas party. Vinnie's idea of a good time was to organise a dwarf-throwing contest. Two dwarfs were hired, with appropriate protective gear, and thrown around the room with wanton abandon.

Another time Jones bit a journalist on the ear. The following 1 January, a friend presented him with a colourful card which read, 'Happy New Ear's Day'.

## Sergeant Wilko

Some players do not react well to being dropped. After signing Gary McAllister, Howard Wilkinson dropped Vinnie Jones from the Leeds side. One day after training, Vinnie burst into the manager's office with a double-barrelled shotgun in his hand. Jones was a keen shot and was off to a shoot directly after training. He jokingly pointed the gun at the shocked Wilkinson and threatened him with both barrels if he did not give him back his place!

In autumn 2002, after Ireland lost 4–2 to Russia, the consensus was that Mick McCarthy was a shoe-in to replace Peter Reid as manager of Sunderland. To everyone's surprise the job went to Howard Wilkinson. Mind you, he didn't have the stiffest competition for the job. One of the few other applicants was a fan whose letter had two main planks: 'My spouse is willing to launder the football kits after each match and my uncle Jack, who has his own allotment and a petrol lawnmower, is willing to cut the grass once or even twice a week.'

Wilko was never known for his sense of humour, but in his first week at Sunderland, he showed a waspish streak. He was unhappy with the general level of fitness in the squad, but particularly with that of Tore Andre Flo. Wilkinson asked him, 'Have you got a boot sponsor?'

'Yes,' said Flo.

'Good. I'll get them to send you some lighter ones.'

As Sunderland found it so hard to win that season, a new riddle was born:

Q: What's the difference between Sunderland FC and a triangle?

A: A triangle's got three points.

## Fanzone

Kevin Baldwin's entertaining manual for fans, *This Supporting Life: How to Be A Real Football Fan* (which suggests that the way to get into Old Trafford for free is to join a parachute team), has an amusing spin on the crass commercialism of clubs that frequently change their jerseys for merchandising purposes. He suggests that the word 'UMBRO', which appeared on Man Utd's kit, stands for 'United's Massively Big Rip-Off'.

He went on to point out that sponsors whose names are initials are usually tailor-made for a club. Witness:

**JVC** *(Arsenal)*: Just Very Cautious

**LBC** *(Wimbledon)*: Long Ball Creed

**NEC** *(Everton)*: Not Even Close

Manchester United fans are known for their ability to dish out wicked little barbs to opponents. In autumn 2002, as the Hammers seemed rooted to the bottom of the Premier League, United fans asked:

'What is the world's best joke?'

'West Ham.'

It is United fans themselves who often dish out the harshest criticism of their team – witness the caption that appeared in Manchester United's fanzine *Red Attitude,* under a photograph showing a plump, elderly nun kicking a football: 'David May Models New Team Strip.'

RTÉ's balancing act to ABU (Anyone But United) Des Cahill is Dustin the Turkey, the strongest champion of Manchester United and Ireland's favourite bird, builder, aspiring politician, pop star, television personality and national institution. Dustin nailed his red-coloured feathers firmly to the mast when he was asked for a prediction of the clash between United and Liverpool. 'I think it will be a close match, so the score will be United 12, Liverpool 0!'

As the following conversation reveals, Irish fans can be very critical of the FAI, particularly in the wake of the Saipan and Sky deal fiascos in 2002:

**Father:** Son, what'll I buy you for your birthday?

**Son:** A bicycle.

**Father:** What'll I buy you for your First Communion?

**Son:** A PlayStation?

**Father:** What'll I buy you for Christmas?

**Son:** A Mickey Mouse outfit.

**Father:** No problem, son. I'll just buy you the FAI!

In autumn 2002 when Stockport County were spiralling down Division Two, having been relegated from Division One the previous season, manager Carlton Palmer bought two pet fish, claiming they would relax the players. One disgruntled fan said, 'They will link up perfectly with the rest of the squad. They're carp.'

## Love and Kerr

In January 2003, Brian Kerr was appointed Irish soccer manager to the delight of most of Irish fans. Kerr is noted for his obsession with soccer. Years ago his wife, Angela, asked him to look after two of their daughters for the afternoon. He brought them to see St Patrick's Athletic's reserves play in Richmond Park. It was raining heavily and he deposited the girls in the stand, telling them he'd be back in 'a few minutes', while he went to talk to one of the St Pat's officials. The pitch was found to be unplayable, so the match was switched to a pitch in Blanchardstown, five miles away. A few hours later, Brian got a phone call from Angela, enquiring how the two girls were getting on. At first he had no idea what she was talking about; then he remembered he had left his two daughters back in Richmond Park. Meanwhile, the girls were patiently wondering why it was taking so long for the two teams to come onto the field and whether this was the longest 'few minutes' in history.

Kerr is one of the nice guys in sport but he's not above pulling a stunt to confuse the opposition. When he heard that representatives from Dynamo Bucharest were watching a St Pat's training session before their European tie, Kerr instructed his players to play Gaelic football for the entire session, leaving the opposition completely baffled!

Kerr has a keen sense of humour. Asked about Damien Duff's legendary capacity for sleep, he replied, 'Damien suffers from adhesive mattress syndrome'.

Kerr also has a rich reservoir of stories about the great personalities of football: 'My favourite story is a true story. It goes back to the under-18 European final against Germany in 1998. We won in a penalty shootout, with the last penalty scored by Liam George. I remember asking Liam afterwards how he was feeling as he made the long walk to take the final kick, knowing that we were going to be European champions and the huge responsibility on his shoulders because of that. When he got close to the ball, he said he could see his father on one of the goalposts and his mother on the other and both were saying to him: "Just put the ball in here and you'll be all right." So he said he picked his mother's side because she was always right. That's where he kicked the ball and he scored. There's a moral there somewhere!'

## Anything You Can Do, We Can Do Better

In 2003, Chelsea FC was taken over by Russian multimillionaire, Roman Abramovich. The club was immediately renamed Chelski. Armed with the new Russian roubles, Chelski spent money on new players as if it were going out of fashion. Any time a big-money player became available Chelski were in like a shot, topping everybody else's bid. According to reports, when Abramovich and his wife were being chauffeur-driven to the opening match at Anfield against Liverpool, they heard on the car radio that the US government had offered a reward of $35 million for Saddam Hussein. As Abramovich's English is not the best, the news item lost something in the translation. Reportedly, he got straight on his phone and told his financial director: 'That guy the Americans want – let's offer $40 million for him.'

# Money Problems

When Peter Ridsdale was made chairman of Leeds in the 1990s, it seemed to be a marriage made in heaven. However, in 2003 he left his post with the club STG£70 million in the red. It was a clear case of 'till debt do us part'.

# What's Love Got to Do With It?

Soccer is the beautiful game but it can ruin a marriage. Joanne Bradley from Kent divorced her husband Neil on the grounds that he was obsessed with Norwich City. Things started to go wrong when he painted their bedroom yellow and green while she was out. Things deteriorated when he took her on a romantic holiday. At first glance this seemed like a good idea. The problem was his idea of a romantic holiday was to take her to watch the team training. The final straw came when he bought her an anniversary present – a pair of Norwich City knickers.

# The Last Word

Some men are more fortunate in terms of having an understanding spouse. Before setting off for the Charity Shield one season, Bill Shankly is reputed to have asked his wife, 'Do you have anything to say before the football season starts?'

Many years ago, when Jimmy Hill was the chairman of Fulham, his club was due to face an FA inquiry after some of their players were involved in a brawl following a match with Gillingham. Hill set out to prove that Fulham should not be held responsible with a video presentation of the game's flashpoints. He was very pleased with his efforts and boasted to friends before the inquiry that the FA should be selling tickets for his presentation. However, when he produced his video as evidence he was shocked to discover that his wife had taped a cookery programme over it!

# Pride Comes Before a Fall

In 1990, Andy Townsend was walking with his wife in Dublin. It was shortly after the World Cup and everywhere they went people were asking for Andy's autograph and requesting to have their photo taken with him. Eventually the couple decided to head for a quieter part of the capital. They were walking down a side street when Andy noticed a woman on the road with a camera. Instinctively, Andy stopped and posed for the camera. After a long pause, the woman screamed, 'You stupid c\*\*\*. Will you get out of the f\*\*\*\*\* way?'

Andy turned around to see a beautiful statue behind him, of which the woman was desperate to take a photo!

## The Milky Bar Kid

Once described as 'George Best without brains', Paul Gascoigne became something of a national icon when he cried after being booked in the 1990 World Cup semifinal against West Germany. Really he should have saved his tears for the Chris Waddle's penalty-taking. The ball from the penalty Waddle missed in that game is probably still in outer space.

In one of his first games for Newcastle, Gazza was faced with West Ham veteran Billy Bonds. Early in the match, Gazza made a robust tackle on the ageing star. Bonds had a reputation for being a hard man and kids like Gazza did not usually mix it with him.

'Are you all right, Billy?' Gazza asked cheekily.

'It's my ankle,' replied Bonds.

'Oh, that's OK then. I thought it might be arthritis!'

Bonds had the last laugh by not giving Gazza a kick of the ball after that, though he did give him plenty of kicks.

One of the many stories told about Gazza goes back to when he was a young player trying to break into the Newcastle team managed by Jack Charlton. Gazza was rooming with an apprentice on an away trip to play in a reserves match. That night the apprentice produced a pack of cards and said, 'At least we can pass the time playing poker'.

According to folklore, Gazza said he had something better and produced a packet of Tampax, 'It says on the packet that you can go riding, swimming, skiing and play tennis with these'.

Gazza was selected to play for England B against Iceland in Reykjavik. The Milky Bar Kid asked plaintively, 'How can I play in a place I can't even say?'

When the England team were playing a match in Russia, Bobby Robson was disappointed that the team hotel was located in such a poor area. The players had few facilities and boredom quickly set in.

Robson walked into a hotel room to see Chris Waddle, John Barnes and Paul Gascoigne hanging out of the window. Their room was twenty floors up. 'What are you doing?' asked Robson. Gazza replied, 'I'm throwing soap at these chickens.'

Gazza's answer was met with disbelief, 'You're doing what?'

'I'm throwing soap at these chickens,' Gazza repeated.

'Can you really hit them from here?'

'Yeah, of course.'

'Show me.'

Gazza took aim with the soap and scored a direct hit on a chicken. Robson just walked out of the room shaking his head.

After establishing himself as an England international, Gazza was offered a lucrative contract to advertise the aftershave Brut on television. A massive press launch was arranged to bring the good news to the great British public. Unwisely, Gazza chose to decline the script that Brut offered him and opted to speak off the cuff. It was a disaster waiting to happen.

Immediately a journalist asked the obvious question, 'How long have you been using Brut, Paul?'

'I don't.'

'What aftershave do you use?'

'None. They bring me out in a rash.'

Gazza arrived at a match midway through the second half. 'What's the score?' he asked his friend Johnny Fivebellies.

'0–0,' was the reply.

'And what was the half-time score?' he asked.

At the height of his fame Gazza was asked, 'Is it right that you earn way more money than the prime minister?'

'Only fair,' said Gazza, 'I've played a lot better than he does.'

Gazza was once said to have gone to Paris for his cousin's wedding. The only problem was that his cousin got married in London. Another apocryphal story told about Gazza goes back to his schooldays. The teacher in the mechanics class spoke to him, 'I'm putting this rivet in the correct position. When I nod my head, hit it hard with your hammer.' Gazza did; the teacher woke up the next day in hospital.

Sport is always inextricably intertwined with the wider culture. In his prime at Rangers, Gascoigne was more than a footballing icon – before kebabs, cigarettes and nights on the town with Danny Baker and Chris Evans saw his star go into rapid decline. According to legend, a Jewish family turned up at a funeral parlour in Glasgow to have one final look at their deceased father laid out. His daughter burst into tears when she noticed her dad had been dressed in a Rangers shirt, white shorts and blue socks. 'What have you done to my father?' she wailed.

I'm very sorry, madam,' replied the undertaker. 'I was informed that his final request was to be buried in the Gazza strip.'

## Posh and Becks

David Beckham is part of the new English royalty. It is difficult to imagine a football star more interested in fashion (especially if the story from the 1998 World Cup is true: the real reason Posh Spice was allowed to visit him for 'morale purposes' was not because he was upset about being dropped for England's opening match but because he missed the Armani summer sale in Bond Street!) In hard times, Beckham favours retail therapy and goes to the shopping mall. When the going gets tough, the tough go shopping.

As a boy, Becks' fashion sense wasn't so well developed. One story told about him goes back to his early school days. As the rest of his class left school at the end of a winter's day, Becks remained behind sobbing. 'What's the matter, David?', his teacher asked.

'I can't find my boots,' Becks cried.

The teacher looked in the cloakroom and found a pair of boots.

'Are these yours?'

'No,' Becks replied.

The teacher and David searched all over the room. Finally, the teacher asked, 'Are you sure these boots are not yours?'

'They aren't mine,' the distraught Beckham replied. 'Mine have snow on them.'

Years later in a poll in Manchester, Becks was voted the sexiest man alive. Are there any sexy dead ones? His mother-in-law was worried that he would develop a roving eye for other women. Becks tried to reassure her by telling her that his marriage was made in heaven.

'So is thunder and lightning,' his mother-in-law replied.

In 2002, there was a daring plot hatched to kidnap Posh, but it was foiled at the last minute. Cynics aware of her many shortcomings as a vocalist remarked that the kidnap was probably prompted by music fans trying to ensure we would never have to listen to her warbling again.

After news of the kidnap attempt broke, a police spokesman stated, 'The Beckhams will now be the subject of intelligence monitoring'. It must have been the first and last time that the Beckhams and intelligence were mentioned in the same sentence.

In April 2003, it was widely reported that Becks was about to sign for Real Madrid. Posh began to prepare for the move by learning Italian!

One of Becks' challengers for the title of pretty boy of football is Ryan Giggs. According to folklore, Ryan has been offered a small fortune to denote his sperm to a fertility clinic. Now he's going to be making money hand over fist! He may as well get loads of money for something most footballers do for free.

A year after the birth of their first son, Brooklyn, Posh and Becks were interviewed by Ali G. He began the interview with a question to Posh, 'Is your little boy starting to put whole sentences together?'

**Victoria**: He's saying little bits and pieces, so yeah.

**Ali G**: And what about Brooklyn?

After Becks' second son Romeo was born, speculation mounted about what advice Dad would give his son when Romeo played his first match. One Shakespeare scholar observed if Becks handed Brooklyn the No. 4 jersey, he could adapt one of the most famous lines in English literature: 'Romeo, Romeo, wear four out there, Romeo?'

On a shopping trip to Harrods, Beckham noticed a Thermos flask. 'What's that for?' he asked. 'It's to keep hot things hot and cold things cold,' replied the salesman. Beckham bought one, and took it home to show Posh. With wonder in his voice, he told her, 'It's to keep hot things hot and cold things cold'. With a gasp of astonishment she said, 'You ought to take it to work'. Becks took the flask to training the following day. 'What have you got there?' inquired Roy Keane.

'It's to keep hot things hot and cold things cold,' said Becks with pride.

'That's a good idea,' said the captain. 'What have you got in it?'

'Coffee,' answered Becks. 'And some ice-cream.'

# Chapter Two
# Ruck and Roll

A SPORT played by women and men with odd-shaped balls is bound to produce great characters and moments of mischief and mirth. In any roll of honour of the personalities in Irish rugby, at the top of the list are Moss Keane and Willie Duggan. Hence the story told at a Lions reunion dinner, 'Moss and Willie read that drink was bad for you. They gave up reading.' Throughout his career Moss lived by the adage that moderate drinkers live longer and it served them right.

In 1982 as Ireland stood on the threshold of winning the Triple Crown, Moss made the ultimate sacrifice and cut his drink in half – he left out the water.

## The Keane Edge

Stories about Moss Keane are more common than showers in April – though few are printable in these politically correct times. Some are even true. Keane has a nice line in self-depreciating humour: 'After I left university, I found I had no talent for anything, so I joined the civil service! I won fifty-two caps – a lot of them just because they couldn't find anybody else.' Keane was once asked to give an after-dinner speech at very short notice. He began by saying that he felt like a dog surrounded by four trees – he didn't have a leg to stand on.

### No Hopers

In 1974 Ireland faced England at Twickenham. Although they were the underdogs, Ireland won the game 26–21. When the Irish players were running onto the pitch before the game, they were stopped in the tunnel by an official who had the archetypal RAF moustache. He said, 'Tally ho, boys. Tally ho. The BBC cameras are not ready for you yet.' The Irish lads were just itching to get on the pitch and found the waiting a pain, particularly when they were joined in the tunnel by the English team. The English were led by their captain,

John Pullin, who was shouting at his team about Waterloo. The Irish players couldn't understand what Waterloo had to do with them.

The English players looked bigger and stronger than their Irish counterparts. As they were always on television, the English players were famous and had superstar-sounding names like David Duckham and Andy Ripley. The Irish players were studiously trying to avoid eye contact with them, because they planned to rough them up a bit on the pitch. However, Tony Neary went over and tapped Moss Keane on the shoulder and said, 'Moss, best of luck. May the best team win.'

Keane growled back, 'I f****** hope not!'

### The Search Party

Keane toured with the Lions in New Zealand in 1977. After their second test victory, the Lions threw the party to beat all parties in the team hotel. It was soon discovered that one of their players was missing. According to legend, when everyone else expressed concern about him, Keane said he knew where the missing person was – next door with his girlfriend. Keane was dispatched to bring the guilty party back – though he was given strict instructions not to break down any doors. (His nickname on that tour was 'Rent-a-Storm', so the decree seemed more than justified.) The rest of the squad listened to a slight flurry next door, and moments later Moss came in the door with the missing player under his arm, completely naked and squirming like a fish on a hook. Under the arm, he held the player's girlfriend in a similar state of undress and embarrassment. Keane in his best Kerry accent boomed out: 'To be sure, did you be wanting the two of them?'

### Moderate Moss

Another classic story about Keane goes back to one of his tours with the Barbarians in Wales. His team went to the bar after a game of golf. Although everybody else was drinking beer, Keane, with commendable patriotism, was drinking Guinness and was knocking back two pints to everyone else's one. As dinnertime approached, it was decided it was time to return to the team hotel. As people prepared to leave, somebody shouted 'One for the road'. Ten pints later for the team at large and twenty pints later for Keane, the team was again summoned to the team bus. Keane was asked if the team should stay for one more drink; he shook his head. When questioned why he was opposed to the idea, Keane replied, 'To be sure, I don't want to be making a pig of myself'.

## Teamwork

Keane paid an interesting tribute to his team-mate Ollie Campbell after the 1980 final trial. (The final trial gives the selectors a last chance to survey the available talent before the Five Nations Championship.) The Probables beat the Possibles 28–12, with Campbell giving a virtuoso performance, scoring twenty-four points, including three tries. Keane scored the other try to complete the Probable's scoring. In the dressing-room, Keane turned around to Campbell and said: 'Wasn't it great that it was only me and you that got our scores, all the same?'

## The New Scotsman

From time to time, Keane's strong Kerry brogue caused some problems for his colleagues. Ballymena were playing a Willie John McBride XV in an end-of-season match. The cast included Gareth Edwards, Gerald Davies and Ian Barnes. Barnes is a second-row forward from the Borders, who speaks with a thick Scottish accent. His scrumming partner was Keane. Both were sorting out tactics before the match but were incapable of communicating through words. By using gestures and amid vigorous nodding of the head, they seemed to have worked something out. The scrum was a total disaster. The touring side was losing by twenty points at half-time. Barnes went to Mick Quinn as his out-half and said, 'Hey Micky, I canna understand what he's saying. I'm pushing on the wrong side of the scrum. Would you think you could get him to swap sides with me?' A minute later, Keane came up to Quinn and said, 'That bloody Scot can't speak f***** English. I'm pushing on the wrong side.' Quinn brokered a compromise; the tourists were a transformed side in the second half and won the match.

## The Warning

When the troubles in the North were at their height, Lansdowne played a match in Belfast. The drink was much cheaper up there, and after the match, the lads stopped in an off-licence for a case of beer for the train journey home. That evening there was a bomb scare, which ruled out travelling by train; after a long delay a bus arrived instead. The problem was that there was no room on the bus for Keane and some of the other players. Keane, who had already disposed of a couple of his beers, was not too happy with the prospect of having to wait even longer. He marched on to the bus and according to folklore said, 'Excuse me; this bus is going to crash'. At first nobody moved, but then a little old man timidly walked up to the towering figure of Keane and said, 'Excuse me, sir, but where did you say this bus was going to?'

## Fast Talker

In Keane's final years on the Irish team, the young players looked up to him as if he were God. New players from the North found his accent particularly difficult to decipher. The senior players devised a little initiation for those new players. When Trevor Ringland was brought onto the team for the first time, they put him beside Keane for dinner; Trevor was in awe of him. They primed Keane to speak for two minutes in fast-forward mode. He was talking pure gibberish, and then he turned to Trevor and asked him what he thought of that. Ringland answered lamely, 'I think you're right' not having a clue what Moss had said. Then Keane launched off again only faster. The panic on Ringland's face was a sight to behold. All the senior players were killing themselves trying to keep a straight face until Ringland found out he was being wound up.

## Labour of Love

One of Keane's team-mates for a period was former Labour leader Dick Spring. In 1979 Spring was capped three times for Ireland. He is probably best remembered (though unfairly, as he was a much better player than he was given credit for) for an incident in a Wales match, when Ireland gifted the home side with fifteen points to lose 24–21. After twenty-two minutes, Ireland led 6–0 courtesy of two lengthy penalties from Tony Ward. In the twenty-fifth minute the picture changed dramatically. The Welsh fly-half lofted a kick towards the Irish posts; Spring was under it and there seemed to be no danger. Somehow the ball slipped through his hands and bounced over the Irish line for Alan Martin to rush on and score a try, which Steve Fenwick converted. While Spring's political career flourished in the 1980s and 1990s, he has never been let forget that incident. Throughout RTÉ Radio 1's enormously popular series *Scrap Saturday*, Spring was consistently referred to as 'Butterfingers'.

Although Spring's international record is not the one he would have wished for, he still has many happy memories of his rugby days. He and Barry McGann went out drinking one night. The next day, they were training for Munster and neither of them was feeling the best. Tom Kiernan was training the side at the time. An awkward, high ball was pumped in between them and they both shouted, 'Yours'. Kiernan intervened immediately and said, 'Gentlemen. There's only one call in rugby: "Mine!"'

Spring linked up on the Irish team with Moss Keane, another distinguished former Gaelic footballer from Kerry. Keane loved his grub. After a match at Twickenham, Spring and Keane returned home after a very late night session in St Mary's rugby club. They stayed in Moss's 'high class' flat in Rathmines. They woke up the next day at midday very much the worst for wear and went to 'Joe's Steakhouse' for some food. Moss ordered a mixed grill. Spring's tastes were more modest and he just asked for plaice and chips. When the food arrived, Moss was feeling a bit queasy. He looked up and said, 'Springer, would you ever mind swapping?' Spring duly obliged. That day has gone down in rugby folklore, because it is said to be the only time Moss turned his back on a big meal!

Another time, Moss and Spring were together for a match in London. On the Saturday night, they were both starving. The two of them crept into the kitchen of their hotel and sought out some food, but were caught in the act by the porter. They expected to have the face eaten off them. However, after a dramatic pause, the porter said, 'Ye know, ye're lucky lads. There's now three Kerrymen in the room.' The two lads got the meal of their lives.

## Cap-ital

Another well-known Kerryman to play rugby was the peerless Con Houlihan, who lined out for his beloved Castleisland. Houlihan took his fair share of heavy tackles. As the man says himself, 'I never got capped for Ireland, but I got kneecapped for Castleisland'.

## Captain Fantastic?

Stories about Willie Duggan abound in rugby circles. Like Moss Keane, Duggan was an Irish national institution. He was a man with little enthusiasm for training; indeed his most celebrated comment was, 'Training takes the edge off my game'. Duggan was one of a rare group of players who always made a point of bringing a pack of cigarettes with him onto the training field. Asked once in a radio interview if this was a major problem for him fitness-wise, he surprised the broadcaster by saying that it was a positive advantage, 'Sure, if it was not for the fags, I would be offside all day long'.

### Smoke Gets in Your Eyes

Another time, Duggan was having a fag in the dressing-room in Twickenham before Ireland played England. The time had come to run onto the pitch but there was nowhere in the dressing-room for Duggan to put out his cigarette. He knew that if he ran out in the tunnel with the fag in his mouth, the cameras would zoom in on him straight away. The Scottish referee, who was making his international debut, was also in the dressing-room, so the Irish No. 8 asked him: 'Would you hold that for a second, please?' The obliging referee said yes, and Duggan promptly ran out on the pitch. The ref had no option but to face the glare of the cameras with a still-lit fag. The first sight the television audience had of him was holding a cigarette!

### Consistency in a World Gone Mad

Duggan was never too bothered about tactics. Asked by a journalist for the reason for a vintage Leinster performance, Duggan answered: 'We had decided to go out in the first half to soften them up and kick the proverbial s\*\*\* out of them. And it went so well for us, that we had a quick word at half-time and decided to kick the s\*\*\* out of them in the second half!'

## *A Snail's Pace*

Fergus Slattery tells a story about Duggan, his partner in the back row. In 1983, some of the Irish team played in a match against the Western Province in South Africa. The match was played in mid-July. Typical of Willie all he took with him on the trip was a small bag with his toothbrush and cigarettes. Willie was never too bothered about training at the best of times, but in the middle of the summer he was always totally unfit. The game passed right by him. At one stage Fergus saw him stamping on the ground. Slatts went over to him and asked him what the hell he was doing. Willie answered, 'Oh, I'm stamping that bloody snail which has been following me around since the match started!'

## *The Scarlet Pimpernel*

Donal Lenihan tells another story about Duggan. Donal called Willie the Scarlet Pimpernel of Irish rugby because he was so hard to find for training. During his reign as Irish captain, Willie was not known for his gentle words of encouragement to the players. One of Donal's clearest memories of Willie's captaincy is of the morning after the Scotland game in 1984, when all the papers had a picture of Duggan with his arm around Tony Ward. The photo was taken just before Ward kicked a penalty. It appeared that Willie was acting the real father figure, but knowing him as Donal does, his guess is that Willie was saying, 'If you miss this penalty, I'll kick you all the way to Kilkenny!'

## Time to Say Goodbye

In 1975, Willie John McBride played his last game for Ireland against Wales in Cardiff, a match in which Willie Duggan won his first cap. The Irish team were badly beaten. Nobody said anything in the dressing-room afterwards because they were so disappointed with their performance. Later, Willie John met two guys wearing green scarves and with their arms around each other. One of them recognised Willie John and said, 'I know this is the centenary year of IRFU but there's no need to play like one of the founding members'.

## The Ould Enemy

In Northern Hemisphere rugby, the enemy is generally England, as Max Boyce demonstrated in this unique rendition of the Last Judgement.

When it comes to the one great scorer,

To mark against your name.

He'll not ask you how you played the game,

But whether you beat England!

## Balls and Walls

In Limerick, they keep their friends close and their enemies closer, as the following parable serves to illustrate: Thomond Park had a 20-foot wall around it, but this was often insufficient to prevent the ball from leaving the ground. When balls were lost, the crowd were wont to shout, 'Never mind the ball, get on with the game'.

## Rest in Peace

On another famous occasion the crowds had been gathering since lunchtime in Thomond Park for the Munster Cup final between Shannon and Young Munster. One of the first into the stand was a man who had presented two tickets on arrival. With only five minutes to go before the match, the seat beside him remained unoccupied. This aroused the curiosity of the person on his other side. 'Are you waiting on someone?' he inquired. 'Ah, no,' replied the Young Munster fan. 'We've had a death in the family since I bought the tickets. In fact, to tell you the truth, it was my wife that died.'

'I'm very sorry for your trouble,' said the other, 'but could you not get anyone else from the family to come along with you?'

'Yerrah, not at all, sure they all wanted to go to her funeral!'

## Big Tom

No one encapsulated the passion for the game in Limerick better than Tom Clifford. Clifford was first capped for Ireland against France in 1949 and was a key part of the Triple Crown victory in that season. His name lives on through Young Munster's ground 'Tom Clifford Park', which had been variously described as 'The Killing Fields', 'The Garden of Get Somebody' and 'Jurassic Park'. It has been said that the club's motto is, 'Kick a head. Kick any head.' A variation is, 'Kick anything that moves above the grass and if doesn't move kick it anyway'.

Tom played for Munster against the Wallabies in 1948. Munster had a very simple way of dealing with touring sides: as soon as possible bring them down to your own level and sure then it's an even match. Tom was in the front row packing against Nick Shehadie, one of the stars of the Australian side. 'Come in here, son,' said Tom. 'You may as well die here as in f****** Sydney.'

### *A Raleigh-ing Cry*

Everybody in Limerick knew Clifford's bike. He never locked it because no one would dare touch it. Once when he was speaking about a big match to an ever-increasing circle of Young Munster fans, he held his bicycle in the air. Asked by an onlooker what he was doing, he replied, 'I'm holding a Raleigh!'

### *The Faithful Departed*

At Tom's funeral the church was teeming with rugby folk. The priest giving the homily had been a lifelong friend of Tom's; he told the congregation how he had invited the giant of Irish rugby to his ordination Mass. After the ceremony, he asked Tom what he thought of it. Tom replied, 'You spoke too long. The next time if you go on for longer than ten minutes I'll set off an alarm clock in the church.' The next Sunday, the priest saw Tom arriving in at the church and noticed he had a bulge in his overcoat. When Tom caught his eye, he pulled out an alarm clock.

## The Life of O'Reilly

In the annals of Irish rugby, a special place is reserved for Tony O'Reilly. O'Reilly is the Roy of the Rovers of Irish rugby. Such was the speed of his progression that he played for the Lions before he played for Ireland. Having first being capped against France as an eighteen-year-old in 1955, he became the undisputed star of the Lions' tour to South Africa in the same year.

As a schoolboy, O'Reilly also excelled at soccer, playing for Home Farm, but he turned his back on the game after an assault. During a match, he made a bone-crunching tackle on an opponent. The boy's mother rushed on to the pitch and attacked O'Reilly with her umbrella. The future Lions sensation remarked: 'Rugby is fair enough – you only have your opponent to deal with. Soccer you can keep, if it involves having to deal with your opponent and his mother.'

Belvedere College provided a nursery for both O'Reilly's rugby and entrepreneurial skills. When he was seven, O'Reilly was the only boy in his class to make his Holy Communion. To mark the occasion, a priest gave him an orange – an enormous luxury during the war years. Like most of his friends, O'Reilly had never seen an orange. He subsequently claimed: 'After I ate the centre, I sold the peel for one penny per piece, thereby showing a propensity for commercial deception which has not left me since.'

### Drink Up

O'Reilly tells a great story about Brendan Behan. Behan turned up totally drunk for a chat show on Canadian television. The presenter was unimpressed and asked him why he was so drunk. Behan replied, 'Well, a few weeks ago I was sitting in a pub in Dublin and I saw a sign on a beer mat which said: "Drink Canada Dry". So when I came over here I said I'd give it a go!' O'Reilly deftly uses that incident to illustrate the need for a positive attitude that says, 'I'll give it a go'. O'Reilly always gave it a go.

### Not My Fault

What people forget was that, a bit like Simon Geoghegan, O'Reilly seldom got the ball when he played for Ireland. In fact, he played many matches for Ireland when he never got a pass. With the ball in his hands though, he was a sight to behold – but he was not above passing the buck! In those days, defences were not as organised as they are now. Normally it was man-to-man marking, with players taking up their opposite number. In O'Reilly's first game against France, his opposite number came through like a rocket between David Hewitt and Kevin Flynn and scored a try. O'Reilly came up to Flynn afterwards and said, 'He was your man!'

## Holy Wit

O'Reilly's quick wit was evident on the tour to South Africa in 1955. O'Reilly was asked what he had been doing looking the other way as Springbok goal-kicking ace Van der Schyff took the kick which would have given South Africa victory over the Lions in the first game of the 1955 test. He replied, 'I was in direct communion with the Vatican'. Van der Schyff missed and the tourists won 23–22.

Such is O'Reilly's flair with words, it is difficult to imagine that he was once out-quipped – but miracles do happen. O'Reilly played in a game in which England beat Ireland 20–0. As he walked off the pitch, O'Reilly turned to Tom Reid and said: '20–0! That was dreadful.'

Reid responded, 'Sure, weren't we lucky to get the nil!'

O'Reilly has such a penchant for witty quips that he is sometimes mistakenly credited with any classic rugby comment. When an English official remarked at a post-match dinner that the soup was tepid, it is believed that O'Reilly replied, 'I thought it was chicken!' In fact, the player responsible for this remark was the Scottish lock Alistair Campbell.

## Lean and Mean?

In 1963 following Ireland's 24–5 defeat at the hands of the French, O'Reilly was dropped for the only time in his career. Although the news came as a shock, O'Reilly had arguably never consistently reproduced his Lions' form in the green jersey. It seemed after twenty-eight caps his international career was over. Seven years later, in an ill-judged move, the Irish selectors persuaded him to come out of retirement for his twenty-ninth cap to play against England at Twickenham in place of the injured Billy Brown. To put it kindly, O'Reilly, now firmly established as a commercial giant because of his work in business, was anything but a lean, mean machine. His shape prompted Willie John McBride to remark: 'Well, Tony, in my view your best attacking move tomorrow might be to shake your jowls at them'.

Ireland lost 9–3 and O'Reilly gave an undistinguished performance. In the final moments he dived boldly into the heart of the English pack. As he regained consciousness, he heard an Irish voice shouting: 'And while you're at it, why don't ya kick his f****** chauffeur too!' The Heinz slogan is: 'Beans Means Heinz'. After the match a wag was heard to say: 'I never realised Heinz means has-beens!'

### *It Says In the Papers*

Although he only played one season with O'Reilly at international level, former Irish flanker Jim McCarthy was best man at both of O'Reilly's weddings. When McCarthy arrived on the scene, he was the darling of the media and could do no wrong. However, after his first match against France, the tables turned: the *Irish Independent* said that Jim had played poorly and had not protected Tony, even though McCarthy wasn't playing in the centre. He was dropped for the next match, and never played another international. Twenty-five years later, Tony put him on the board of the *Irish Independent*, just to make up for their injustice to him all those years ago.

## McGann the Man

Barry McGann was one of the great Irish rugby fly-halves and a great soccer player. He was also a little 'calorifically challenged'. One of the great expressions about McGann was, 'He had two speeds – slow and very slow'.

Around the time he was first capped for Ireland, McGann moved from Cork to Dublin and was persuaded to play for Shelbourne FC. The club had some tremendous players at the time, such as Ben Hannigan and Eric Barber. McGann always got a great slagging whenever he went back to play in Cork. One time Shelbourne were playing Cork Celtic. As he ran onto the pitch, Barry heard a voice from the terraces: 'Who's that fella?'

'That's McGann the rugby player.'

'Oh, wouldn't you know it by his stomach!'

An even more damning indictment of McGann's bulk was subsequently provided by Tony O'Reilly's quip: 'Twice around Barry McGann and you qualify as a bona fide traveller!'

### *An Error of Judgement*

McGann was one of the greatest kickers in the history of Irish rugby. Towards the final days of McGann's international career, Syd Millar was coaching the team. Barry had the reputation of being a very laid-back player, but he was serious when he needed to be. McGann was late for a training session because of work, although he got there as quick as he could. The training session at Anglesea Road was in full swing when he arrived. McGann went over and apologised to Millar for being late but he had a strong feeling Millar didn't believe he had made much of an effort to be there. McGann asked Millar what he wanted him to do and was told to warm-up. Instinctively McGann rubbed his hands together, blew on them and said, 'Okay, coach, I'm ready'. Moss Keane was in stitches but no one present will ever forget the bemused look on Millar's face. McGann remains convinced that incident probably cost him ten caps.

## Donal's Doughnuts

Put-downs were a particular speciality of Donal Lenihan. During the 1989 Lions tour of Australia, the second string team acquired the nickname of 'Donal's Doughnuts' – doughnuts because they played to 'fill the hole in the middle of the week', and Donal's because they were captained by Lenihan. Lenihan's ready wit was to the fore on a number of occasions on that tour. Bridgend's Mike Griffiths once inquired, 'Can I ask a stupid question?'

'Better than anyone I know,' answered Lenihan.

Another time, the touring party were driving through Sydney when they passed a couple coming out of a church after being married. In all earnestness, Jeremy Guscott asked: 'Why do people throw rice at weddings?' Lenihan replied immediately: 'Because rocks hurt.'

Scott Hastings grew impatient when his brother Gavin seemed to prefer playing tennis or going windsurfing with Ieuan Evans than with him. Lenihan commented: 'Ieuan's like the brother Gavin never had.'

'What about me?' asked Scott.

'You're the brother he did have,' responded Lenihan.

## Family Ties

The capacity for put-downs seems to be a common trait in the Lenihan family. After Ireland lost to Australia in the World Cup in 1987, Lenihan rang home. As a result of the time difference the match was shown live on Irish television at 6 am. His mother had seen the match and knew the result already. Instead of offering him sympathy she said, 'Anyone stupid enough to play rugby at 6 o'clock in the morning deserves to lose!'

## Calling...

Although Lenihan was a great lineout jumper, he was occasionally thrown by the calls. When Ireland faced England to win the 1985 Triple Crown, Ireland had a lineout on the halfway line. Ciaran Fitzgerald had come up with a coded system for the calls to confuse the English. Ciaran held the ball high and barked out, 'Limerick, hurling, women, drink, 1916'. As the English forwards frantically wondered who the ball was going to be aimed at, Donal Lenihan exclaimed loudly, 'Holy God, me again'.

## Bless Me Father

In 1982 after Ireland won the Triple Crown, the team travelled to France hoping to win the Grand Slam. The Irish team bus entered the stadium and was surrounded by French supporters who were going crazy, thumping the side of the bus and shouting abuse at the team. The Irish team were very tense and everyone was silent. Lenihan was sitting beside Moss Finn. The French fans were screaming: 'L'Irelande est fini. L'Irelande est fini.' Finn stood up and said, 'Christ, lads. Isn't it great to be recognised.'

After the Lions 27–11 victory over Australian Capital Territories in 1989, Lenihan brought the touring Lions party to the Friends of Ireland bar where they were greeted by a priest. After much liquid refreshment, it was time for the team to return to their hotel. The priest bade them farewell. Slightly under the influence, Andy Robinson, one of the 'star players', told the clergyman he was wearing his collar back to front.

'I'm a father, Andrew,' said the priest.

'I've got kids myself,' replied Robinson.

'No, I'm the father to hundreds of people in this area,' explained the priest.

'Really? In that case, it's not your collar you should be wearing back to front, it's your bloody trousers!'

The Irish team at the 1987 World Cup were coached by Mick Doyle. Doyler decided he was going to get into shape on the trip because he was two stone overweight. He started to train with the backs, but the lads stepped up a gear. At the end of the session, Doyler was in bits. Later that night Lenihan heard that he had been taken to hospital. As captain, Lenihan went to see him that evening in hospital. In the taxi on the way there, Lenihan was in the front seat and Syd Millar and Mick Molloy were in the back. At one stage in the conversation, Syd said Doyle's wife, Lynne, had been on the phone and was very concerned about him and wanted to come 'down under' to see him. Then he said Doyle's girlfriend, Mandy, was very worried about him and she too wanted to travel to see him. The Maori taxi-driver turned to Lenihan and said with real feeling, 'That stuff about holy Catholic Ireland is a load of crap!'

When Lenihan got back from the hospital, Brian Spillane asked, 'Did he have a girl or a boy?'

Some years later, at a dinner, Lenihan told this story to a charming woman with an English accent whom he had never met before. He had no idea who she was except that she was very well versed in rugby matters. It turned out to be Doyler's ex-wife, Lynne!

## Doyler

Mick Doyle famously coached Ireland to the Triple Crown in 1985. Although he played upon his 'give-it-a-lash' image, he was a very shrewd coach. Before getting the Ireland job, he had been coach of Leinster. The province played Romania when they toured Ireland in 1980. The home side arrived at the ground well over an hour before the game. Players thought they had mistimed the arrival; they hadn't. The previous week Romania had hammered Munster, and Doyler had noticed that in the lead-up to the match the Romanian players were constantly in and out of the toilet. Being the cute Kerryman that he was Doyler gave a newspaper and a match programme to each of the Leinster substitutes and told them to lock themselves in the toilets until the game began. Leinster demolished the Romanians in the match. The next day the phrase that was used in the newspapers was, 'The Romanians were strangely heavy and leaden-footed'. Was it any surprise?

### The Limerick Leader

As a player, Doyler had a distinguished career, though from time to time he had problems with some of the other boys in green, notably Mick English. In 1952 English was tickled by a letter written to him by the late Mai Purcell of the *Limerick Leader* when he won his first cap. The letter read:

> *Mick,*
>
> *I should like to impress on you that I'm spending a whole week's wages to visit Dublin just to see you play and I beseech you not to make an idiot of yourself on this occasion.*

Doyler and English played their first match together for Munster against Connacht. There was a downpour throughout the game. Munster were on top and English was kicking everything. Doyler was going mad for a pass and eventually English passed to him but Doyle dropped the ball. Connacht broke right up to the other end of the field. English screamed out, 'Doyler that's the last f****** time I'm passing to you until you can drop it further than I can kick it'.

### Political Influence

After his career as Irish coach ended, Doyler wrote his autobiography, which was described by one observer as 'a good love guide'. Doyler rang up Charlie Haughey to see whether he would be willing to launch the book. CJH asked him what it was about. Doyle told him 20 per cent was about rugby and 80 per cent was pornography. The then Taoiseach said, 'You got the balance just right!'

Charlie opened his speech on the night by saying, 'I always like people who expose themselves in public!'

At a book signing, a few men arrived dressed up as nuns. The costumes were not totally inappropriate: one of the scenes in the book relates how a nun had caught Doyler in a state of undress after performing the 'marital act'.

Some time later, Doyler was doing a book signing in O'Mahony's bookshop in Limerick. Garret Fitzgerald had been there the night before promoting his autobiography. In the front window they had photographs of both Doyle and Garrett. As he prepared for his signing, Doyler noticed a religious brother in his white collar walking up and down past the shop shouting, 'Get that b****** off the window'. One of the shop assistants went out and asked him, 'What's wrong with Mick Doyle?'

'Nothing. He's a grand fella. It's that other so-and-so that I can't stand!'

## Jim'll Fix It

Rugby tours have a number of striking similarities with religious pilgrimages: uniformity in dress codes, the chanting of familiar songs and a feeling of community and fellowship. The analogy does not hold true for the Wasps tour to Malaysia in 1992, when some of the tourists bared their posteriors for the world to see. Not surprisingly in a Muslim country, this cheeky behaviour caused outrage and the offenders were severely fined and deported.

In 1980, the year Jimmy Carter had arranged a boycott of the Moscow Olympics because of Russia's invasion of Afghanistan, Leinster, under Mick Doyle and Mick 'the Cud' Cuddy, toured Romania. One of the players on the tour was Jim Glennon, who in 2002 was elected a TD. A vivid memory for Glennon is of going with Phil Orr and George Wallace to see Romania play Russia. The Russians were staying in the same hotel as Leinster but on a different floor. That night, the three amigos met up with the Russian captain and invited him and his colleagues up to their room for a jar. They had stared disaster in the face earlier when they discovered that there was only one bottle of whiskey in the hotel. Worse still, that bottle was in the Cud's room and was not intended for public consumption. The Cud was annoyed, to put it mildly, when he discovered it 'missing'.

The next morning the manager of the Russian team came in to the lobby, asked to speak to 'the leader of the Irish delegation' and invited Leinster to tour in Russia. It was a pretty strange spectacle because the Russians had KGB types following them everywhere, watching their every move. Glennon thought this invitation might provide the key to a rapprochement with the Cud, so he headed in before the Russian delegation to explain the situation. The Cud was not impressed. He said, 'Look, Glennon, would you ever bleep off and tell them Russians to bleep off and while you're at tell them to bleep off out of Afghanistan as well!'

## Golden Oldies

Old rugby players never die – they simply have their balls taken away. Even after his retirement Glennon, to his own surprise, continued to grace the world's playing fields. When he finished playing in 1988, he got the most unexpected invitation to tour as part of a Golden Oldies team. He got a phone call from Moss Keane in June of that year, inquiring whether he was free for the last weekend in August. Jim forgot all about it until the last Wednesday in August when he got another call from Moss. Moss told him that he had been invited to play in an exhibition match for a Lions' Golden Oldies side against a junior team across the water. Although Moss had been given the plane ticket, he was unable to travel. He said he was going to ring the organiser and tell him he couldn't make it, but that he would be meeting Jim later that day and would attempt to persuade him to travel.

Shortly afterwards, Glennon got a phone call from a panic-stricken secretary, apologising profusely for the short notice, but wondering whether he would be willing to play instead of Moss. A delighted Jim 'reluctantly' agreed. On the plane over, he was joined by Phil Orr, Willie Duggan and Fergus Slattery. They had a great weekend.

Glennon was the only 'non-Lion' on the team. His partner in the second row was Alan Martin of Wales. After the match, the pair were chatting in the bath when Martin asked him out of the blue, 'What about Stockholm?' Martin went on to explain that there was a Golden Oldies match there the following weekend, Thursday to Monday, but that he couldn't travel. 'Would you be interested?' Martin asked.

On the Monday, Jim rang Moss to thank him for the wonderful weekend and asked him why he had left it so late to tell organisers he couldn't make it. Moss answered, 'Because I didn't want some hoor from England to take my place'.

Two days later, Jim got a phone call from a different panic-stricken secretary, apologising profusely for the short notice, but wondering whether he would be willing to play in Stockholm, instead of Alan. This time, Jim made the secretary sweat a bit more and told him he wasn't sure if he would be able to make it because he had other commitments. However, he rang him back less than an hour later and agreed to the trip. On the plane over, he was again joined by Orr, Duggan and Slattery. Also on the trip were J.P.R. Williams and Jim Renwick, among others. It was an absolutely brilliant weekend.

On the Tuesday morning, Jim rang to thank Alan for putting it his way. When he asked him why he had left it so late to tell them he couldn't make it, Martin replied, 'Because I didn't want some hoor from England to take my place!'

## Wish You Were Here?

Not all rugby tours are pleasurable. Dissatisfaction with facilities is an occupational hazard for rugby tourists. The story is told that on the Lions' tour to New Zealand in 1993 the secretary of the touring party, Bob Weighill, asked for an extra pat of butter to accompany his bread roll. He took umbrage when he was told this would not be possible. 'Do you know who I am?'

'No, sir.'

The waiter listened impassively as Mr Weighill listed his auspicious catalogue of titles. Then he softly replied: 'And do you know who I am?'

'No.'

'I'm in charge of the butter.'

### *Eggs-actly*

One of the most famous tours in rugby history was the Lions tour in 1974 and one of the greatest stars on the tour was the Welsh prop forward Bobby Windsor. Windsor had some memorable exchanges with waiters during the trip. One went as follows:

**Windsor**: I want one egg boiled for exactly 26 seconds and I want another one boiled for 25 minutes 14 seconds. And I want three slices of toast which are pale gold on one side and burned pure black on the other.

**Waiter**: But, sir, that's simply not possible. We can't go to all the trouble to fill an order like that.

**Windsor**: Oh yes you can, sonny boy. That's exactly what you dished up to me yesterday!

At another meal the players were tucking into a big steak dinner. Bobby was feeling a bit under the weather and just asked for an omelette. The waiter asked, 'What kind of omelette would you like, sir?' Bobby just looked up at him and barked, 'A f****** egg omelette!'

## Painting a Picture

Windsor was one of the game's great raconteurs. One of his favourite stories was about a Welsh Valleys rugby club on tour in America. On coming back from a night on the town, two of the players could not find their rooms. They decided to check for their team-mates by looking through the keyholes. They came upon an astonishing sight. There in her birthday suit was a Marilyn Monroe look-alike. Close by was a man who was chanting out with great conviction: 'Your face is so beautiful that I will have it painted in gold. Your breasts are so magnificent that I will have them painted in silver. Your legs are so shapely that I will have them painted in platinum.'

Outside the two Welshmen were getting very excited and began jostling each other for the rights to the keyhole. Hearing the racket, the man inside shouted out: 'Who the hell is out there?' The two Welshmen replied: 'We're two painters from Pontypool.'

## Back from the Dead

On the Lions' flight to South Africa in 1974, Windsor was taken ill with food poisoning. He was so ill that he was taken to the back of the plane and told to suck ice-cubes to help him cool down. The team doctor, former Irish international Ken Kennedy, came to take his temperature without knowing about the ice-cubes. When he looked at the thermometer, he shouted out, 'Jaysus, Bobby, you died twenty-four hours ago!'

### *Hanging on the Telephone*

In the golden age of amateurism, Alan Thomas was the manager of the Lions 1974 tour. Thomas tended to lose things, especially room keys. He had a phone in his room but each player on the team was only allowed one phone call a week. Bobby Windsor spotted Alan's keys and held on to them. Every evening, he used it to sneak in to Alan's room and phone his wife. As the tour concluded and the team were leaving the hotel, Alan came into the foyer and addressed the entire squad in a crestfallen voice, 'I'm very disappointed. I have been handed a phone bill for a thousand rand. One of you guys has been using the phone every night behind my back. The Lions are supposed to be the cream of rugby but one of you has let the side down. Sadly the guy who did this is a countryman of my own. He's been ringing Pontyprid.'

At this point Bobby Windsor jumped up from his seat and started waving his fists menacingly, as he said, 'Which of you b******* has been phoning my wife?'

### *The Riot Squad*

One night on the tour, a group of players were partying and disturbed all the guests in their hotel in the middle of the night. An undiplomatic war broke out. The tiny hotel manager tried to keep the peace. Two scantily clad players were parading around the corridors, and he roared at them to get back into their rooms. Not liking his attitude, the players told him, with all due lack of politeness, what he could do with himself. The manager's threat to ring the police met with no reaction. At this point, along came Willie John McBride. The manager thought his problems were solved at the sight of the Lions captain arriving. When McBride seemed to be ignoring the matter, the manager repeated his threat to call the police. McBride called him forward with a tilt of his head. The manager breathed a sigh of relief, believing his threat had worked. He was in for a big disappointment, as McBride bent down to him and whispered, 'How many will there be?'

McBride went back to the party. Some time later, a group of riot police arrived with their dogs. Again Willie John intervened decisively. He went down to the coffee machine and bought some milk and gave it to the dogs and then invited the police to join the party. They did and had the night of their lives.

During the tour, McBride had been trapped at the bottom of a ruck, when a few players kicked him on his head. After the game, he was asked did he remember the pounding on his head. He answered: 'I do. I heard it.'

When the Lions won the series in 1974, a magnificent party was staged in the hotel. The festive spirit got a little out of hand and every fire extinguisher and water hose in the hotel was set off. The problem was that nobody thought to turn them off. The next morning, the hotel could have done with the services of Noah's Ark. The touring manager was summoned to explain the actions of his team. Thomas had gone to bed early and had no idea what had happened until he discovered himself thigh-deep in water. He half-walked, half-swam up to Willie John's room and prepared to knock on the door only to discover that the door had been a casualty of the flood. To his astonishment, McBride was puffing contentedly on his pipe and calmly sitting on his bed, as it bobbed around on the water. The manager lost control and launched into a vicious tirade. Finally, Willie John replied, 'Alan, can I ask you one question?'

'What?'

'Is there anybody dead?'

### The Accidental Tourist

Another famous tourist on the 1974 Lions tour was Fergus Slattery. An auctioneer by profession, Slats was not sold many dummies on the field. A product of Blackrock College, he was capped more than sixty times for Ireland as an open-side wing forward (a world record for a flanker), between 1970 and 1984, scoring three international tries. The classic story told about Slattery goes back to an African trip. After a British Lions' tour fixture in Rhodesia, there was a celebratory dinner organised. The then Rhodesian prime minister, Ian Smith, arrived to make a speech. Shortly after, Slatts and another Irish player, Dick Milliken, decided to return to their hotel. Having consumed beverages stronger than orange juice, they were feeling particularly adventurous. As they walked out, they noticed a beautiful Cadillac with black-tinted windows just outside the entrance to the club. They decided to 'borrow' the car and go for a drive. After driving around for a few minutes, the partition behind the front seats slid across and the prime minister asked: 'Are you gentlemen looking for a job?'

## Anyone for Golf?

In 1981, Ireland controversially toured South Africa with a depleted side, despite the vigorous opposition of the anti-apartheid movement. The tour saw one of the great wind-ups of Irish rugby. One Saturday, Freddie McLennan was 'duty boy'. (A duty boy is the player in charge of informing other players about travel arrangements, etc., for a particular day during a tour abroad. Each player takes it in turn.) The squad had been given the day off and had to decide how to spend it. McLennan, himself a keen golfer, offered two choices. They could either go for a game of golf or take a trip around Johannesburg harbour. Eighteen players favoured the harbour trip: they could play golf at any time, they argued, but would not always get the chance to do some sightseeing in Johannesburg. The next morning the players were ready at 8 am for their trip around the harbour. However, McLennan informed them that, as the city was 5,000 feet above sea level, it did not have a harbour and that the nearest seaside was a massive bus trip away. The team went golfing.

McLennan was a great personality. Once when Ireland played England, McLennan and John Carleton were having a real jousting match. At one stage, Carleton sent McLennan crashing to the ground in a tackle. As he was going back to his position Freddie shouted at him, 'John, John. Is my hair all right?' The video of the game shows John cracking up with laughter and Freddie straightening his hair.

## O'Desperate Measures

John 'O'Desperate' O'Driscoll is the consummate gentleman, but he liked to enjoy himself on tour. He toured with the Lions to South Africa in 1980. The only unpardonable sin on a Lions' tour is to miss training. No matter how awful you feel or how low your morale is, you simply must get out to the training field at the appointed hour. Sunday was a day for total relaxation. To pass the afternoon Ray Gravell and O'Driscoll played a card game with a difference. The penalty if you lost a hand was to take a drink – a mixture of spirits and orange juice. When John lost, he noticed that Ray was adding extra spirits to his drink. John thought he was being very clever by saying nothing and adding a lot of extra juice. What he didn't know was that Gravell had laced the orange juice with spirits as well. The next morning, O'Driscoll had the mother of all hangovers and had to miss training.

O'Driscoll was a very committed, driven player but was a real Jekyll and Hyde character. His party piece was to hang out of windows late at night. During Ireland's tour of South Africa in 1981, this got a bit boring after a number of weeks. For the sake of variety, O'Driscoll decided he would hang someone else out of the window; one night he held Terry Kennedy by the legs and he dangled him outside the hotel window – seventeen storeys up. It was the only time the Irish players ever saw Kennedy quiet. Then Willie Duggan came into the room, puffing on his cigarette, with a bottle of beer in his hand and with his matted hair that hadn't being combed since the tour started. As Duggan was such a senior player and a close friend of O'Driscoll's, everyone assumed he would talk some sense into him. All Duggan said to O'Driscoll before turning and walking out was, 'O'Driscoll, you don't have the guts to let him go'. He was right, too.

## Top of the Props

Another famous Irish tourist was prop forward, Phil O'Callaghan. Prop forwards get a hard time in rugby, particularly from backs. The standing joke is, 'Prop forwards don't get Valentine cards for religious reasons – God made them ugly!'

O'Callaghan toured three times with Irish parties: to Australia in 1967, to Argentina in 1970 and to New Zealand and Fiji in 1976. As well as his fire on the pitch, he was also noted for his quick wit. The most oft-quoted story about him is of the day a referee penalised him and said: 'You're boring, [the term used to describe the way a prop forward drives in at an illegal angle into an opposing prop forward]

O'Callaghan.' Philo's instinctive retort was: 'Well, you're not so entertaining yourself, ref.' The referee penalised him a further 10 yards.

During another match, O'Callaghan put out his shoulder. The former Irish captain and leading gynaecologist, Karl Mullen, attended him. Dr Mullen said: 'I'll put it back in but I warn you it will be painful.' He did and it was. According to the story, Philo was screaming his head off with the pain. The doctor turned to him and said: 'You should be ashamed of yourself. I was with a sixteen-year-old girl this morning in the Rotunda as she gave birth and there was not even a word of complaint from her.' Philo replied: 'I wonder what she bloody well would have said if you tried putting the f****** thing back in.'

One of the highlights of O'Callaghan's career came in 1967, when Ireland became the first team from the Northern Hemisphere to beat Australia. The Irish party stopped off in Hawaii on the return journey. At one stage, they were standing at the side of a swimming pool. Philo had his back to the deep end and was pushed in by a now popular, or infamous, journalist. Philo was not able to swim and went under. The guys thought he was faking it when he didn't surface. Terry Moore dived in and lifted him out of the water long enough to give him the air he needed before he went down again. The late, great Jerry Walsh found the pole for cleaning the pool and extended it to Philo and eventually he hauled himself out of the pool. He asked Jerry later why he had not dived in. Walsh replied, 'Why ruin the tour by having both of us drown?'

## Sounds a Bit Fishy

When Ireland toured New Zealand in 1976, the squad included Brendan Foley, father of current star, Anthony. At one stage on that tour, Brendan came down to the hotel's foyer, which had a big fountain. He went into the middle of the fountain to do some fishing. He didn't catch anything. After that he was known as 'Foley never caught a fish'.

## Glory Days

The most famous Irish fly-half of all was Jack Kyle, star of the team that won back-to-back Triple Crowns in 1948 and 1949. Shortly after the 1949 win, Kyle drove down to Cork to get away from it all. On the way he came to a to a railway station, but the level crossing was halfway across the road. He sat in the car for ten minutes and then got out and found the stationmaster and asked, 'Do you know the gate is halfway across the road?'

'I do,' replied the stationmaster. 'We are half expecting the train from Cork.'

### The First Noel

Noel Henderson was another of the giants of Irish rugby in the golden era of Jackie Kyle. A radio commentator once slated Henderson's performance in an Irish international match. Noel's father was so outraged at the stream of insults that he threw the radio out the window!

Henderson's most famous pronouncement was, 'The state of British sport is mostly serious, but never hopeless. The state of Irish sport is usually hopeless, but never serious.'

### And as for Fortune and as for Fame

One episode which proves the veracity of that remark came in 1951, when Ireland toured South America. It was a total success off the field and a disaster on it. Ireland became the first international team to be beaten by Argentina.

When the Irish team arrived in Argentina, they were told they couldn't play any rugby because Eva Peron had just died. The Argentinians sent the boys in green down to Santiago in Chile to teach the cadets how to play. After eight days the cadets beat the Irish. The players didn't take the tour very seriously. Paddy Lawler went missing for a few days and nobody had a clue where he was. When he returned, a team meeting was hastily called. The team manager solemnly announced that he had been talking by phone to Dublin, which was a big deal in 1952, and then looked around menacingly and said, 'I'm deciding whether or not to send some players home'. Paddy stood up straight away and replied, 'We've been talking among ourselves and we're deciding whether or not we should send you home'.

### Keep off the Grass

Des O'Brien captained Ireland in the 1950s. Before an international match, Sean T. O'Kelly, the first Irish president to attend a rugby international, was being introduced to the teams. He was a man who was, shall we say, small in stature. The match was being played in October so the grass was long. As captain, Des was introduced to him first. O'Kelly said, 'God Bless you, Des. I hope you have a good game.' Then O'Brien heard a booming voice in the crowd, 'Hey, Des, would you ever get the grass cut so we'd bloody well be able to see the president!'

## Amazing Grace

By the time Tom Grace became Irish captain, the grass problem was resolved but other problems remained. Grace made his international debut on the wing in the high-pressure zone at Stade Colombes in Paris. To soothe his frayed nerves, he sought consolation from an old hand. At the team talk, captain Tom Kiernan traditionally spoke with each player individually. He spent a lot of time talking with the wingers. He was almost frothing at the mouth he was so fired up! Kiernan warned Grace and his partner on the wing about the way the French would bombard them with high balls. However, he assured them he would be there beside them to take the pressure off them.

The match had barely started when the French out-half kicked an almighty ball up in the air between Kiernan and Grace. To Tom's horror he heard Kiernan shouting, 'Your ball'. So much for all that brothers-in-arms talk. Grace caught the ball and nearly got killed as half the French team jumped on top of him.

### Grey Matter

During his playing days, Grace had jet-black hair and a Beatles haircut, so it came as an enormous shock to him when his hair went grey. He was up in Donegal with his family before one of the international matches. RTÉ were showing some highlights from previous seasons. When they started to show a few of Grace's tries, his wife called their six-year-old son, Conor, to come and watch his dad in his prime. When Conor came in, she pointed excitedly at the television, where Grace was in full flight. Conor shook his head and said, 'No, it's not him. My dad has grey hair.' Then he turned on his heels and ran out to play soccer.

## Suds

Peter Sutherland was captain of one of the UCD sides Grace played on. 'Suds' is probably more famous in rugby circles for his after-dinner speeches than for his achievements on the pitch. One of his favourite stories was about two former famous internationals from Cork who were on a trip to England. The pair passed a shop and saw a notice on the window which read: 'Trousers £2. Shirts £1.50.' Tom and Noel were thrilled. They decided they would make a killing: buy clothes cheaply in England and sell them off at a proper price back home in Ireland. Wanting to play it cool, they decided to speak in English accents. They walked up to the counter and said to the manager, 'We'll buy all the trousers and shirts you have'. The manager looked at them with astonishment. Despite their feigned accents, he asked, 'Excuse me, gentlemen, are you both from Cork?'

Noel and Tom asked in unison, 'How did you know?'

'Oh, call it an inspired guess. You probably didn't notice, but this is actually a dry-cleaners!'

The two principals in this tale were also involved in another famous story. Tom Kiernan was a great motivator. Before Munster played Australia in 1967, the team met in the Metropole hotel. Noel 'Noisy' Murphy limped in before the match and said, 'My leg is shagged and I can't play'. A sub was duly called for and informed of his selection. Then Kiernan cut loose with his motivational speech. Everyone was ready to tear into the Aussies afterwards. Noel Murphy was so caught up by Kiernan's emotion that he said, 'Ara, f*** it, Tom, I'll play'.

## Johnny Come Lately

Johnny Moloney was a very single-minded player. In a schoolboy match, he was charging through for a try when a despairing dive by his marker robbed him of his shorts. True to form, John raced on for the try in his underpants before worrying about getting new togs.

### Don't Be Too Formal, but…

As a young player, Moloney introduced himself to Leinster manager, Ken Ging, by saying, 'Mr Ging, my name is John Moloney. I'm the scrum-half.'

Ging replied, 'Don't call me Mr Ging, call me Kenneth'.

### Surprise, Surprise

Mick Quinn looms large in Moloney's comic reminiscences of his days with Ireland. Ireland were playing England away. Stewart McKinney went through the pages of *Mayfair* magazine and saw the number of an escort service. He rang it up and booked a lady of the night for Quinn, who was usually the perpetrator of practical jokes rather than the victim. Moloney had to play his part by keeping Quinn in his room and slipping out just before she was due to arrive. The lady of the night was wearing a raincoat, with nothing on underneath except suspenders and some very skimpy underwear. Quinn had to pay her £25 just to get her out of the room. After she left, Quinn went out the corridor and everyone in the squad was looking out from their rooms, laughing at him. It was the only time they ever saw him lost for words.

Quinn would sometimes involve Moloney as his practical joke partner-in-crime. Quinn had a trick he played on every player gaining his first cap. Before their debut, a lot of players feel that they are a bit sluggish and not at their best. Quinn would pretend to be very sympathetic and tell them he had the solution. He would inform them, in the strictest confidence, that the top players always took a freezing cold bath to give them an edge in a big match. The only reason why this was not generally known was because it was a trade secret. The biggest casualty in all of this was Freddie McLennan. Quinn and Moloney put McLennan in a cold bath and added buckets of ice. They told him he had to wait in there for twenty minutes, otherwise the treatment would do him no good. Freddie was squealing like a pig. When his time was up, he couldn't move and had ice on his legs.

# The Mighty Quinn

'Mine has been an eventful career.' This is Mick Quinn's summation of his life in rugby, which brought him ten caps for Ireland at out-half. Whereas Ollie Campbell would probably be regarded as his generation's crown prince of Irish rugby, Quinn is more likely to be seen as the clown prince.

Quinn doesn't remember much about the build-up for his Irish debut, except that he fell asleep during Willie John McBride's team talk. In his first game, it was pay for play with a difference: he had to pay for his jersey. Ireland beat France 6–4 and Quinn's opposite number was the great J. P. Romeau.

As it was his first cap, there was no way Quinn was going to part with his No. 10 jersey but he still really wanted Romeau's. He went back into the dressing-room and asked Ray McLoughlin for his No. 1 jersey. McLoughlin is a very successful businessman, heading up the James Crean Company, and not short of a few bob. He sold Quinn his jersey for £10. Mick rushed out and swapped jerseys with Romeau. Quinn was thrilled with himself when he returned, but suddenly the Frenchman came into the Irish dressing-room. With Romeau's dreadful English and Quinn's awful French, communication was a problem but it didn't take Mick long to see that the problem was that Romeau wanted a No. 10 jersey. Mick used sign language to tell him, 'Zero fello offo'.

Quinn enjoyed his rivalry with Ollie Campbell and Tony Ward for the Irish No. 10 jersey. In his biography, *The Good, The Bad and the Rugby*, Ward jokes that if it hadn't been for Ollie Campbell, Ward would have got forty caps. When Quinn read that, he rang Tony and said if it hadn't been for Ward, Mike Gibson, Barry McGann, Campbell and Paul Dean, he would have won eighty caps.

## *The Naked Truth*

One of the highlights of Quinn's career was at Lansdowne, where he won his third consecutive Leinster Cup in 1981. Lansdowne beat Old Belvedere in the final, and it was nice for Quinn to put one over on Ollie Campbell on the pitch. After the match, the team bus was bringing the Lansdowne team on to the victory celebrations. Quinn suggested to his colleagues that they should 'lob a moon' – display their bums out the window – to the people of Dublin. This proposal was enthusiastically agreed to. When the posteriors were on display, Quinn turned around and saw that there was a car travelling alongside the bus. To his horror the occupants were his father, mother and sister. His mother told him afterwards that she had recognised his bum because it hadn't changed since the time she used to change his nappies! Quinn told her he found that hard to believe.

### What's the Name of the Game?

Perhaps Quinn's most enduring legacy to the rugby fraternity is the number of players to whom he gave nicknames. He called former international scrum-half, Tony Doyle, 'Gandhi' because he had less meat on him than a cheese sandwich. He called the Wesley player, Dave Priestman, 'Vicarman' because he told him it was a ridiculous for a Protestant to be called priest. He called Brendan Mullin 'Bugs Bunny' because of his smile. He also christened Harry Steele 'Stainless' for obvious reasons; Rory Underwood 'The Chinese Takeway' and Jean Pierre Rives (now a noted sculptor, and the living proof that you don't have to be big to be a world-class forward), 'Je t'aime' because he had such a way with women.

### A Humbling Experience

Quinn is also willing to tell stories about himself. After one international match, he was accosted by a young autograph hunter: 'Can I have your autograph please, Johnny?' Mick didn't have the heart to tell him he had got the wrong man, so he signed it: 'To Bert, Best wishes, Johnny Moloney.' As he was leaving, the young boy looked up and said to him, 'How do you keep playing with Mick Quinn? He plays like s***!'

## From Naas to Here

Willie John McBride and Mick Quinn were invited to South Africa to play for a World XV against the Springboks. Quinn was interviewed on South African TV and was asked who he thought were the main contenders for the Springbok's No. 10 shirt. Quinn mentioned that he had been taken by this new kid called Naas Botha, whom he had seen play on television. The next day, Quinn was training when Botha came over to him to thank him for his compliments.

Naas was a hugely controversial figure in South Africa. The public either loved him or hated him. Quinn got on very well with him and subsequently invited him to come over and get some experience in Lansdowne. He thought nothing more about it until some months later, when he got a phone call. It was Naas. He said he would like to take up Quinn's offer of hospitality. Quinn told him that he would be very welcome and asked him when would he be travelling over. Botha answered, 'Well, Mr Quinn, I'm ringing you from a place called O'Connell Street in Dublin!' Botha brought his brother, Darius, with him. Darius went on to become a Dutch Reformed Minister, and he used to organise prayer meetings in Quinn's house.

Naas Botha was one of the most prodigious goal-kickers of all time, but he attracted a lot of controversy in South Africa because of his apparent reluctance to pass the ball. After he kicked his club side's twenty-four points to give them victory in a cup final, he was sitting beside another man on the plane. Botha was a bit surprised that his companion said nothing to him. After a half an hour of total silence, he turned around and said, 'I don't think you realise who I am; I'm probably the most famous rugby player in South Africa'. His companion quietly said: 'I don't think you realise who I am. I play for your team. I'm your first centre!'

## Murphy's Law

Johnny Murphy was a great captain of Leinster. He had a bus and hearse business and turned up for training one night in his hearse with a coffin inside. Some of the Leinster players found it disconcerting to be doing their press-ups beside a coffin and grumbled to Murphy. He just said, 'She's not going anywhere and doesn't mind waiting'.

Murphy's speeches were memorable not least because he was great at taking off posh accents. His opening sentence in a speech after a Connacht match was, 'Mr President of Leinster, Mr President of Connacht, players and the rest of you hangers on'. Not surprisingly he was carpeted afterwards and told to clean up his act when making speeches.

The next week Leinster played Llanelli and beat the pants off them. Everyone was dying to know what Murphy would say. He began, 'Well, lads, I've got to be very careful what I say this week. It was a great honour for us to have the privilege of playing against such a famous side. My only regret is that BBC's *Rugby Special* wasn't here to see us beating the s*** out of ye. I know people will say ye were missing some of yer star players but don't forget we were missing one of our greatest stars – Hugo MacNeill. He couldn't get his f******* place – I have it.' The whole place was in stitches and Ray Gravell had to be picked off the floor he was laughing so hard.

## Water Works

Gravell, like a lot of the Welsh players, is very nationalistic. Once before an international in which Mick Quinn was a sub, he went into the toilet and heard Gravell in the next cubicle singing arias about the welcome in the hills in Wales. Quinn told him that the only reason they welcomed people in the hills was that they were too mean to invite them into their homes.

There was a limit to the amount of Gravell's singing Quinn could take, so he asked him to give it a rest but Gravell went on and on. To shut him up, Quinn filled a bucket of cold water, threw it over Gravell in the cubicle and fled. When the Welsh team came out, some of the Irish players remarked that Gravell must have gone through an awfully heavy warm-up because the sweat was rolling off him.

## Religious Affairs

Mick Quinn claims the credit for Mike Gibson's great displays for Ireland. Quinn always blessed himself with Lourdes holy water before matches and always splashed some on Gibson's legs when he wasn't looking. Gibbo went out and played like a genius.

It wouldn't be accurate to say the Irish team were an ecumenical bunch, but there were times religion brought them together. In 1976, the team was on tour in New Zealand on a holy day of obligation for Catholics. The team doctor, Dr Bob O'Connell, arranged for a priest to say Mass for them, and it was decided that the whole team should attend. The Catholics in the team knew to bring change for the collection, but the Protestants didn't. As a result, the priest got a silent collection from them. He was thrilled and wrote to all the Irish papers, declaring what a wonderful bunch the Irish squad were, such fabulous ambassadors for their country.

## Faux Pas

Sean Lynch was on the Irish tour to Argentina in 1970. All the players were attending a dinner. A Lord somebody was to be the main dignitary. Before he arrived, the players were warned that he had Parkinson's disease and that it would take him a long time to walk to the dinner table. After what seemed like a half an hour, the Lord eventually made it to his seating position. He was sitting beside Lynchie and said, 'Well, Mr Lynch, are you enjoying your tour?' Lynchie replied, 'Yes, Mr Parkinson, I am!'

Sean Lynch is said to have a deep-rooted terror of spiders. One day on the bus going to a match, a kind friend and team-mate threw a rubber insect at him; Lynchie leapt so high in the air in terror, his head went through the baggage rack.

## A Star is Born

No Irish sport star, apart from George Best, has filled more newspaper columns than Tony Ward, as is illustrated by the following story: During his time as national rugby coach, Mick Doyle was guest speaker at a luncheon of the Irish Business Association in the London Metropole Hotel. He was quoted as attacking newspaper reporting of rugby as 'insensitive', 'wildly inaccurate' and 'pseudo-aggressive'. Doyle made particular reference to the harsh treatment given by newspaper reporters to the Irish selectors because of their failure to pick Tony Ward. As an example of the distortions in the print media, Doyle told the 'parable' of an Irishman who fell under a tube train in London and was killed. The London *Times* reported it straight, the *Sun* that an Irish terrorist had disrupted British Rail schedules, the *Irish Independent* that a Scotsman had been killed at Heathrow, the *Irish Press* that British Rail had murdered an innocent Irishman and *The Irish Times* that Tony Ward had his travel schedule disrupted because of a mishap on British Rail.

## For Whom the Bell Tolls

Ward exploded onto the sporting scene in 1978, the year he first played for Ireland. Already he was a local hero in Limerick, where he was training to be a P.E. teacher in Thomond College, because of his displays for one of the city's top teams, Garryowen. Ward was the unnamed culprit in a story that did the rounds just as he broke onto the Irish team. The story involved two conversations between a Young Munster (Garryowen's great rivals) supporter and his parish priest.

**Priest**: 'Tis a long time since your face has been seen in this sacred house, my son. Anyway we cater for all types here. Can I be of any assistance to you at all?

**Fan**: I don't know if you can, Father. You see, this could be a job for the bishop. I am in an awful way. My state of mind is such that all communications with the wife, both verbal and otherwise, have temporarily ceased.

**Priest**: My son, confession is good for the soul. What is the terrible secret that you bear?

**Fan**: Father, the truth is... I... I... am in danger of becoming a supporter of the Garryowen team.

**Priest**: I see. That's bad; in fact, it's very bad.

**Fan**: I knew you would understand, Father. All my life I thought that rugby consisted of rucks, scrums and line-outs with a few fights thrown in for good measure. Where I come from, shouts of 'ahead, ahead' have a different meaning than that employed elsewhere. To be candid, Father, I was happy in my ignorance, but now tis all jinking and running, reverse-passing and blind-side moves. And to make matters worse, Father, I am being entertained by it all. Tell me... Do you think I could be losing the faith?

**Priest**: My son, the ordinary, everyday problems of life – wife-swapping, divorce, drinking – are but minor difficulties compared to your dilemma. Come back to me tomorrow; I shall have spoken with a higher authority by then.

**The next day:**

**Priest**: My son, you can put your mind at rest. A solution to your problem exists and where else was it to be found but in... religion. Within a year or two, the blackguard most responsible for Garryowen's madness and for your unhappy state of mind will be plucked from our midst and transported away. Normality will return.

**Fan**: But how can I be sure of this?

**Priest**: My son, the bells of St Mary's will ring out for him... and he will answer their call.

Shortly afterwards Ward transferred to St Mary's club in Dublin.

## Lucky Numbers

Ward was one of the stars when Munster famously beat the All Blacks in 1978. After the game, a local journalist asked the coach, Tom Kiernan, whether it was a one-off. In all earnestness, Kiernan is reputed to have replied, 'You could play the All Blacks two or three times and they would beat you nine or ten times!'

## The Odd Couple

Playing for Ireland, Ward immediately struck up an instant rapport, on and off the field, with his half-back partner, Colin Patterson. It was said that they went together like ham and eggs, and that Patterson could find Ward in a darkened room. The scrum-half was heard to proclaim that Ward was not the first person he would want to meet in those circumstances!

'Patty' landed Ward in big trouble when he and the golden boy of Irish rugby appeared on *The Late, Late Show* together. Ward was involved in a serious relationship at the time and Gay Byrne asked him whether he had a girlfriend. Knowing it was completely untrue, but wanting to land his friend in trouble, Patty quipped immediately, 'One in every town'. Ward had a lot of explaining to do to his young lady after that! Ward was also asked whether he had thought about defecting to Rugby League. When Tony rejected the idea out of hand Gay turned to Patty and said:

'Tony is looking down on Rugby League, Colin, how about you?'

'When you are only 5 feet, 5 inches you can't afford to look down on anything,' Colin replied.

## The Good, the Glad and the Ollie

After he was sensationally dropped by the Irish rugby selectors on the tour to Australia in 1979, Ward became embroiled in one of the most keenly disputed controversies in the history of Irish sport. For three years a fierce debate raged: who should wear Ireland's No. 10 jersey, Ward or Ollie Campbell? Campbell thought he had finally resolved the issue with a series of stunning performances that ensured Ireland broke a thirty-three year famine and won the Triple Crown in 1982. A few weeks later, Ollie was leaving Westport one morning when he picked up an oldish lady who was visiting a friend in Castlebar Hospital. After an initial flurry of small talk, the conversation unfolded as follows:

**Her**: And what sports do you play? Do you play Gaelic?

**Ollie** (*as modestly as possible*): No, I play rugby?

*Long silence.*

**Her**: Do you know there's one thing I'll never understand about rugby?

**Ollie** (*with all due modesty*): What? I might be able to help.

*Short silence.*

**Her**: The only thing I don't understand about rugby is why Tony Ward is not on the Irish team!

In 1981 Tony Ward was brought back onto the Irish team at out-half and Campbell was in the centre; just before the game, O'Driscoll went out with Campbell for a walk through Stephen's Green. Suddenly O'Driscoll told Campbell that he was delighted he was playing in the centre. Campbell's morale lifted straight away and he inquired why. O'Driscoll replied, 'Now at least we will have somebody at out-half who can make a tackle!'

Unlike most rugby players, Campbell is renowned for his politeness. When the team were checking into their hotel in Perth, during the 1979 tour to Australia, Campbell said to the lift attendant, 'I'd be grateful if you could let me off at the sixth floor – if it isn't out of your way'.

## Supermac

One of Campbell's closest friends on the Irish team was Hugo MacNeill, who was capped thirty-seven times for Ireland. MacNeill scored eight international tries, a record for a full back, arguably making him Ireland's greatest attacking full back of all time. When he burst onto the Irish team, MacNeill was in awe of Willie Duggan, but following Duggan's retirement in 1985, their relationship was more like that between two equals. MacNeill promised to get Duggan tickets for a Scotland match. He was sharing a room with Brian Spillane and the phone rang the night before the match. Hugo answered with the words, 'The Spillane–MacNeill suite'. Immediately he heard Duggan respond, 'You might as well be sleeping together you spend so much time together on the pitch!'

Hugo got his revenge later that evening. He went out for a walk and when he came back he saw Willie, all dressed up, with a number of business friends. Duggan called Hugo over: 'Willie, it's a great thrill for me to see you here.'

'Why's that, Hugo?'

'Well, in all the years I've known you it's the first time I've seen you in the team hotel the night before a match!'

## Speaking Proper

After a sojourn in Trinity, MacNeill won two Oxford Blues, captaining them in the Varsity match. Despite his stay abroad, MacNeill maintained close contact with his colleagues on the Irish side. In his time at Oxford, he invited Ollie Campbell over to speak at one of their dinners. What did Campbell do but tell a story about him?

An American tourist had come up to MacNeill in Oxford and asked, 'Scuse me, where is the library at?'

MacNeill allegedly made no effort to conceal the contempt in his voice when he answered, 'This is England. Here we speak the Queen's English. We do not end a sentence with a preposition.'

'OK,' said the tourist 'Where is the library at, a******?'

MacNeill did get his own back on him, though. Campbell's biggest problem is that he can't say no when people ask him to do them a favour. One night, MacNeill rang him up and, putting on an accent, told him he was Mick Fitzgerald from Irish Marketing Ltd, which was organising a beauty competition. 'Fitzgerald' asked Campbell to be one of the judges, knowing full well that he would hate that kind of thing. Campbell sighed and sighed, struggling to come up with a plausible excuse. Eventually he asked what date the contest was. When 'Fitzgerald' gave him the date, Campbell replied, 'Oh, that's an awful shame. I'm really sorry but I have another function on that night. It's such a pity because I always wanted to judge a beauty contest.'

'That's no problem, Ollie. You see, one of the prizes we are going to offer is a night out with Ollie Campbell. We'll pay for everything and it'll be first class all the way.'

'Gosh, I'm afraid I'm going to have a lot of commitments around that time. I won't have many nights free.'

'But that's the beauty of this, Ollie; we'll arrange it for any night that suits you.'

The panic was getting ever more noticeable in Campbell's voice and MacNeill could visualise him writhing in his chair as he tried to find a way out of it. Eventually, Campbell explained that he was backing away from that type of thing. Then MacNeill asked him if there were any of his colleagues who would be willing to judge the show. Campbell blurted out MacNeill's name immediately and provided his phone number faster than you could say Tony Ward!

### It's Not Over Till the Subs Are Picked

MacNeill was once down in Cork with Moss Finn, Donal Lenihan and Michael Kiernan. They were having lunch with five or six rugby fans. In any other place in Ireland, sports fans would have passed the time by picking their greatest-ever Irish team. Not so in Cork. They picked the worst-ever Irish team. MacNeill kept his head down as they discussed the merits of three of his predecessors for the full back position, expecting to have his name mentioned at any minute. After they made their choice for full back, he remarked with relief, 'I suppose I can relax now'. Quick as a flash one of the fans said, 'Hang on boy, we haven't picked the subs yet!'

In 1982 MacNeill was at a festival in Malahide with Ollie Campbell. It was not long after the Triple Crown victory and they had a very high profile then. At one point MacNeill became conscious of a group of girls looking at them. He heard murmurs of, 'Yes, it is', 'No, it isn't'. Shortly afterwards, he felt someone tap him on the shoulder. It was a young lady who asked him whether he was Hugo MacNeill, the Irish rugby player. When MacNeill said he was she went back to her friends. MacNeill heard her whisper, 'Jaysus, I've never been so disappointed in all my life. He's nowhere near as good looking in real life as he is on television!'

## Theory and Practice

While Ireland had the good fortune to win two Triple Crowns in the 1980s, the 1990s were a barren decade for Irish rugby. Tactically Ireland were often exposed in key games. While Jimmy Davidson was coach, the Irish squad had a running joke about tactics: 'That will work brilliantly in practice but does it stand up in theory?'

At the end of a weekend squad session on a Sunday afternoon at Lansdowne Road, the Irish captain Terry Kingston was the butt of jokes about Plan A and Plan B. Asked to explain in the course of a television interview what that meant, Kingston said that Plan A was for the Irish side to kick the ball high at the opposition and chase after it. 'And Plan B?' asked the interviewer, Fred Cogley.

'Plan B calls for us is to kick it even higher!'

## Early Baths and Cold Showers

In the early 1990s, Bath were the kings of rugby, largely because of head coach Jack Rowell who transformed them from a team of virtual no-hopers into the cream of the crop. Rowell was renowned for his straight talking. He once described the former England prop, Gareth Chilcott, as 'green around the gills and a stranger to the lavatory'. Rowell was also a hard taskmaster. Shortly after Chilcott got married Rowell called his wife into the office and instructed her that there was to be no lovemaking before the Pilkington Cup final. Rowell handed her a bottle of sleeping tablets to ensure that her husband had a quiet night. 'How many is he to take?' she asked. 'They're not for Gareth. They're for you,' he replied.

One story typifies the pressure he put on Bath's players: Jim Waterman's son was doing his biology homework and asked his seemingly perpetually exhausted father if he knew what a condom was. Waterman's answer was, 'Of course I do; I've bloody well been carrying around one in my wallet for months!'

## Simon and Glassful

Bath star Simon Geoghegan lit up Irish rugby in the early 1990s. His performance has not always been enhanced by his Irish team-mates, however. Geoghegan was rooming with Neil Francis the night before the Fiji game in November 1995, which was Murray Kidd's first outing as team coach. Francis got thirsty during the night and drank of a glass of water he discovered in the bathroom. The next morning when Geoghegan went to retrieve his contact lenses, he discovered that Francis had unwittingly drunk them and the glass of water they were in.

## Judge and Jury

Few international players in recent years have got more media coverage than England's Austin Healey. His abrasive personality guarantees that he gets under the skin of many people, none more so than some of his team-mates. Healey had a major disappointment in 2001 when he failed to make it onto the Lions starting team. His anger was largely directed against the Lions coach, Graham Henry. Shortly after he returned home, Healey bumped into Ian McGeechan, who had coached the Lions to glory on their previous tour. McGeechan asked, 'Austin, how did the tour go?'

'Oh terrible, terrible. Yer man, Henry, took an instant dislike to me. An instant dislike.'

'Why did he take an instant dislike to you?'

'I suppose he just wanted to save time.'

Before Healey, the England player with an exceptional capacity to rub people up the wrong way was Will Carling. Carling went up to play for Harlequins in a league match that was being filmed by *Rugby Special*. After the match, Carling was set upon by a Leicester fan, who punched him on the chin. It was widely reported afterwards that it was the first time the fan had hit the s***.

# Don't Cry For Me Argentina

Willie Anderson will probably always be remembered as the player who precipitated an international diplomatic incident. Anderson was on a tour of Argentina with the Penguins in 1980 and took a shine to the Argentinian flag and decided to claim it as his own. The only problem was that he was caught and spent a few harrowing months in prison.

Anderson met Dennis Thatcher some years later and told him that he could have informed Maggie Thatcher that the Argentinians were scrapping for a war. There was an amusing postscript to the incident many years later. Willie was attending the Bermuda Classic and the Argentinians were playing the Americans. The ball went out of play and came in his direction. As he went to retrieve it, he heard one of the Argentinians say, 'Give us back the ball there, Willie, and while you're at it give us back our flag!'

## The After-dinner Speaker

In the late 1980s, Anderson was chosen as captain of Ireland. The flip side of the coin was that he had to make the speeches at the dinner. A lot of drink is consumed on those occasions and not everyone wants to listen to a speech. One of his earliest dinners as captain was after a Scottish game. During his address he looked down and he could see Kenny Milne with his hand over his mouth trying to hold back the vomit. He could only hope it was from drink and not from listening to his speech.

Anderson seemed to have an effect on Scottish players. At another Scottish dinner, he was sitting beside Craig Chalmers all night. At the end Chalmers had to be carried away on one of the tables.

## Thy Will Be Done

After captaining Ireland to a defeat against England, Anderson was talking to Will Carling at the dinner in the Hilton Hotel. It was a very sombre atmosphere, so he asked Carling to go downstairs with him for a 'wee drink'. Anderson nearly dropped dead when the barman charged him £10 for two gin and tonics. The barman wouldn't let him charge the drinks to his room. He also refused to accept Anderson's two Northern Ireland £5 notes.

Carling, who was not renowned as a big spender, had to pay for the drinks. Anderson claims there was a combination on Carling's wallet. Although Ireland lost the match, at least Anderson had the satisfaction of making the English captain buy him a drink, which was said to be a more difficult task than beating England.

## *Let's Dance*

As Irish captain, Willie Anderson was renowned for a piece of sporting theatre: Before a game against the All Blacks, Anderson led the Irish team literally up to the noses of the All Blacks in an attempt to intimidate them. Years later when Ireland played New Zealand in the Bermuda Classic, the Irish players knew Anderson would have something special planned for the 'haka'. The New Zealanders were led in the haka by their female physiotherapist. Anderson kept his hands behind his back until they had finished; he then walked up to the physiotherapist and pulled out a big bunch of flowers.

At another game, the Irish players theatrically swung over their legs, just as the All Blacks started the haka. The All Blacks weren't sure what the Irish were up to until they started singing, 'You put your left leg in and your left leg out'. The whole place cracked up.

## *The Famous Five*

In 1994, Anderson travelled to Australia as assistant coach to the Irish touring side. When the Irish seconds played the Australian thirds, Ireland were lucky to keep the defeat down to sixty points. Ken O'Connell had just joined the Irish touring party. Afterwards, Anderson went into the dressing-room where the Irish players were in a state of shock at such a hammering. He told them not to worry; they would get another chance. Anderson then asked O'Connell how he had got on. O'Connell answered, 'I sidestepped one guy five times. The only problem was that he had the ball each time!'

## *Run for Cover*

Anderson once played in the Hong Kong Sevens. He decided he would go out for an authentic Chinese meal with Jonathan Davies.

After they had finished, Davies said he was going to do a runner. Anderson told him not to be crazy because there were six guys at the door, all armed with machetes precisely to discourage people from leaving without paying their bill. Davies could do the 100 metres in about 10.5 seconds. Anderson could do it in 16.5, so sprinting off was not a realistic option for him. When Davies ran out, Anderson carefully considered his options and eventually decided to pay for both of them. When he went out, he found Davies hiding behind a dustbin!

### A Ripe Old Age

In 1985 after Ireland famously beat England to win the Triple Crown, Anderson's wife, Heather, met Seamus Heaney's wife, Marie. This was a big thrill for Heather, as she is an English teacher. A few weeks afterwards, the Andersons were at the dinner to mark the Triple Crown victory. It was the night of one of Barry McGuigan's big fights and Anderson went upstairs to watch the contest on the television, leaving Heather on her own. She was trying to make polite conversation with Ciaran Fitzgerald. However, she made a bit of a faux pas by telling him that she had met James Joyce's wife after the English match. Fitzie turned around and asked Hugo MacNeill what age would Mrs Joyce be. MacNeill answered, 'About 150!'

## Observe the Sons of Ulster Marching on

In 1999, Ulster won the European Cup final in Lansdowne Road. All of Ireland got behind Ulster team, who were bidding to become the first Irish side to win the competition. A number of prominent Ulster Unionist politicians were at Lansdowne for the occasion. One found himself in the proximity of a staunch republican, a person very much on the opposite end of the political spectrum. The Unionist turned to this staunch nationalist and said, 'How does it feel to belong to a thirty-two county Ulster?'

## More than Words

Different personalities employ a wide variety of strategies to motivate teams. Phil Bennett psyched up his team against England with the invocation, 'Look what these f*****s have done to Wales.

They've taken our coal, our water, our steel; they buy our houses and they only live in them a fortnight every twelve months. What have they given us? Absolutely nothing. We've been exploited, raped, controlled and punished by the English – and that's who you are playing this afternoon.' Wales won handsomely.

In 1984, England coach Dick Greenwood's speech to his team before their match against Australia at Twickenham was simply two words, 'England expects'. England lost 19–3.

## Matt-er of Fact

In 2003, Matt Williams led Leinster to the Heineken Cup semifinals. Williams is one of the increasing number of coaches who have made the journey from 'down under' to Ireland. Williams once described the cultural differences between Ireland and France: 'In Ireland they take you to parties and give you loads of free drink in the pubs, and then kick the daylights out of you on the pitch. They do the same in France except they don't take you to parties or give you free drink in the pubs.'

## Lights Out

One of the key players on the Leinster team is Reggie Corrigan. All around him were thrown into chaos when the floodlights failed during a Leinster match in the European Cup, plunging the ground into total darkness. Corrigan calmly said, 'It's a bit dark, isn't it?'

## The Claw

Peter 'The Claw' Clohessy is one of the legends of Irish sport. Once when Clohessy was playing for Munster, he got a bad knock on his knee and had to be carried off. It was the strangest sight the players ever saw in a match, because the stretcher-bearers were wearing wellingtons! Mick Galwey turned to the Claw and said, 'Don't worry; the fire brigade are coming'.

In 2002, Galwey and Clohessy were denied the Heineken Cup that all Ireland felt they deserved by Neil Back's infamous 'hand-of-God' backhander. The controversy spawned a new joke:

Q: What's the difference between Tim Henman and Neil Back?

A: Neil Back is much better with his backhand.

### Get Your Retaliation in First

Mick Quinn tells a story about Clohessy which dates back to Ireland's win over England in Twickenham in 1994. The Irish players decided to start a fight with the English team early in the match, in order to throw the English guys off their stride. In the dressing-room beforehand, the question arose as to who should start the fight. Everyone's eyes turned to the Claw. When the match started, Clohessy was looking around for a suitable person to fight with. He first considered Jason Leonard but he thought Leonard might be a bit of a handful, so his eyes fell on the English hooker, Brian Moore.

Moore is not the most handsome man in the world. In an alcohol-induced moment, one of his team-mates said of him, 'His front teeth are in the back of his mouth and the back teeth are in the front' and 'He was born so ugly that his mother thought his face was on fire and she decided to put it out – with a shovel!'

The Claw said to Moore, 'Listen pal, what are you going to do for a face when Saddam wants his a******e back?' Moore immediately started a bust-up, and because he struck the first blow Ireland were awarded a penalty and three easy points.

The Claw's toughness is illustrated by the suggested epitaph for his tombstone: 'What the f*** are you looking at?'

## Translations

When Warren Gatland was Irish coach, the Claw sometimes had problems deciphering Gatland's Kiwi accent. On tour to Australia, the Claw was having trouble sleeping and Gatland suggested he take a sleeping pill before the second test. The morning of the game, Gatland asked the Claw how he had slept. Claw replied, 'Great'.

'Did you take a pill?' asked Gatland.

The Claw looked very sheepish as he replied, 'Yeah, yeah, I did'.

'Did you get one off the doc?'

'What?'

'Did you get a sleeping pill off the doc?'

'Aw, f***, is that what you meant? I thought you'd asked me if I'd had a pull, not a pill.'

Warren Gatland tells the story of how one day Trevor Brennan told him he was feeling a bit tired and wondered if he had any suggestions. Gatland replied, 'Take four or five bananas and that should help'. The next morning, Brennan went up to apologise profusely, 'Gats, I'm sorry I could only manage twenty-nine bananas'. Gatland shook his head as he said, 'Trevor, I said four or five bananas not forty-five!'

## Tactical Insight

Brennan was once asked to share his thoughts on tactics. He said, 'They're cool, minty and freshen your breath'.

Another story told about Brennan is that he was walking through the city centre when he saw a man dead on the street. He pulled out his mobile phone and rang the guards. Brennan explained the situation to the guard and the boy in blue replied, 'Okay you're there in Exchequer Street. Spell Exchequer Street.'

Brennan started, 'E-x-c, no E-x-h, no....' He paused and said, 'Hang on a second. I'm just going to drag him round to Dame Street and I'll ring you back then.'

## Sleeping Beauty

Keith Wood has one blemish. During the 1997 Lions tour to South Africa, Woods shared a room with the English winger, John Bentley. As a result of his shoulder problems, Woods could only sleep in one position, with two pillows propped under both shoulders. As soon as he fell asleep, Woods started snoring loudly. After seven sleepless nights, Bentley could take no more and sought medical advice. On the eighth night as soon as Woodie started sleeping, Bentley kissed him on the cheek. For the next three nights, Woodie lay awake in case Bentley would make further advances on him.

### Knock on Wood

For years English players have been the butt of Irish jokes. In recent years though, the English lads have started taking their revenge. Invariably their prime target is Woodie. Wade Dooley tells the story of Ireland touring Japan, when the team hotel was destroyed by a massive earthquake. Searching for survivors, the local police heard a faint voice from under the rubble, 'It's Keith Wood, the Irish captain. Is anyone there?'

'Keith, Keep talking. Where are you? We're going to get you out.'

'Yes, it's me. I can hear you. I'm okay. I'm in room 247.'

English winger Dan Luger tells the story about a man who loved his garden. One day the gardener's world almost ended when he woke up to see that his pride and joy was scarred by a proliferation of molehills. The poor man was distraught, but he soon wiped his tears and got out the Yellow Pages. He saw an ad which read: 'For the best mole catcher in town, call Keith Wood – simply the best.'

As this was in the time of amateur rugby, Woodie's days as a rugby pro were still ahead of him. He was on the job instantly. He promised the man he would solve the problem. He stood on watch all night, hoping to catch the mole but with no luck. The next night he repeated the vigil but again with no sign of the mole. By now the garden owner was raging and said to Woodie, 'When you catch this damned mole, make him die the worst death you can imagine – really nasty'.

The next morning Wood was jubilant, 'I caught him, just as I promised'.

'That's wonderful news. How did you kill him?'

'Horribly,' replied Woodie. 'I buried him alive.'

## Just in Case

Justin Bishop was celebrating his first cap for Ireland on tour to South Africa. Bishop qualifies to play for Ireland under the parentage rule and as a true Londoner is not up to speed on Irish accents. An Irish fan with a strong brogue approached Bishop in the bar after his debut match and congratulated him on his performance. Bishop replied, 'Sorry, mate, I don't speak Afrikaans'.

## Fogra

Former Irish international Gary Halpin was playing for London Irish in a key cup semifinal match at Sunbury. The match was building up to a tense climax when a message came over the tannoy: 'Could the owner of car reg. No. T235 OUN please move their car?' Apparently, the car was blocking an ambulance.

Halpin was forming a scrum at the time but he ran to the sideline and admitted that it was his car that was blocking the ambulance. The match was held up for five minutes as Halpin got his keys.

## The Life of Brian

The undisputed star of the Irish team is Brian O'Driscoll. O'Driscoll has been in thrall to the game of rugby for as long as he can remember. It helps that his father, Frank, played for Ireland, as did his cousins Barry and John. Ours is an age wedded to an almost mystical concept of celebrity. O'Driscoll's mother, Geraldine, is all too aware of this. The France game in 2000, when Brian scored three tries, changed everything for Brian and, indeed, for his family. Geraldine first realised that when she was introduced to someone after the match and they said, 'This is Geraldine O'Driscoll. She used to be Frank O'Driscoll's wife. Now she's Brian O'Driscoll's mother!'

Geraldine noticed just how big Brian had become the following Halloween. She knew there would be lots of kids calling to the house trick or treating. She put bowls of sweets on the table and left Brian in charge of them. When she came back, she was shocked to find all the sweets still there and to see a bundle of pieces of paper lying beside the bowls. She asked Brian what had happened and he replied, 'The doorbell hasn't stopped ringing all evening but none of the kids want the sweets. They just want my autograph!'

After his hat trick of tries for Ireland against France, Brian's nickname became 'God'. Everybody loves a winner. When Ireland travelled to Rome to play Italy in 2001, the team was granted an audience with the Pope. Injury forced O'Driscoll to miss the trip. Pope John Paul II is said to be still eagerly awaiting his audience with Brian O'Driscoll!

# Chapter Three
# Hookers and Swingers

GOLF IS a game in which purple people pursue white balls over green hills. It has a long and colourful history. On 6 March 1457, Scotland's James II banned playing of both 'Fute-ball and Golfe'; they were interfering with the practice of archery and thus threatened the defence of the realm!

## The Haig

*Sugar, Sugar*

The game of golf has produced many great characters – none greater than Walter Charles Hagen. The Haig won eleven major championships: four British Opens, five US PGA titles and two US Opens. In the light of his achievements, it is surprising that his name does not feature more prominently in golfing parlance – particularly as his off-the-course activities were the stuff of legend. The Haig was the sort of man you wouldn't invite home to meet your mother even if you were certain she was out. He explained the secret of his success with women: 'Call every woman "Sugar" and you can't go wrong.'

*A Healthy Lifestyle*

Off the course, the Haig was seldom seen without a cigarette in the one hand (he got through fifty a day) and a large Scotch on the rocks on the other. He was careful to preserve his 'tearaway' image – so much so that on the few evenings he allowed himself the benefits of an early night he instructed his caddy, Spec Hammond, to crumple up his tuxedo so that the next morning everyone in the clubhouse would think he had spent the night painting the town red.

Not that Hagen often needed such deception. He once lost a seventy-two-hole challenge by a whopping eighteen and seventeen, owing to the mother of all hangovers.

## A Royal Occasion

The Haig was something of the *bête noire* of the British golfing establishment; like the majority of his American professional colleagues he was barred from attending most of the leading clubhouses. On one occasion, Hagen was invited to dine with the Prince of Wales at Royal St George. As they prepared to order their meal, a stuffy member approached the prince and drew his attention to the rules. The furious prince roared, 'If you don't stop this nonsense I shall take the "Royal" out of St George's'.

During the 1920 British Open, Hagen thumbed his nose to the clubhouse ban by booking a suite at the Ritz and driving to the course every day in a Daimler limousine, accompanied by his butler. The Haig was served in the most public way possible, with a five-course lunch using the most exquisite china and the most immaculate crystal for drinking vintage champagne.

## The Perfect Arrangement

Edna Hagen, the Haig's second wife, explained her divorce on the perfectly reasonably grounds: 'The only place I can find him is on the sports pages.' Before the break-up Hagen joked, 'My wife and I still have romance in our lives. We have candle-lit dinners twice a week. She goes on Tuesdays and I go on Thursdays.'

## A Picture Tells a Thousand Words

Hagen turned his hand briefly to painting. After painting a picture of the eighteenth at Royal St George, he asked his friend, 'Go on, be honest with me and tell me what's your opinion of my painting?'

'It's not worth anything.'

'I know, but I'd like to hear it anyway.'

## The Road to Damascus

Hagen made history in 1922 at Sandwich, when he became the first American-born winner of the British Open, on foot of an epic confrontation with George Duncan. The following year, he came second. His response to the disappointment was to invite the crowd of spectators to the local pub, where he paid for drinks for everyone.

Shortly afterwards, Hagen publicly announced to the media that he had given up drink. His Pauline conversion lasted all of three days, and he was horrified later that week to discover that he had put two empty whiskey bottles into his dustbin. He explained to his friend, 'You can imagine my embarrassment. I got rid of them fast because I didn't want the binman to let the world know I was back on the drink again so quickly.'

'So what did you do with them?' asked his friend.

'Oh, I put them in the priest's dustbin down the road. Everyone knows he doesn't drink.'

The Haig was once asked, 'If you had to give up wine or women, which would you choose?' He thought for a moment, 'That would rather depend on the vintage of each'.

### Erections

Hagen didn't always have the best of relations with his neighbours. One of them was a DIY enthusiast and was putting up a monument. Hagen commented, 'The person next door has a large erection in his back garden which is unsightly and dangerous'.

### Beauty Sleep

Hagen made a trip to Scotland to play in a tournament. He was staying in a plush hotel. The next morning, the manager inquired how he had slept. Hagen replied, 'Okay, but the people in the room above me are very annoying. Last night, they stomped and banged on the floor until midnight.'

'That's terrible,' said the manager. 'Did they keep you awake long?'

'No. Luckily I was still up, playing my new bagpipes.'

### Sweet Revenge

Hagen once approached an attractive woman sitting alone in a busy bar. 'Excuse me,' he said, 'may I buy you a drink?'

'What, to a motel?' she screamed, trying to embarrass him.

'No, no,' protested the Haig. 'You misunderstood. I just asked if I could buy you a drink.'

'You are asking me to go to a motel?' she screamed, even louder.

Completely bewildered, the Haig retreated to a corner table while everybody glared at him indignantly. After ten minutes the young woman came over to explain. 'I'm, sorry to have created such a scene,' she said. 'I'm a psychology student studying human behaviour in unexpected situations.'

The Haig looked at her and shouted, 'What? A hundred dollars?'

### *A Last Wish*

The Haig, who was suffering from throat cancer, died at the age of seventy-six, following an operation to remove his larynx. The manner in which he reacted to his illness encapsulated his approach to life. On the way to hospital for the surgery, he stopped in no less than ten bars and when they finally reached their destination he made a pass at one of the nurses! Asked about coping with old age, the Haig answered, 'You know you're getting old when your back goes out more often than you do'.

A few years previously, Hagen underwent a very complicated operation and afterwards kept complaining about a bump on his head and a terrible headache. Since his operation had been an intestinal one, there was no reason why he should be complaining of a headache. Eventually, the nurse, fearing that he might be suffering from post-operative shock, spoke to the doctor about it. The doctor assured the nurse, 'Don't worry about a thing. He really does have a bump on his head. About half way through the operation, we ran out of anaesthetic.'

## Uncle Sam

Q: What do golfers have in common with President George Bush?

A: They are not always the most up to date on international affairs.

The great Sam Snead was asked in the course of a crisis in the Middle East, 'What do you think of Iraq?' He responded, 'I've never played it. Who's the pro there?' Asked later that week what he thought of Beruit, he replied, 'I think it's a great aftershave lotion'.

An excited woman once told him, 'I got a set of clubs for my husband'. Snead replied, 'Lucky you, what a swap!'

A female journalist once asked Snead, 'Are all top golf players conceited?' He replied, 'I don't really know but I'm not'.

During a recreational game, Snead was so puzzled to see his partner taking so much care before driving from the fifth tee that he asked, 'Why this intense concentration?'

'I'm very anxious to make this shot a good one,' said his partner. 'My mother-in-law is down there in the clubhouse watching me.'

'Impossible,' said Snead. 'You could never hit her from this distance.'

## A Close Shave ·

Lee Trevino's career nearly ended when he was struck by lightning during the Western Open in 1975. Trevino's comment was, 'I should have been carrying a 1-iron that day. Even God can't hit a 1-iron.' Bob Hope had a different take on it, 'If I'm on the course and lightning starts, I get inside fast. If God wants to play through, let him.'

### *Lee and Love*

Trevino famously said at the US Open in 1974, 'I have to win this tournament. My wife bought $50,000 worth of furniture last week. And you should see the house she built around it.' Many top golfers, particularly those who have experienced a costly divorce, would empathise. Rex Caldwell spoke for all when he said, 'I'm not winning, but I think my ex-wife is the twelfth leading money winner on tour'.

Golf widows don't like staying home alone indefinitely, and many golfing marriages go through problems. Lee Trevino experienced this at first hand in 1983 when his wife, Claudia, left him. Trevino commented, 'It was a complete surprise to me, but, on the other hand, it didn't surprise me at all. That'll happen when you haven't been home in eighteen years.'

Trevino remained impressed by one of her talents: 'My ex-wife is great at bird imitations. She watches me like a hawk. She hasn't spoken to me for a few months now. I don't want to interrupt her.'

Nonetheless, every cloud has a silver lining. Trevino remarried a different Claudia. He saw the practical advantages immediately. 'Same name; that way I won't forget it. And I don't have to change the towels. I got a $1.4 million home with my initials all over it, so I might as well live with someone whose name begins with a C.'

After all the publicity about his marriages, Trevino was walking to tee off in a tournament when he heard two women discussing his love life. The first asked, 'How many wives has that man had?'

The second replied with another question, 'You mean apart from his own?'

Trevino was well able to joke about his life of domestic bliss. 'My wife gave me ten oysters last night to get me in the mood for a night of passion. I think only nine of them worked out.'

## Seeing the Woods from the Tees

Tiger Woods was a golf prodigy to end all prodigies. Yet when Sandy Lyle was asked his opinion of Tiger in 1992, he replied, 'I don't know. I've never played there.'

Tiger was once nicknamed Urkel by his friends because he was so geeky. Tiger does not like distractions. With his 'Tiger Slam' in reach, Woods strode purposefully and proudly towards the eighteenth green of the 2000 British Open. However, the limelight was sensationally taken off him when Jacqui Salmond, an attractive thirty-three-year-old lapdancer, streaked on the green and seemed to mistake the flag for a stripper's pole. Unlike the crowd, Tiger was unimpressed. He said, 'It's a shame because I wanted to walk up there and have a special moment. I don't think running down the fairway without your clothes on showed the proper respect.' Most of the fans though were more than happy with her barefaced cheek.

### Eye of the Tiger

During one of Tiger's victories in the Masters, a crowd of golfing worshippers were watching television in the pub, marvelling at his genius. Two Cork hurling fans in the audience were less than impressed as the crowd went wild when Tiger sank a 30-foot putt. The elder Cork fan shook his head clearly unmoved: 'Sure twas asy for him do that, boy, cos there was no one to mark him.'

## I'm Alright, Jack

Before the emergence of Tiger Woods, Jack Nicklaus bestrode the world of golf like a Colossus. At one stage, Nicklaus was invited to attend a major corporate event on the theme of motivation. He sat at the back of the conference hall while the opening speaker gave an incredibly boring speech. Halfway through his speech, he noticed his distinguished guest and said, 'If you can't hear me at the back, there is a vacant seat at the front'.

Nicklaus replied, 'I can't hear you, but I'm quite happy where I am, thank you.'

During the height of Nicklaus' powers, the *Cork Examiner* sought an interview with him. When their request was put to Nicklaus' PR person, he shook his head firmly saying, 'My client would have no interest in being interviewed in a publication that is about nothing but corks'.

## Nasty Nick?

Nick Faldo often had strained relations with the media. *Sports Illustrated* famously said that his idea of an evening out was 'dinner for one on the hotel balcony'. Faldo didn't do much to court their favour and try to reverse this situation. In 1992 he burst into tears after a brave and hard-won victory at Muirfield. The media might have turned him into a Gazza-style hero, as they done to Paul Gascoigne after he cried at Italia '90. Before a *rapprochement* occurred, Faldo scuppered the deal in his acceptance speech when he thanked the media, 'from the heart of my bottom'.

Faldo was frustrated that he had to spend so long waiting for his dinner to be served in a posh restaurant. When the meal finally arrived he said, 'You tell me, you're the same fellow who took my order. Somehow, I expected a much older waiter.'

### Frugal Comforts

Some of his critics portray Faldo as being a bit tight with money. One wag suggested that his idea of a Christmas treat for his children was to take them to Santa's grave!

One of the stories told about Faldo, always behind his back, goes back to early in his first marriage. He had been away a long time on the tour and thought it would be good to bring his wife a little gift. 'How about some perfume?' he asked the girl in the cosmetics department. She showed him a bottle costing £100, 'That's too much,' he said. The girl then said, 'We do have this smaller bottle for £50'.

'That's still too much,' he said. The girl bought out a tiny £20 bottle, but even that was too costly for him. 'What I mean is,' he said, 'I'd like to see something really cheap'.

The girl handed him a mirror.

Early in his career Faldo's caddy was trying to persuade him to give him a rise. When Faldo saw his caddie, who was a little portly, eating a cottage cheese salad he asked, 'Are you trying to lose weight?'

'Oh, no,' the caddie replied. 'I'm on a low salary diet.'

### Always Keep Your Head

Faldo tells the story of the golfer who was so bad that he threw his clubs into a pond. Then he dived in himself. His caddie thought he was going to drown, but then he remembered the golfer couldn't keep his head down long enough.

### The Perfect Partnership

Faldo's most famous caddie was Fanny Sunneson. This spawned an obvious joke: 'Some days Faldo like to play with a Fanny. Other days he like to play with himself.'

### Expert Advice

Faldo was practising one day when a fan came up and asked if he could stand and watch him. Faldo hit four perfect balls and then paused to take a practice swing. The fan said, 'Did you know that your practice swing is not the same as your actual swing?'

## The Great White Shark

Apart from his skill on the course, Greg Norman is also known for his habit of crumbling at the wrong times in major championships, and for occasionally putting his foot in his mouth. Norman tends to be as spectacular in defeat as in victory. In 1986, he led all four majors after three rounds but ended up only winning the British Open. Norman has lost a play-off in each of the four majors. In the wake of his wonderful last round in the 1993 British Open, he was making all the right noises about how thrilled he was to win against a leader board packed with great players and about how much it meant to him to win golf's most historic tournament for a second time.

Then his humility deserted him and he said, 'You know, I'm not usually one to brag, but I was in awe of myself out there today'.

In fairness, Norman can also tell stories about himself. After the 1979 US Open, he boarded a flight in Toledo, when his eyes caught sight of the flight attendant, Laura. He told his friend, 'I bet you I'll marry that girl'. By the end of the flight, Laura had gone into the cockpit and told the captain, 'I think I've just fallen in love with a golfer'.

'A golfer,' said the captain, an ardent golfing disciple. 'Which one?'

'I think his name is Greg Norman,' she said.

'No way,' the captain answered. 'There's no golfer named Greg Norman.'

Norman generally practiced at Bay Hill, near Orlando, Florida, where he and Laura built a home. Before John Daly emerged on the scene, Norman was considered a big hitter. One of the jokes told about him is that one day he was hitting some tee shots in the general direction of the Atlantic Ocean. One of his shots was so hard that Cuba fired back!

Norman tells the story of the golfer whose ball had stopped near the edge of a lake. The golfer hit the shot and when he followed through too far, he tumbled into the water. As the golfer was going down for the third time he had one hand sticking out of the water. His caddie nudged the other caddie in the group and said, 'I think he wants a 5-iron'.

## The Fully Monty

Colin Montgomerie tells the story of the golfer who barked at his caddie, 'Will you please stop looking at your watch all the time? It's very distracting!' The caddie replied, 'It's not my watch, sir, it's my compass'.

Another of Monty's stories is of a groom who said to his bride just after they got married, 'I've got a confession to make: I love golf. I sleep, eat and breathe golf. I'm obsessed with golf. You must realise that it completely dominates my life.'

The bride turned to her new husband and said, 'Thank you for being so honest. Now I have something to tell you: I'm a hooker.'

'No problem,' the groom said, taking her wrists. 'You hold your left hand just a little higher than the right, with your thumb down there...'

## Viva El Spania

Severiano Ballesteros was born on 9 April 1957, in the tiny Spanish town of Pedrena. The youngest son of a peasant farmer, Seve grew up running barefoot and free in the wild and rugged beautiful country of northern Spain. His brother fashioned Seve's first golf club from the head of an old three-iron and a stick.

Seve fell in love with Carmen Botin, the daughter of one of Spain's wealthiest bankers, but was denied her hand for twelve years because her parents didn't think a man with his peasant background was good enough for her. Only when he had amassed a fortune and earned a reputation consistent with their own high standards, did they relent. Perhaps because of his humble origins, Seve earned a reputation for demanding high appearance fees. Accordingly, when Seve's first child, Baldomero, was born after Carmen had gone through a long labour, it was rumoured that the baby was delaying his birth because he was demanding appearance money.

## Penny Wise and...

Brian 'Save A Shilling' Shurrock played on the tour in the 1970s. Shurrock was very, very careful with money. At one point, he was given the choice of flying or driving from Madrid to the south of Sardinia for the Italian Open; he decided to drive. Shurrock set off for Marseille one Friday afternoon, only to discover on arrival that there was no ferry to Sardinia for three days. He had to fly after all, but the only flight available was one to the northern tip of Corsica. When he arrived in Corsica, he hired a car and drove the length of the country in a manner of which Eddie Irvine would have been proud.

Shurrock stayed overnight in a hotel but was down at the harbour as the dawn was breaking the next day to get a boat to Sardinia. He eventually secured a boat trip but at a king's ransom. When they landed, the captain of the boat flagged down a passing Mini, and had an intense conversation with the driver, not a word of which Shurrock understood. The conversation concluded with both men loading Shurrock's luggage into the car. The golfer breathed a sigh of relief. The driver smiled at Shurrock as he got into the car and Brian thought at last his luck was turning. His joy was short-lived. After about 500 yards the driver stopped beside a bus stop, dumped a stunned Shurrock and his luggage on the side of the road and fled away even faster than Brian had driven in Corsica.

The bus arrived a full three hours later, by which time Shurrock's blood pressure was at a dangerous level. The bus only went as far as the town centre. Shurrock then caught a train to Is Molas, the tournament venue, just before midnight on the Sunday. By this time he had spent a small fortune. If he was to simply recoup his expenses on the trip, he needed to finish well in the tournament. Tragically, he took a wrong drop at a water hazard in the very first round, the next day, and was promptly disqualified!

### Share and Share Dislike

Another time Shurrock was playing in a pro-am with a wealthy banker, who was taking a drink at every tee but never asked Shurrock if he'd like a sip. On the fifth hole it started to rain, and on the ninth hole, as the rain teamed down, the banker looked at Shurrock and said, 'Aren't there any dry spots around here?' Shurrock replied, 'Well, you could start with the back of my throat'.

## There's No Show Like a Joe Show

Joe Carr was perhaps the greatest amateur international golfer Ireland ever produced. After his retirement, Carr was appointed captain of the Walker Cup team but did not initially get the respect he was entitled to. The players were arguing amongst themselves about the best tactics to deploy, as if their captain were the invisible man. Carr came up with an imaginative method to get them back on track. He said, 'Anybody who's won one championship stand up'. Six players stood up.

'Anyone who has won two.' Fewer stood up.

'Anyone won three?' Fewer still.

'Anyone won four or five?' There was dead silence.

'Anyone, other than me, won thirty?' Everybody looked at their shoes. Then Carr established his authority by simply saying, 'Okay, this is what we'll do?'

One of the players that Carr found most difficult to deal with was Ronan Rafferty. Rafferty once showed up twenty minutes late for a meeting. Carr said, 'You should have been here at nine o'clock, Rafferty.'

Ronan replied, 'Why, what happened?'

Late in 1990, Carr was invited to become captain of the Royal and Ancient Golf Club of St Andrews, one of the most prestigious posts in golf; in the process he became the first Irish captain of golf's ruling body. He first went over to St Andrews in his official capacity in spring 1991. He brought with him a speech that had been lovingly crafted with the help of top public relations guru and speech writing expert, Tom Savage. The speech discussed the way in which golf was a unifying force in Ireland, north and south. Carr had gone over and over it like a Leaving Cert student swotting for the Honours Maths paper. After Carr was officially announced as captain, he turned around to the MC and asked, 'When do I speak?'

The man replied, 'Next September'.

## Mr Darcy's Pride and Present

Eamonn Darcy has long been one of the most popular golfers on the Irish circuit, but at one stage he was the victim of a wind-up in Barcelona. The culprit was Chris Moody, one of the tour's great mischief-makers. Moody was having a drink in a bar with another golfer, Donald Sterling. The centrepiece of the bar was a huge magnum of champagne. Moody said to Sterling, 'I could nick that'. Sterling bet him that he couldn't nick the champagne. Moody kept his eyes peeled on the bar and for a brief moment both barmen went missing. With a speed that the Artful Dodger could never have matched, Moody went around the bar and had the champagne tucked underneath his jacket.

That amount of devilment would have been enough for most people, but not Chris Moody. He walked up to Eamonn Darcy, who was having a quiet drink with friends in the corner and said, 'We've had our differences in the past, but I'd like to show you that there's no hard feelings'. With that, he presented Darcy with the champagne.

Darcy had missed Moody's activity behind the bar and was gobsmacked at such apparent generosity. He thanked Moody profusely. Moody withdrew modestly and gracefully. Darcy was about to open the champagne, when he was set up on by two barmen screaming incomprehensibly in Spanish as they tried to wrestle it away from him. Sterling was watching with concern as the dispute showed all the signs of turning ugly. He said, 'Chris, you'd better say something'. He turned around to plead with Moody, but by then Moody had vanished. Darcy was left hanging high and dry.

## My Business

Moody was once in a busy office when a computer crashed and began to make a strange noise, like a heart monitor. Moody asked, 'Does anyone here know how to do mouse-to-mouse?'

## Directions

Another time, Moody went into a bus depot with a friend and said to the clerk, 'I want to buy a ticket for Norwald'.

A puzzled look came over the clerk's eyes, and he began frantically to search through his destination book. The clerk said, 'I don't see Norwald listed here, and for the life of me I can't find it anywhere on the map. Where is Norwald exactly?'

'Over there,' Moody replied cockily. 'He's my brother-in-law.'

## Padraig's Parade

### A Good Result Spoiled

It is said that when a prominent former Irish golfer, who shall remain nameless because of the libel laws, dies, the presiding clergyman will have to break with liturgical convention. Such is this man's liking for publicity that instead of saying 'May perpetual light shine upon him' the vicar will probably say, 'May perpetual limelight shine upon him'.

Padraig Harrington is cast in a very different mould. For this reason everybody hopes that the one award he will never win is the NPNTHWAM – the Nicest Player Never To Have Won A Major. His popularity was wonderfully captured by Ted Walsh's proud boast, 'I must admit that I do be delighted to bulls*** that I know him'.

### Sauce for the Goose

In October 2002, South Africa's Retief Goosen and Harrington were locked in battle as to who would win the Order of Merit. At the start of the Madrid Open, Goosen complained that Harrington was 'the slowest player in Europe'. Harrington replied, 'That's the pot calling the kettle black'. The next day, Harrington shot 65, while Goosen received a slow play warning. The *Star* reflected the irony of the situation with its headline, 'What's Good For The Goose....'

### *Almost Perfect*

One of the stories told about Harrington goes back to his time in college. It was mischievously claimed that, because of golf practice, Harrington attended only one lecture in a long course but subsequently sat the examination and obtained a mark of 95 per cent. When the astounded tutor asked him to explain this, Harrington is said to have replied, 'Well, sir, I had hoped to get 100 per cent, but the lecture confused me'.

## Don't Play It Again, Sam

In 2002, Harrington was part of the European team that reclaimed the Ryder Cup. The team captain was Sam Torrance. As a player, Torrance was famous for sleepwalking around hotels as naked as the moment he was born. In 1993, Torrance withdrew from the English Open after bruising his chest sleepwalking into a flowerpot. He said, 'I remember waking up and seeing this thing, and I thought someone was in my room. I ran at it and cracked my sternum.'

## Hopelessly Devoted

Golf has always attracted celebrities, the most famous of which is probably Bob Hope. In an effort to improve his game, Hope went for a lesson and made the mistake of asking, 'Should I bend my knees more?' The pro replied, 'Yes and pray, brother, pray!'

Hope claimed that he once hit an alligator so hard that it became his golf bag. He was famous for his remarks about the former American president Gerry Ford's shortcomings on the golf course: 'His golf is improving; he's hitting fewer spectators.'

Hope was playing with a friend one day when his partner said, 'Did you hear about Bill?'

'No,' replied Hope curiously, 'what about him?'

'He went mad last week and beat his wife to death with a golf club.'

Hope shuddered. 'God, that's awful.'

They paused for a moment's reflection, and then Hope asked, 'How many strokes?'

After a dismal performance on the course, Hope asked his caddie, 'So what's my score?'

'Fifteen, sir.'

'Could be worse. Let's try the second hole.'

### Man and Wife

Hope told the story about one of his friends who was a keen golfer. On one particular afternoon, he was joined by his wife and was having a disastrous time. Teeing off on the fourteenth, he pulled his shot so badly it spun off towards a groundsman's hut. Unfortunately, the hut was obstructing the line. However, his wife noticed that the hut had two doors, and that if both doors were opened it was possible to play through.

The man asked his wife to go around the back and open the far door. Sure enough, there was a clear path through to the green, although the ball needed to keep flat. He pulled out a wood, lined up and took the shot. As the ball cracked off, his wife looked around the doorway. Tragically, the ball hit her in the centre of the forehead, killing her stone dead.

A few weeks later, the new widower was playing the same course with a friend. Again, he pulled his shot at the fourteenth, and ended up in front of the hut. 'Hey, you might be able to play through if we opened both doors,' observed the friend. The man shuddered and went pale. 'No way. Very bad memories. Last time I did that, I ended up with a seven.'

## The Rat Pack

The galleries always flocked to see Hope play, especially when he brought his showbiz pals. At one pro-am Dean Martin was five up on Bing Crosby, and that was before they left the bar. *Kojak* star Telly Savalas was another regular; he had played a cop so long that when he struck a wild shot he screamed 'Freeze!' instead of 'Fore'. During his Dirty Harry phase, Clint Eastwood was easy to spot on the course. He was the only one who carried his putter in a holster.

Another regular was Sammy Davis Jr, who had a penchant for wearing jewellery. Whenever he hit the ball 80 yards, his jewellery flew 100. Sammy was asked on the golf course about his handicap. He replied, 'I'm a one-eyed Jewish Negro. What's yours?' After a terrible round of golf Davis was asked how it went. He replied, 'I missed a spectacular hole in one – by only five strokes. At least I hit two good balls today. I stepped on a rake.'

### An Unhappy Coincidence

One day Davis was having a very bad round. He was thirty over par after four holes, had lost fourteen balls in the same piece of water and had practically ploughed the rough trying to get a ball out. Then, on the green of the fifth, his caddy coughed just as he took a 10-inch putt, and he sliced it. Davis went wild. 'You've got to be the worst damn caddie in the whole wide world.' The caddie looked at him sourly, and replied, 'I doubt it. That would be too much of a coincidence.'

### When Two and Two Make...

After that, Davis chose his caddies more carefully. His interview for the successful applicant for the post as caddie went as follows:

'Ok, caddie, can you count?'

'Certainly, Mr Davis.'

'So what is four plus five plus three?'

'Nine, Mr Davis.'

'You're hired.'

### A Pair Like No Other

Davis once agreed to play a foursome with Burt Reynolds but the two other players didn't turn up. Davis was frustrated, but Reynolds told him not to worry about it because he would sort out their problem. Mindful of her two most famous assets, he simply called Dolly Parton.

### All in the Game?

It was said that when Arnold Palmer hit the ball the earth shook. Bob Hope asked him how he liked Hope's game. Palmer replied, 'Well it's okay, but I still prefer golf'.

Bing Crosby once asked Palmer to help him with his game. Palmer replied, 'I've already seen your game. I think you should take up tennis.' Crosby got his retaliation in by saying on one of his television shows, 'Arnold Palmer shot three eagles yesterday. Unfortunately, he was in his plane at the time. Arnold has also gone on a fitness programme. He started jogging and gave up smoking. He only coughs now when his opponent is putting.'

### Etiquette

Crosby's wife asked him why he no longer played with the bishop. Bing replied, 'Would you play with a man who swears and curses with every shot, who cheats in the bunkers, who alters his scorecard when you're not looking and who never buys a drink in the bar afterwards?'

'Certainly not,' his shocked wife replied.

'Well, neither will the bishop.'

### What a Drag

Another row between Crosby and his wife occurred when Bing arrived home from the golf course several hours late. 'We had a problem,' he said. 'Bill collapsed and died on the second hole and from then on it was play the ball, drag Bill, play the ball, drag Bill....'

### On Thin Ice

Bing Crosby and Bob Hope were playing near the edge of a course one winter's day. Hope looked over the fence in amazement and said, 'Look! Those idiots over there are out skating on the pond in this blizzard.'

## Amateur Corner

An amateur stepped up to the tee and drove off. The ball sailed down the fairway, leaped off the green and rolled into the hole. He did a dance of delight. 'Have you gone stone mad?' asked his wife, who was trying to learn the game in the interest of improved marital relations.

'I just got a hole in one,' screamed the golfer, with a glint in his eye.

'Did you really, dear?' his wife asked placidly. 'Do it again, dear – I didn't see you.'

A novice golfer was frantically trying to get out of the bunker: 'I'd move heaven and earth to break 100.'

'Try heaven,' suggested his partner. 'I think you've already moved enough earth.'

A frustrated golfer who was on course for a huge score said, 'I'm certainly not playing the game I used to play'.

His disgusted caddie replied, 'What game was that, sir?'

A golf pro, employed by a club to give lessons, was approached by two cheeky chappies. 'Do you want to learn to play golf?' the pro asked them.

'Not me,' said one, 'it's Peter here. He wants to learn. I learned yesterday.'

A golf professional was struggling to keep his patience: 'Now, suppose you just go through the motions without hitting the ball.'

'But,' protested the pupil, 'that's just the difficulty I'm trying to overcome'.

A bad golfer kept losing balls and his caddie said to him, 'Don't you think it would be better and cheaper if you played with some old balls?'

The player replied, 'I have never had a ball long enough for it to be old'.

One old golfer could still hit the ball pretty well but the problem was he couldn't see where it went. Accordingly, he had a hard time getting a game. One day the club pro told him, 'Peter, I've got just the right partner for you. Paul's about your age and he's got eyes like a hawk.'

The two guys got together and on the first tee Peter hit his drive, turned to Paul and asked, 'Did you see it?'

'Yes.'

'Where did it go?'

'I forgot.'

## True Passions

A husband came home from work and found his wife sobbing in front of the television set. 'How in the world can you get worked up over the troubles of people on *Coronation Street*?' he asked.

'I suppose it's the same as your shouting and getting excited when you see men you don't even know grab a little ball and chase up and down a golf course with it.'

Most golfers don't really believe that there are golf widows. An ardent golfer was talking to one of his friends on the tenth hole: 'For years I couldn't imagine where my wife spent her evenings!'

The friend was expecting to be told about an affair and asked, 'And what have you found out?'

'Well, one evening I went home… and there she was.'

Another golfing widow was furious that her husband was spending so much time on the golf course. Her husband smiled beatifically at her and replied, 'But, darling, didn't you hear what the doctor said? He told me that I needed more greens.'

A middle-aged couple had played golf together for most of their married life. One night over the evening meal, she mused: 'If I die before you, will you get married again?'

Although he was absorbed in the evening newspaper, he muttered, 'I guess so'.

'Would you play golf with her?'

'I guess so,' he mumbled.

'Would you take her to our club?'

'I guess so,' he said.

'Surely you wouldn't let her use my clubs?'

'No, of course not. Anyway, she's left-handed.'

## Simply Delicious

In Papua, New Guinea, the membership of the first golf club was made up almost exclusively of cannibals. There was a special dinner to mark the end of the first captain of the club's year of office. During the course of the meal, one member turned to his neighbour and said, 'You know, I don't really like the captain'.

'Really?' said the neighbour. 'In that case, why don't you just eat the vegetables.'

## Legal Eagles

American society is notoriously litigious. One golf club in California was sued by a member whose wig blew away during eighteen holes. A committee was formed to establish whether this amounted to loss of limb, loss of personal property or loss of golf accessories.

## Nothing but the Best

In one street in a Swedish town there were three golf shops. The sign outside the first read, 'Best golf shop in the world'. The second proclaimed, 'Best golf shop in town'. To which the third replied, 'Best golf shop in the street'.

## A Golfer's Best Friend

Caddies are an integral part of the golfing landscape. One of the game's most lovable stars was the great Max Faulkner. Appropriately his caddie was an equally colourful personality, who rejoiced in the name Mad Mac. Regardless of the weather, Mac wore a selection of topcoats. Beneath these layers, he wore several ties but curiously no shirt. He always carried a pair of opera glasses from which the lenses had long since disappeared. After peering through this unorthodox device at the line of a putt, he would offer the following gem of advice, 'Hit it slightly straight, sir.'

A beginner observed, 'Golf's a funny old game'.

A Scottish caddie replied, 'It's not intended to be funny and the way you play it, it's downright tragic'.

A golfer with a history of poor scores, shot an 86 in a pro-am. It was one of the best results of his career. He was so excited that he almost wet himself, and tried to impress some of the gallery and imply that he was having an off day and said, 'I wasn't myself today'.

His caddie took the wind out of his sails and gave the game away, 'I noticed that all right. You were much better than usual.'

Golfers though don't always give the respect to their caddies they deserve. Many golfers seem to think that a caddie's role is to keep their clubs clean and their balls warm. The great Bobby Jones famously said, 'If I needed advice from my caddie, he'd be hitting the shots and I'd be carrying the bag'.

A golfer said to his caddie, 'This is a terrible course. I've never played on a worse one.'

The caddie replied, 'But this isn't the course. We left that more than an hour ago.'

## Foreplay

An old married couple, no longer able to play a full round of golf, still managed a round on the putting green every day, following which they dozed off to sleep in chairs on the club veranda. One day, the woman woke up, picked up her putter and walloped her sleeping husband across the shins. He woke up in a state of shock, 'What's that for?'

'Forty-eight years of lousy sex.'

Back they went to sleep. This time, he woke up, grabbed his putter and smashed her on the shins.

'What's that for?' she asked.

'For knowing the difference.'

## Heaven's Above

A golfer was playing in the rain. The water was up to his knees and along came a rowboat and a voice asked, 'Can I help you?'

The golfer replied, 'No, I'm fine. I made a deal with God'.

The rains were soon up to the golfer's chest and along came a helicopter and a voice asked, 'Can I help you?'

The golfer replied, 'No, I made a deal with God'.

The water was soon over the golfer's head, and he drowned. When he got to heaven, the golfer ran into God and asked, 'What happened to our deal?'

God answered, 'I don't know – I sent a rowboat and a helicopter for you'.

# Strokes for Cavan Folks

Two Cavanmen, Mick and Joe, were out playing golf, and they decided to put some competition into the game by staking some serious money on the round – €1. With such a sum at stake, both men were concentrating fiercely, and they were perfectly matched for the first nine holes. On the tenth, though, Mick drove into the rough and couldn't find his ball. He called Joe over to help and the pair searched around. Finally, desperate to avoid the four-stroke penalty for a lost ball, Mick popped a new ball out of his pocket when Joe wasn't looking. 'Joe, I've found the ball,' said Mick.

'You filthy, cheating swine!' exploded Joe. 'I never thought that any friend of mine would stoop so low as to cheat in a game that had money on it.'

'I'm not cheating!' protested Mick. 'I've found my ball, and I'll play it where it lies.

'That's not your ball,' snarled Joe. 'I've been standing on your ball for the last five minutes.'

# Knowing the Score

Three men assembled for a round of golf on Mother's Day. All three were quite surprised at having been able to escape from the family for the day, and so they compared notes on how they managed it. The first bloke, who was from Roscommon, said, 'I bought my wife a dozen red roses, and she was so surprised and touched that she let me go'.

The second, who was from Sligo, said, 'I bought my wife a diamond ring, and she was so thrilled that she let me go'.

The third man, who was from Cavan said, 'Last night I had a big feed of garlic. When I woke up this morning, I rolled on top of my wife, breathed with gusto onto her face and asked, 'Golf course or intercourse?'

She blinked and replied, 'I'll put your clubs in the car'.

# Answered Prayers

While playing golf, a man found a corked bottle on the green. Upon opening it, a genie appeared and granted the fellow one wish. After thinking about it for a while, the man said, 'I'd like to shoot par golf regularly'.

'No problem,' said the genie. 'But understand that your sex life will be greatly reduced as a side effect.'

'I can handle that,' the man replied. Several months later, the genie reappeared on the same golf hole and asked the man how his golf was going.

'Fantastic!' said the man. 'I'm now carrying a scratch handicap.'

'And what effect has it had on your sex life?' the genie inquired.

'I still manage to have relations a couple of times a month.'

The genie said, 'That's not much of a sex life.'

Well,' the fellow responded, 'it's not bad for a middle-aged priest with a very small parish'.

## When a Man Loves Two Women

Two men, who played a regular game of golf every Saturday, usually on different courses, were playing round a majestically wooded course when they ran into two ladies playing ahead and doing so very slowly. After two or three holes, one of the deadly duo decided to ask the women if they could play through. He went forward, disappeared behind trees and bushes and returned a few minutes later.

'Can we play through?' asked his companion.

'No! I never asked them. I discovered that it was my wife and my mistress.'

'Gosh, that was a narrow escape,' said his friend. 'I'll go and ask.'

He disappeared behind the bushes, only to return a few minutes later looking very red in the face. His friend asked, 'Can we play through?'

'No.'

'Didn't you ask?'

'No. Those two women are also my wife and my mistress!'

## Girl Friday

A golfer was shipwrecked on an island for three months. He looked out and saw what he thought was a mirage – a stunning woman coming towards him in a canoe. Eventually, he realised it really was a beautiful woman in a canoe. She walked up on the beach, very scantily clad, and asked him, 'How long have you been here?'

The golfer replied, 'Three months'.

The lady said, 'Would you like a cigarette?'

'Would I ever?' the golfer replied wistfully.

She took a cigarette out of her bra and handed it to him. Then she asked him if he would fancy a little Scotch. The golfer again replied wistfully, 'Would I ever?' So she took a little bottle of Scotch out of her bra and handed it to him. As he smoked the cigarette and sipped the Scotch, the woman slid up beside him, pouted her lips provocatively and whispered seductively into his ear, 'Would you like to play around?'

The golfer leapt to his feet incredulously and asked, 'Don't tell me you have a golf club in there as well?'

## For Whom The Bell Tolls

A golfing mad vicar was so keen to maximise his time on the golf course that he hired a young lad to take over his bell-ringing duties. Obviously, some training was necessary for the job, so the vicar demonstrated how to ring the bells. The only problem was that the large bell had its clanger missing. 'It's quite easy,' said the vicar. 'All you have to do is swing it and hit it with your head.' He gave a demonstration, swinging the bell and heading it. The new assistant nodded his head with a certain amount of apprehension.

The following Sunday, the vicar was still on the eighteenth hole as the young man went to ring the bell to let the parishioners know that it was almost time for the service. However, when he swung the bell and headed it, he was hit with such force that he fell out of the belfry and onto the pavement below. Within minutes, the police were on the scene. They arrived just as the vicar returned from the golf course. One of the constables asked the clergyman, 'Do you know this boy?'

The vicar replied, 'No, but his face rings a bell'.

# Chapter Four
# Football Frolics

## Are You Watching, Pat Spillane?

Despite his unique insight into Gaelic games, which comes from being one of the greatest footballers of all time and winning eight All-Irelands, Pat Spillane does not always get his predictions right. At half-time in the 2002 All-Ireland final, Spillane was 'sceptical' about Armagh's chances of beating Kerry. He caused consternation among Armagh fans when he said, 'My mother has arthritis but even she has more pace than the Armagh full back line'.

In the second half, Spillane was left eating humble pie, as Armagh outplayed Kerry. Understandably, one banner featured prominently in the subsequent media coverage. Against a backdrop of the Armagh colours it said simply, 'Are you watching, Pat Spillane?'

Three days later when Armagh played Louth in the GOAL challenge, a large man – dressed up in drag in the Kerry colours, and wearing a placard stating 'Pat Spillane's Ma' – challenged each of the full back line to an individual race. 'She' won each time. The players weren't trying.

Getting predictions wrong does not faze Spillane unduly. On such occasions he always quotes the lines of the Declan Nerney song:

If I knew then what I know now,

I'd be a wiser man.

He is philosophical about his errors: 'The great thing is that RTÉ pay me to come and tell the nation what I think will happen. Then when I make a dog's dinner of it and get it badly wrong, the *Sunday World* pay me the following Sunday to explain why I got it so wrong!'

### *The Tourists*

Pat Spillane was one of the many players who made trips to America to play in the New York championship. It was an ideal opportunity to make a few dollars and have a holiday. Big name stars over from Ireland were always subject to 'robust' play on the field. On one occasion, this necessitated Spillane visiting the medical room with blood pouring from his nose. An Italian doctor was on duty and was more interested in reading the *New York Times* than attending to Spillane. Without looking up from his paper, he asked Spillane what was wrong. The Kerry star said, 'I think I've broken my nose'.

With no concern in his voice, the doctor told him to go over to the mirror and clean off the blood. When this task was completed the doctor inquired, 'Does it look different than it did this morning?'

Spillane replied, 'Yes, it's crooked'.

The doctor calmly replied, 'You probably broke your nose then'.

Thus ended the medical consultation.

Exotic tours abroad were a feature of Spillane's life with the great Kerry teams of the 1970s and 1980s. In 1986, Mick O'Dwyer brought them on a holiday to the Canaries. It was mainly for rest and recreation, but there was a small element of training. Every evening at 5 pm, the players met for a run along the sand dunes of Playa del Ingles. Part of the beach was reserved for a nudist's section. Spillane remarked that when the Kerry players reached that section of the beach the pace dropped alarmingly!

Four years earlier, O'Dwyer brought the Kerry team for a run on a beach in San Francisco the day after they had given a horrendous performance against the All-Stars. The display was the legacy of a day-long drinking session by some of the squad at Fisherman's Wharf on the eve of the match. The most revealing evidence of the commitment of the Kerry players' to the cause was that the first man home on the beach run was the president of the GAA, Seán Kelly, then chairman of the Kerry County Board.

In 1982, Kerry planned a holiday to Bali in the Far East to celebrate what they had expected would be their fifth championship in a row. After sensationally losing the final to Offaly, the Kerry players were saying that the only Bali they would be going to was Ballybunion! Another said, 'It won't even be the Canaries this year. All we'll get is the Seagulls.'

## Technical Adjustments

In 1981 after completing the historic four-in-a-row of All-Ireland titles, the Kerry team went on a holiday of a lifetime to America, Hawaii and Australia. They were booked into a hotel in Adelaide in Australia after a long overnight flight. Shortly after checking in, an irate member of the Kerry delegation rang down to complain about the lack of air conditioning in his room. He threatened to pull the entire Kerry party out of the hotel if the problem was not fixed immediately. A member of staff arrived up to the room. He took a quick glance around, before looking the complainant in the eye and coolly saying, 'Why not try plugging it in, buddy?'

## Tip Off

After a drinking session one evening on that tour, Spillane was reputed to have taken a taxi with a few of the other players back to the team hotel. The taxi-driver was a bit obese and was also 'hygienically-challenged', with a less than enticing aroma emanating from his body. He recounted a tale of woe about his lack of success with the opposite sex. After the Kerry lads paid their fare the taxi-driver said, 'How about a tip?'

Before anyone could even thinking of reaching into their pockets for a second time, Spillane is said to have interjected, 'Certainly. Start using a deodorant and you might have some chance with the women.'

## Solicitous

Later that evening, Spillane was propositioned by a 'lady of the night'. She said, 'Would you like to sleep with me for $20?' Spillane is said to have replied thoughtfully, 'I'm not very tired but the money will come in handy'.

## Ah, Ref!

Spillane was wont to complain to referees. After a series of bad decisions from one ref, Pat approached him and said, 'If I called you a stupid old goat who didn't know the first thing about football, what would you do?'

'I would report you and you would be in front of the GAA authorities,' said the ref.

'What if I didn't say it, and just thought it?'

'Well, nothing could be done about it.'

'Okay,' said Pat. 'We'll just leave it at that, then.'

### Missed Opportunities

During his college days, Spillane was less than impressed by a player on the Thomond team. He said to him, 'It's a pity you didn't take up the game sooner'.

'You mean I'd be better now?'

'No, you would have given up the game long ago.'

### Choose Your Words Carefully

Spillane's ability to tell it like it is doesn't always have the results he anticipates. He was in a hotel one evening, when a party of women descended upon the venue. Anxious to find out the nature of the occasion, he asked one if it was a hen party. 'No,' she answered, 'it's a Weight Watchers convention'.

'Oh, not been going long?' he inquired casually. That was the moment she floored him with a cracking right hook.

### Talk Is Cheap

In recent times, Spillane's talents are increasingly deployed as an after-dinner speaker. He did initially have a few prejudices to overcome. A club in Louth was considering him for their function. The chairman asked, 'Why don't we have Pat Spillane as our after-dinner speaker?'

The treasurer replied, 'Don't be silly. He couldn't wait that long.'

The secretary butted in, 'He'd be no good at it. I bet he'd even stuff up the minute's silence.'

After one of his longer speeches at a club function, Spillane asked the chairman, 'Did I put enough fire into my speech?'

The chairman replied, 'I don't think you put enough of your speech into the fire.'

Spillane was the main speaker at a major gala of a prominent club in Ulster. At the end of the night a spectator went up to Adrian Logan from UTV, the MC for the evening, and said, 'Twas shocking to hear all that filthy language here this evening. That kind of talk has no place in the GAA.'

Adrian nodded and just to make conversation asked the man what he thought of Pat Spillane. Logan was surprised with his response: 'I can't stand that f***** c***. He only talks s****.'

Spillane, though, was not the famous Kerry footballer of yesteryear, who was the guest speaker at a dinner of a major club in Mayo. The star launched into a passionate speech as to why the club he named was one of the top clubs in the country. A few minutes into his speech, he noticed that the audience reaction was much less warm than he anticipated. He discovered that he was talking about the wrong club! He excused himself and said he had to go the toilet. He never returned.

### On the Castlebar Express

After the 1996 and 1997 All-Irelands when Mayo let titles slip through their fingers, Spillane poured scorn on the Mayo forwards. His comments were not appreciated in Mayo to such an extent that the mere mention of Spillane's name in Mayo was as welcome as a nun in a brothel. One of the most memorable train journeys this writer ever experienced was shortly after the 1997 All-Ireland. I found myself sitting beside a man of mature years, who was puffing away on his pipe. Given his disposition I thought at first he might be a parish priest. The conversation quickly turned to football and he gave an incisive critique of the problems of Connacht football. Then he turned to the media reportage of teams from the West. Immediately he had a transformation of Jekyll and Hyde proportions. He reeled off a litany of journalists and pundits. What he proposed to do with them cannot be reprinted on the grounds of public order and morality. After his vicious tirade, he paused for deep breath. A pregnant pause ensued before he said, more in sorrow than in anger, 'F*** them all, bar Spillane.'

I nearly fell of my seat. I was wondering what he would say about the Kerryman that hadn't already been said about toxic waste. I heard myself ask incredulously, 'Why do you say "bar Spillane"?'

'Ah sure, young fella, Spillane is f***** already.'

# Are You Right There, Michael?

From the beginning, the GAA has had a history of abrasive characters, who have the gift of rubbing people up the wrong way. Michael Cusack will always be remembered for his role in founding the GAA in 1884. Yet, having given birth to the Association, Cusack almost strangled it in its infancy. People often miss out on the historical significance of the 'Athletic' in the title of the GAA. In the early years, it was envisaged that athletics would play a much greater role in the life of the GAA. One of the people trying to ensure this was John L. Dunbar. He wrote to Cusack in December 1885 suggesting that the GAA and the athletics organisation should meet 'with a view to a possible merger'. Cusack did not mince or waste his words in his response. The letter in reply read as follows:

> GAA,
> 4 Gardiners Place,
> Dublin.
>
> Dear Sir,
> I received your letter this morning and burned it.
> Yours faithfully,
> Michael Cusack.

# O Stony, Grey Soil of Monaghan

Another abrasive personality was Patrick Kavanagh, one of Ireland's greatest poets of the twentieth century. Kavanagh had an inglorious career as a Gaelic football goalkeeper in Monaghan. His most famous contribution was wandering off to buy either an ice cream or a drink, depending on whose version of events you listen to, while the opposition scored a goal between the deserted posts. The final ignominy came when he conceded the match-losing goal in the county final by letting the ball roll between his legs. His own supporters shouted, 'Go home and put an apron on you'.

Kavanagh's career as a sporting administrator fuelled even more venom. As club treasurer, he kept club funds under his bed, a situation that prompted some nasty rumours. Kavanagh's own response to the innuendo was, 'It is possible that every so often I visited it for the price of a packet of cigarettes, but nothing serious'.

Kavanagh always maintained that a high level of skill was necessary to decipher comments about footballers. Some of his footballing critics, strangely known as 'hurlers on the ditch', were brutally blunt: 'Sure, he couldn't kick snow off a rope'.

Others were more subtle: 'He always makes the ball do the work', which is code for 'he is lazy'.

'He could get more out of the ball', meaning 'he is stupid'.

'He has to train a little bit harder' – 'he is completely unfit'.

'In fairness he has a powerful shot' – 'he never hits the target'.

'He is a grafter', meaning he is a carthorse, a player with no skill, to be brought on as a sub at corner forward, usually when the team is four goals down and playing against the wind and without a chance of winning.

The most grave allegation levelled against Kavanagh was that he was 'a great minor', suggesting he had not played a good game since he was sixteen.

Kavanagh once took time off work on the 'stony, grey soil of Monaghan' to attend the county final. He was asked to predict the outcome of the match. After a dramatic pause, he responded, 'The first half will be even. The second half will be even worse.'

## Holy Wit

The long relationship between the GAA and the Catholic Church is a rich and complex one. Culturally and in many respects spiritually, the GAA and Catholic Church are very close and the Church was to the forefront in promoting the GAA. Nonetheless, the Church banned its priests and seminarians from actually playing inter-county football for years. Seminarians and priests had to assume false names to allow their footballing careers to continue at the highest level, a curious case of men preaching the truth but practising deception. Everybody knew who they were, including the bishop, but a blind eye was turned. It was a Jesuitical solution to a uniquely clerical problem.

Kerry is the only county that has produced a bishop who was the holder of an All-Ireland medal. In 1924, Kerry faced Dublin in the

All-Ireland final. Kerry's Mundy Prendville was a student priest in All Hallows College in Dublin at the time. He was spirited the short journey down the road to Croke Park, just in time to play and helped Kerry to win. Christianity is all about forgiveness, but they took football seriously back then. Mundy was refused re-admission to the college after that! He had to find a new seminary to continue his studies and subsequently became Archbishop of Perth.

Although Mundy forgave All Hallows for their actions, he did enjoy telling a story about a conversation he claimed happened in his time there. Following rigidly the rules whereby one must not complain about one's food, a young seminarian found a mouse in his soup, so he attracted the attention of the server: 'Please, Brother! The student next to me has no mouse in his soup.'

## Brevity is the Soul of Wit

Archbishop Prendville was well able to tell a story against himself. During the course of a long-winded Sunday sermon, he explained why he had a plaster on his face, 'I was concentrating so much on my homily this morning, while shaving, that I cut myself'. As he was counting the money in the collection plate after the service, he discovered a note which read, 'In future, Reverend, concentrate on the shaving and cut the sermon!'

## I Can See Cleary Now

In 1955, the late Michael Cleary was in line for a place on the Dublin team to play Kerry in the All-Ireland football final. The problem was that he was also attending the diocesan seminary in Clonliffe at the time. Under college regulations, there was no way he would be freed to play the match. It was a straightforward choice. Which was the more important to him: playing in the final or becoming a priest? He chose to become a priest, but as the final was being played he could practically see the ball from down the road in the college. After his ordination, he played for Dublin under the name of Mick Casey.

Years after his ordination, Fr Michael bumped into a well-known footballer who was clearly the worst for wear because of alcohol. He went up to reproach him, 'I'm sorry to see you are back on the drink. Haven't I told you before that the drink is your worst enemy?'

'Yes, but remember Fr Mick, the Church is always telling us to love our enemies.'

'That's true. But I can't ever remember them saying to swallow them.'

### Window Shopping

Another time Fr Michael went to the local prison to visit a former club team-mate, who had fallen foul of the law. He asked the man what he was charged with.

'Doing my Christmas shopping early,' he answered.

'But that's no offence,' Fr Mick replied wide-eyed. 'How early were you doing this shopping exactly?'

'Before the shop opened,' admitted the convict.

### Sobering

While he was in the prison, Fr Michael remembered the words from Matthew's Gospel, 'I was in prison and you visited me', so he decided to visit some other inmates. One had such sad eyes and looked so lonely that Fr Michael felt really sorry for him.

'Does your mother visit you often?' Fr Cleary asked.

'Never.'

'Your father?'

'Never.'

'Your brothers or sisters?'

'Never.'

'Why is that?'

'I killed them all,' the prisoner said with a whisper.

Fr Mick made a hasty retreat.

### What God Has Joined Together

Fr Michael gained a reputation for his fast driving. Once his car broke down on the way to a wedding ceremony and he was an hour late on arrival. The wedding party was beginning to panic when he arrived, and he was so embarrassed he never forgot the incident. Twenty years later, he met the husband, a prominent former footballer, at a function and said, 'I'm so sorry about that horrible fright I gave you on your wedding day'.

'So am I,' said the GAA star. 'I've still got her!'

### Say Cheese

Fr Cleary was a regular visitor to Croke Park. Once he was accompanied by a well-known, but cantankerous bishop. They were having their photograph taken by a press photographer. The photographer had a lot of trouble trying to get the bishop to pose properly. Eventually, after much bickering, he was about to take the picture. 'Look pleasant for a moment,' said Fr Mick. 'Then you can be yourself again.'

One of Fr Mick's favourite stories was about the woman who went to confession. She asked, 'Father I was looking into a mirror and I decided I was beautiful. Was this is a terrible sin?'

The priest answered, 'Certainly not. It was just a terrible mistake.'

### Run

Fr Mick claimed to have broken the 100 metres world record. The circumstances were rather bizarre: In the mid-1960s, when Galway reigned supreme, the singing priest (as Fr Mick was known, having recorded an album) was invited by a club in Galway to be their 'pretend Santa Claus' in a charity fund-raising event in the local school. Fr Mick donned a white beard and red cloak in the normal way. He took his place beside a Christmas tree but was a bit puzzled to see that someone had decided to light a number of candles behind his chair. He started giving out presents and was really getting into the spirit of things when a young girl started screaming hysterically, 'Santa's dress is on fire'. Fr Mick looked down to see that his cloak had brushed against one of the candles and was, indeed, on fire. The singing priest became the racing priest as he fled into the bathroom at great speed with a trail of smoke in his wake and a hall of children in hysterics and his dignity in shreds.

## Blessings

Dermot Earley is now a high-ranking army officer, but for twenty years he was the undisputed star of Roscommon football. Traditionally, the army held a mission every Lent. In 1979, the mission was given by Fr Michael Cleary. In one of his talks, Fr Mick spoke about determination. Much to the amusement of the rest of the congregation, he compared determination with Dermot Earley going through with the ball for the goal. On that Ash Wednesday, Earley was going up to receive the ashes when Fr Cleary revised his blessing somewhat. Instead of 'Remember man thou art but dust and into dust thou shalt return,' his blessing was: 'Up the Dubs!'

## A Ref's Best Friend

Dermot Earley was one of the greatest players never to win an All-Ireland medal. The closest he came was the controversial 1980 All-Ireland final when Roscommon lost to Kerry. The Roscommon fans were irate about the refereeing of the game. Legend has it that one of them approached the referee immediately after the game and said, 'Hi, ref, how's your dog?'

The ref is said to have replied, 'What do you mean? I don't have a dog.'

The fan responded, 'That's strange. You're the first blind man I've ever met that doesn't have a guide dog!'

## Earley to Rise

After he retired from football, Earley managed the Roscommon team for two years. During the winter, he trained the Dublin-based players in the Phoenix Park. One night they were training there, a day or two after Earley had substituted a player in a game the previous Sunday. The player in question was unhappy with his substitution. After training, the squad normally went to the Ashling Hotel for a meal. However, before joining the others, Earley and the player were sitting outside the hotel in the car having a very serious discussion about the player and his future with the team. There was a loud rap on the window. They turned around to see a lady of the night asking them, 'Would you like a good time?'

## Excuses, Excuses

During Earley's stewardship of the Roscommon team, a fringe member of the squad missed a number of training sessions. Earley tried to make contact with him but to no avail. He had to resort to leaving him messages in all kinds of strange locations. A few days later, he got a message on his answering machine, 'Dermot this is X. I'm sorry I missed the last four training sessions. My reasons were compelling and indescribable.' So ended the message and his brief and undistinguished career as a Roscommon footballer.

### Reach for the Stars

After his stint in charge of Roscommon, Earley took over from Mick O'Dwyer as manager of the Kildare team. Kildare's problem has always been the lack of scoring forwards. Shortly after his appointment, Earley was up on the roof of his two-storey house in Newbridge painting his chimney, when a Kildare fan passed by on his bicycle and shouted up at him, 'Are you looking for forwards?'

## Supermac

Tony McManus was the other star of the Roscommon team that Earley played, not just because of his skill but because of the intelligent way he played the game. A revealing insight into the sharpness of McManus's mind came in a county final between his club Clann na nGael and Kilmore. At one point a Clann player grabbed the ball. One of his opponents called him by his Christian name. Instinctively, the Clann player passed the ball to him and the Kilmore player raced up the field. Shortly afterwards, McManus won possession and the same Kilmore man yelled, 'Tony, Tony, pass the ball'. McManus swung around and said, 'If I was playing with you, I wouldn't pass you the ball!'

## Brought Down to Earth

A Roscommon football star of the 1950s, Gerry O'Malley was also a wonderful hurler. In 1961, O'Malley played for Connacht against Munster in a Railway Cup match. At the time, the balance of power in hurling was heavily weighted towards Munster but Connacht ran them close enough. On the way home, O'Malley stopped off for a drink with the legendary Galway hurler, Inky Flaherty. Given the interest in hurling in the Banner County, the barman recognised Inky straight away and said, 'Ye did very well'.

'Not too bad,' replied Inky.

'I suppose if it wasn't for O'Malley, you would have won,' speculated the barman.

Flaherty answered back, 'Here he is beside me; ask him yourself'.

***Post-match Verdict***

In 1962, O'Malley played in his only All-Ireland football final, a game the Westerners lost heavily to Kerry. O'Malley was injured and had to be taken to hospital after the match. He was in a bed beside a man he had never met before. His neighbour knew who O'Malley was and they got talking. The next day, a fella came in with the newspapers, who didn't recognise O'Malley from Adam. The bed-ridden man asked his friend, 'How did the papers say O'Malley played?'

'Brutal,' came the instant reply and it certainly left O'Malley feeling even more brutal.

## Pub Talk

The glory years of Roscommon football came in the 1940s; the county had its only All-Ireland successes in 1943 and 1944, both under the captaincy of Jimmy Murray. Murray's pub-cum-grocery in Knockcroghery is arguably the spiritual home of Roscommon football, with memorabilia from the two All-Ireland victories, including the football from the 1944 final.

The football survived a close shave some years ago when Murray's premises were burned down – a fact he recalls with mixed feelings. The ball was hanging from the ceiling and, of course, the fire burned the strings and the ball fell down and rolled safely under the counter. The fire occurred on a Saturday night and when the fire brigade came one of the firemen jumped off and asked Murray, 'Is the ball safe?'

As Murray was watching his business go up in smoke, the ball wasn't his main priority! But the fireman came out later with the ball intact. The next day Murray got calls from all over the country asking if the ball was safe. He was bit annoyed at the time that all people seemed to be concerned with was the safety of the ball and nobody seem to be too bothered about what happened to his shop.

## Lovely Leitrim

Another man concerned about warped priorities was a gentleman of the cloth at an emergency meeting of a club in Leitrim. Sixty of the club's players had gone on a weekend tour of Amsterdam for a sevens tournament, at which they were ignominiously dumped out of in the first round. This had occurred one short week after the club had failed to drum up fifteen players to play Carrick-on-Shannon twenty miles down the road. A member of the touring party to Amsterdam responded to the priest's criticism: 'Well, Father, to the best of my knowledge, there are no ladies of the night in Carrick-on-Shannon.'

A club team from Leitrim travelled 200 miles to a tournament game in Waterford. At half-time, they trailed, 7–2 to 0–5. A crisis meeting was held in the middle of the pitch at half-time. Recriminations were flying until the captain called for silence and an end to the bickering. A hush descended. One player said, 'We need some positive encouragement'.

After a short delay the manager-cum-trainer-cum-club secretary-cum groundskeeper said, 'Come on now lads. Let's go out there and show them up. It's plain to be seen; they can't score points!'

## Fat Larry

Anthony 'Fat Larry' Finnerty played for Mayo in the 1989 All-Ireland final. Finnerty earned his nickname because he was fat in the winter but lost a lot of weight in the summer. Three days after Mayo lost the 1989 final to Cork, everyone was feeling very blue in Fat Larry's local pub, Mitchells. Fat Larry had scored the goal that had brought Mayo back into the match, but he had missed a goal chance late on, which might have turned the game for the Westerners. Someone asked him to say a few words to cheer them up. Fat Larry said, 'If I had got that goal I missed ye'd have been talking about me all winter, but now that I missed it ye'll never stop talking about me.'

Some years later during Brian McDonald's controversial tenure as trainer of the Mayo team, McDonald was taking a training session. Twenty-three or twenty-four players were jogging around the pitch. McDonald told them that every time he blew his whistle they were to jump high in the air and imagine they were catching a famous ball. This drill went on until they got level with the dressing-room. Finnerty started to zoom towards the dressing-room. The irate trainer shouted at him, 'Where are you going?'

Fat Larry replied, 'I'm just going in to get my gloves. That blady ball you want us to catch is awful slippy!'

# Where's Your Trousers?

It has become a cliché for journalists and broadcasters to refer to a particular player's 'cultured left foot'. Yet every cliché has its origin in truth. From the days when he first sprang to prominence with St Jarlath's College, Tuam, where he won All-Ireland College's senior medals in both 1960 and 1961, there was never any doubt that John Morley's left foot merited this soubriquet.

Morley was always getting slagged about his right leg, but he always defended it by saying that without it he couldn't use his left!

The most famous incident in Morley's illustrious career came in the 1970 League Final clash, when Mayo defeated Down. Morley was playing at centre-half back, when a Down player grabbed him and tore his shorts. Just as he was about to put his foot into a new pair of shorts, the ball came close by. Morley abandoned his shorts, and, in his briefs, fielded the ball and cleared it heroically down the field to the adulation of the crowd.

## Salmon Leap

In the early 1990s, Connacht footballers were invariably free in August and September and many took on the role of weekend tourist for trans-Atlantic games. Galway were knocked out early in the championship one year. Jackie Salmon, a famous man in the GAA in New York, rang Val Daly and asked him to travel over to line out for the Connemara Gaels the following Sunday and to bring a couple of other good players with him. Daly rang around and persuaded former Galway full-forward Brian O'Donnell to travel with him. O'Donnell had never played in a match in New York. The two lads flew out on the Friday evening and on the plane Daly briefed his colleague on how to get through the weekend. He said, 'Now, Brian, they do things differently over there. It's not like at home, so just enjoy the weekend, play the match and don't mind what anyone says. Whatever you do, say nothing.'

The Tribesmen enjoyed the first part of the weekend but the match went less well. At half-time the Connemara Gaels were seven points down. Jackie Salmon gave a team-talk and said, 'Ye're the most disgraceful shower I ever saw. Ye're a disgrace to the Connemara Gaels jersey. As for the big shots from over in Ireland

I'm sorry I brought ye out at all. Daly you were hopeless and O'Donnell you were even worse. You didn't even catch one ball.'

O'Donnell forgot Daly's advice and retorted, 'Sure how could we play football out there? There wasn't a single blade of grass on the pitch.'

Salmon turned around to him and asked, 'Did you come out here to play football or to graze?'

## Bonus Point

Some Gaelic football stories that have taken hold in popular mythology have just the faintest touches of credibility. A case in point was the story of a match in 1957, when a new pitch was being opened in St Brendan's Hospital. As reigning All-Ireland football champions, Galway were invited to play the home team and duly were awarded a penalty in the game. A Galway player, Mick Ford (who once scored a goal in a club hurling match in Dublin directly from a puck-out) is said to have hit the ball so hard that the lace of the ball came undone and the leather part went over the bar and the bladder went into the net. It is said Galway were awarded a goal and a point!

## The West's Awake

Under the stewardship of John O'Mahony, Galway have reacquainted themselves with the Sam Maguire Cup. Galway won the All-Ireland in 1998, thereby ending a thirty-two-year famine. A couple of days later, the Tribesmen played in the GOAL challenge. Some of their players hadn't slept for three days. After the match started, O'Mahony was going to give a run out to some of the subs. When he got to the subs bench, a few of them were asleep and one of them was snoring loudly. One of the mentors had to shout to wake him up. The groggy footballer didn't know where he was.

## Johnny Come Lately

One of the stars of the Galway team in the 1970s was Johnny Hughes. Although he doesn't have the All-Ireland medal his great talent deserved, he has many happy memories from his time with Galway, as well as some hair-raising experiences.

When the Galway team were training in Tuam, there would always be fellas looking for shampoo afterwards. Hughes always had shampoo but Tomas Tierney and Tommy Joe Gilmore were always swiping his. At the time, Hughes was working for a chemical company, which manufactured a light oil that looked like Clinic shampoo. Hughes poured some of this oil into an empty bottle of shampoo, which he left outside his shower in the dressing-room. He hid a bottle of shampoo in his bag and he went in to the shower with some of it in his hand.

A few seconds later, he saw Tierney coming over and taking the bottle of shampoo. Tierney rubbed it into his hair and passed it on to Tommy Joe. A few minutes later all hell broke loose. The incident stopped them from stealing Hughes' shampoo for a long time after that.

When his inter-county career finished, Hughes found a new outlet for his skills, through his involvement in charity matches with the Jimmy Magee All-Stars. Magee really enjoyed playing in those All-Star games with him. Hughes always did a running commentary as he was playing, much to Magee's delight.

One day before a match, Magee was giving the team-talk to boost morale. He put his hand on his wing-back Fr Brian Darcy's shoulder and said, 'Brian, in years to come GAA people will be sitting around their fires and they'll be talking about the great wing-backs of all time….' He paused and Brian's chest began to swell with pride. 'And you know something, Brian? When they do, you won't even get a mention.'

## A Master Class

Galway's Seán 'The Master' Purcell is often spoken of as the greatest player of all time. According to legend, after Galway won the 1956 All-Ireland, Seán Purcell was waiting in Galway for the bus to Tuam, unaware that the last bus had gone. A driver was on his way back to the garage with an empty bus when he spotted 'the Master'. Although it was against all regulations, he stopped and asked him where he was going. When Purcell told him Tuam, the driver told him to hop on. Four miles from Tuam, the poor driver nearly had a stroke when he saw an inspector standing in the middle of the road, waving him down. The inspector was a seething mass of anger and demanded to know where the driver was taking the bus.

'I have the Master here,' answered the driver meekly.

'The Master. You can't be serious!' said the inspector, boarding the bus to verify the fact.

When he saw the evidence with his own eyes, he turned angrily to the driver again.

'How could you be so stupid? Turn around and get back to the garage straight away. How could you drive the Master in just a single-decker bus? Get him a double-decker straight away, so that he can go upstairs if he fancies a cigarette.'

## Jack's Back

Jack Mahon starred for Galway in the 1950s. Mahon was well able to tell stories against himself. He once bumped into a young fella in Galway and was a bit disappointed to discover that the youngster had never heard of him. Mahon hoped he might impress his new acquaintance when he told him that he played at centre-half back on the Galway team that beat Cork in the 1956 All-Ireland final.

'Gosh, that's shocking,' said the youngster.

'Why? asked a bemused Mahon.

'Because I've just discovered my dad's a liar. He's always said that when Galway won that All-Ireland they never had a centre-back!'

## Survival Plan

Micheal Kearins' first Railway Cup game was against Leinster in Ballinasloe. As he was moving into position before the ball was thrown in, Kearins noticed his immediate opponent, Paddy McCormack, digging a hole along the ground with his boot.

He said, 'You're young Kearins from Sligo. I presume you expect to go back to Sligo this evening.'

'Hopefully,' Kearins replied.

'If you don't pass the mark, you have a fair chance of getting back.'

## The Iron Man

Paddy McCormack, The Iron Man from Rhode, was a tough man who marked tighter than Kylie Minogue's famous hotpants. However, the story goes that when he made his debut for Offaly his mother was concerned about the physical nature of the exchanges. She turned to her husband and said, 'Poor Paddy will break a leg'. Her husband looked at her reproachfully and said, 'He might, but it won't be his own'.

Another story told about McCormack goes back to the time he had a terrible leg on him, returning to the dressing-room, after a bruising encounter in a National League match. The leg was covered in cuts and bruises and had a massive gash from the top of the thigh to the knee. McCormack had no idea whose it was.

## A Compromise

Derry's Jim McKeever was the prince of midfielders. McKeever's happiest memories are of the club scene. His club, Ballymaguigan, were playing Coleraine in a club game. Coleraine's pitch wasn't very well marked. The crossbar was only a rope and there weren't any nets. The ball was bobbing around and somebody swung a kick at it. One umpire gave it a goal, the other a point. Both umpires gave the decision against their own team. The referee split the difference and awarded two points.

The really comic part of the story was that one of Ballymaguigan's best players, the late Michael Young, did not want to play as he had hay ready for baling and the weather forecast was not good. However, he was persuaded to play. When the controversy emerged, Young went up to the referee and told him that he should hurry up and make a decision, as he had to go home to bale the hay!

### The Twilight Zone

McKeever played with Ballymaguigan in a seven-a-side match one evening. Before the match finished, darkness was falling quickly. There was a flambouyant player in the Ballymaguigan side at the time. His team-mates suddenly saw him tearing up the sideline with the ball. They couldn't believe the speed at which he was going. They discovered afterwards the secret of this newly found speed: as he was running, he wasn't bothering to solo the ball, but it was so dark that nobody could spot him.

## Change for the Better

In Derry they take their club football seriously. If you fail to meet the required standard, you will be told in no uncertain terms. During a half-time pep talk, a player who had not distinguished himself in the first half was abruptly told by the manager, 'We're taking you off but we're not bothering to put on a sub. Just having you off will improve our situation!'

## Rubbing People Up the Wrong Way

In the 1990s, Derry football produced one of the great figures in the history of the game, Joe Brolly. Brolly never really surrendered to authority and was never short of self-confidence, which did not always endear him to his managers. One manager was heard to say of Brolly, 'He's down there now letting people know how good he is playing'.

Brolly wasn't always complimentary about his team-mates. After a club game, a disconsolate new recruit to the team said, 'I've never played so badly before'. Brolly appeared surprised, 'You mean you've played before?'

After a county game, one of his colleagues said proudly, 'That was the best game I ever played'. Brolly replied, 'Well, you mustn't let that discourage you'.

## Meat in a Meath Sandwich

One of the many stories attributed to Brolly is of his experiences playing against Meath, and marking Kevin Foley in particular. A high ball came in between them; Brolly fielded it and in his own words 'danced around' Foley before blasting the ball over the bar. A second high ball came in between them with the exact same result. Brolly was aware that the Meath crowd had gone very quiet and he noticed Foley and Liam Harnan exchanging signals. As the next ball that came in, Brolly saw both Foley and Harnan coming at him at top speed, so he ducked, causing Harnan to catch Foley with his elbow. Foley was stretchered off unconscious. Brolly claimed that he became a hero in Derry not because off any score he got but because he was the man who 'floored' Kevin Foley!

## Paying the Penalty

Armagh cornerback John McKnight started off playing junior football when he was sixteen years old. At that stage, it was hard to field a team. In desperation, a man was roped into play for the team and he was provided with boots, socks, a jersey – the lot. McKnight's side were thrashed and, of course, when that happens everybody blames everybody else. When unflattering comments were put to their new recruit, his riposte was, 'Well, you can't blame me. I never got near the ball!'

McKnight played with many wonderful people down the years, including the late Pat Campbell. In those days there wasn't the subs system that there is today. The only way a player could come off was if he were injured. The only way around that system was to feign injury. One day, Campbell was 'injured' and taken off. His right full back, Gene Morgan, was a very droll character. His crack to Campbell was, 'That's the first time I've seen anybody limping off with a sore finger!'

## Seeing Double

Clashes between Armagh and Roscommon have provided many memorable incidents down the years. In 1982, the two teams met for a series of three matches in America. Before the first match, some of the players had partied too hard and went onto the pitch in something less than the full of their health. At one point, the ball was coming in towards the Armagh goal. Their accomplished full back, Jim Kerr, went for the ball, but he was experiencing a form of double vision. Kerr went up for the ball but caught an imaginary one, toe-tapped it and cleared it. Meanwhile, a Roscommon player had caught the real ball and stuck it in the net. When interrogated about the mishap, Kerr's response contained no admission of guilt, 'I got the ball I went for!'

## Jack the Lad

Armagh finally reached the Promised Land, winning the championship in 2002. One of their great characters is their goalie, Benny Tierney. In 2003, Tierney went to San Diego with the All-Stars. As part of the trip, some of the tourists went to see a NBA basketball match. Among the attendance was legendary actor Jack Nicholson. At one point in the game, there was a controversial call and Nicholson was incensed. He rose to his feet and started screaming at the officials. When the torrent of abuse died down, Tierney rose to his feet and reprised one of Nicholson's most famous roles, in *A Few Good Men*, when he shouted, 'You want the truth? You can't handle the truth!'

# Nudie

One test of fame is whether you are known simply by your first name – Bono, Gay, Packie – no further introduction required. In Gaelic football circles, the name 'Nudie' elicits instant recognition, as that of Monaghan's most famous footballer, Eugene 'Nudie' Hughes. Nudie helped Monaghan to three Ulster Senior Football Championships in 1979, 1985 and 1988.

Nudie was well able to hold his own in any company. One player who gave him a lot of problems, though, was the Kerry forward, John Egan. Ulster were playing a Railway Cup match against Munster and Nudie was marking Egan. They were standing talking – Nudie always talked to opponents even though he was always told not to. At one stage Egan said, 'What's that man writing down on that piece of paper? He's a right looking eejit, isn't he?' As Nudie turned to answer, Egan was sticking the ball into the net.

In 1988, Nudie used that same trick on Cavan's Damien O'Reilly, whom he was marking in the Ulster final. At one stage in the game, Nudie said, 'Jaysus, there's an awful lot of people up on the hill. How many people would you say is up there?' As O'Reilly looked up to make his guess, the ball came in between them. Nudie caught it without any obstruction and stuck it over the bar. O'Reilly was taken off him immediately.

## *Too Many Murphys*

Nudie also made his mark on foreign shores. He was playing in England but his club game with Round Towers in New Eltham was cancelled. A few enterprising men came up and got Nudie to play for Bristol against Gloucester in a league final, totally illegally. He was the last sub to be brought on and was about to hand his name, 'Brian Murphy' to the ref. The official from Bristol called him back and said, 'I'd better change that, as the other two I sent in were Brian Murphys and the ref would surely spot it'.

They changed it to Aidan Dempsey and Bristol went on to win the match.

# Clare and Present Danger

Monaghan were playing against Clare in a League match in Ennis. Some young lads started throwing stones at Monaghan's goalie, Bubbles McNeill. True to form, Bubbles started throwing stones back at them. The only problem was that he got so caught up with the stones that he completely forgot about the match. A Clare forward pumped a hopeful ball in from midfield and it went into the empty net. Monaghan lost the match by a point.

# Delayed Reaction

The toughness of Monaghan football is epitomised by the old joke: 'A late tackle in Monaghan is one that comes the day after a match!'

Ulster Championship matches are renowned for their roughness. In 2002, former Monaghan manager Seán McCague, in his role of president of the GAA, expressed his unhappiness at the violence in the first International Rules test between Ireland and Australia. Reporting on McCague's disaffection on *Morning Ireland*, Des Cahill observed, 'He said he wasn't going to support the continuance of the series'. Mindful of the intensely physical exchanges in Ulster football, Cathal Mac Coille quipped, 'Do you think the Ulster championship is in danger?'

# Musical Interlude

In 1979, Monaghan qualified for the Ulster final against Donegal. The match is best remembered for an infamous incident. The referee threw in the ball. Donegal's Seamus Bonner won possession, sent the ball in to the forwards, one of whom popped it over the bar. The only problem was that the band were still on the far side of the pitch playing the National Anthem! The referee had to re-start the game and the Donegal point was disallowed.

# Famous Seamus

Over his lengthy career, Seamus Bonner was involved in some bizarre events. Bonner was playing against Monaghan one day in a League match in Ballybofey and was soloing in with the ball, 20 yards out from the goal with the defence beaten. He had 'goal' on his mind but he had his mouth open and a fly flew into it. Bonner swallowed the fly and nearly choked. He was clean through, but came to a sudden, staggering stop with nobody near him. He let the ball fall out of his hands and lost it. The Donegal fans didn't know what happened. Bonner was not sure what they were thinking about but he's sure it wasn't complimentary. He believes that the moral of the story is when you're on a football field you should keep your mouth shut!

## Everybody Needs Good Neighbours

Donegal and Monaghan 'enjoy' a great rivalry on the football field with Cavan. Their fans are never slow to invoke the stereotypical image of Cavan people, epitomised by the story of the Cavan husband who gave his wife lipstick for Christmas every year so that at least he can get half of it back.

One story they tell in this context is about the Pope. Il Papa was severely ill but had a very, very unusual blood type. The doctors could find only one person in the whole world who had the same type, Paddy O'Reilly from Cavan. So, Paddy donated a pint of blood and the Pope recovered. As a gesture of goodwill, the Pope sent Paddy €20,000. The Pope got ill four times in successive years after that, and each time he received a pint of Paddy's blood. For every donation, he sent Paddy €20,000. The sixth time he got Paddy's blood, the Pope sent him a holy medal. Paddy was devastated and rang the Vatican to ask why he was not sent any money this time. The Pope's secretary took the call and answered, 'Well, Paddy, you have to understand; he has a lot of Cavan blood of him at this stage!'

That may be why when the Cavan football team went on a short holiday, the hotel they stayed at put their Gideon Bibles on chains.

## Revised Orders

Three times All-Ireland winner Mick Higgins captained Cavan to their All-Ireland final victory in 1952. The first match ended in a draw. It was the first time the GAA brought the two teams together for a meal after the game. When Higgins and some of the Cavan boys got to the hotel they ordered drinks – just bottles of ale and a mineral. Higgins went to pay for it, but the barman told him that drinks were on the GAA. Higgins double-checked if he had heard correctly. Quick as a flash, once this was confirmed, one of his colleagues said, 'Forget about the ales and get us brandies'. For the replay, though, there was no free drink!

### Gentleman Jim

The New York–born Higgins found that management was a more frustrating experience than playing. He often told the story of taking charge of Cavan for a championship match against Armagh. As the match reached its climax, Cavan's dominance was threatened as Armagh took control of midfield. Corrective action was required urgently and Higgins decided to send on a sub, Big Jim O'Donnell, whose high fielding prowess was just what Cavan needed.

However, O'Donnell didn't seem to realise the urgency of the situation. After going on to the pitch, he strolled back to the sideline seeking a slip of paper with his name on it for the referee. Moments later, O'Donnell was back again seeking a pair of gloves. Higgins forcefully told him to get back into position immediately and not to mind about the gloves. A minute or two later, he was back a third time to ask, 'Mick, would you ever mind my false teeth?' As he calmly handed the manager his molars, Higgins blood pressure hit record levels.

## King Size

In more recent times, the giant of Cavan football was Stephen King. King played for Ireland against Australia in the compromise rules. The series provided him with one of the most bizarre sights in his career. Ireland were coming off the pitch and one of King's opponents was chastising him and giving him fierce abuse. It didn't really bother him, but Brian McGilligan was coming up behind him and he wasn't very impressed. McGilligan went up and knocked out the loudmouth Australian's gum-shield and stamped on it with his foot. Nobody has ever seen a player shut up so fast.

## Peter the Great

Mick Higgins was the Ulster manager when arguably Fermanagh's best-known player, Peter McGinnity, played his first match for the province against the Combined Universities. There were two other Fermanagh players on the team with him, Kieran Campbell and Phil Sheridan, which was their highest representation ever. Finn Sherry was also playing for the Combined Universities. Four Fermanagh lads playing inter-provincial football on one day was big news.

When the three Fermanagh players went into the Ulster dressing-room, Higgins said to Peter, 'Here you are, Kieran, here's the No. 3 jersey'. He then he turned to Kieran and said, 'Here's your No. 10 jersey, Peter'. It certainly pulled them down a peg or two not to be recognised by Mick Higgins.

### Body Check

One of the funniest incidents in McGinnity's career happened in a club game when he was marking Barney O'Reilly. O'Reilly enjoys a rare distinction of having won senior county championship medals in four different decades: the 1960s, 1970s and 1980s with Fermanagh's Teemore and the early 1990s with Navan O'Mahonys in Meath.

O'Reilly and McGinnity both played for Fermanagh Under-21s and they came up the ranks together. In one club match, the ball went up between McGinnity and O'Reilly's brother, also called Peter, and a kind of ruck developed. McGinnity snatched the ball as Barney O'Reilly came charging in to give his brother some 'assistance'. Happily, for McGinnity, in the ensuing mêlée and confusion, Barney struck his own brother instead of his illustrious opponent. McGinnity headed up the field with the ball. Before he started chasing McGinnity, Barney said, 'Sorry, Peter', to his brother, who lay stretched out on the ground.

## Dub-le Trouble

In the 1970s, Dublin brought new aura of glamour to Gaelic football. The Dublin players had the same status as pop stars and accordingly some of them had great appeal for women. One Saturday night, one of the players took a young lady in his car up the Dublin Mountains and got involved in a passionate embrace. What they had forgotten was that this was during the Don Tidey kidnap investigation and the guards were on the look out for suspicious activities and 'vehicles'. When the couple were in an advanced stage of undress and the car windows were very steamy, there was a knock on the window. The Dublin player hadn't time to react before a flash lamp was beaming on him. The guard was so embarrassed when he recognised the Dublin star that all he could say was, 'Can I see your driver's licence, please?'

## Doctor, Doctor

Another star of that Dublin team was David Hickey, who went on to become a distinguished medical doctor. Hickey joked that he had overheard one of his female patients complaining about him. She said, 'I've been under my doctor for six months but he hasn't done me any good'.

Before the 1977 classic All-Ireland semifinal between Kerry and Dublin, the Dubs were bemused when Hickey yelled in the middle of a training session, 'Typhoid! Tetanus! Measles!'

Kevin Heffernan asked, 'Why are you doing that?'

Hickey replied, 'Oh, I want to be the guy that calls the shots round here'.

## Sleepy

Apart from their contribution on the field, the Dubs added to the lore of the game through players like Mick Holden. Holden furnished the game with some wonderful stories. Coming up to an All-Ireland final, Kevin Heffernan spoke to the Dublin team about diet and proper preparation. He told them if they had any problems sleeping before the final they should get tablets from Pat O'Neill. The first person in the queue was Mick Holden. Heffo said to Holden, 'I never thought you'd have any problems sleeping'. Holden answered, 'Oh, these are not for me. I sleep like a baby. These are for my mother. She can never sleep the night before a big match!'

## Creative Excuses

One Saturday morning, Holden was seriously late for training much to Heffo's chagrin. The manager curtly demanded an explanation. Holden responded by saying, 'I was coming across town and I was stopped by the guards. They said I was a match for one of the guys that pulled that big bank robbery yesterday.'

A bemused Heffo asked, 'Really?'

Holden answered, 'No, but it sounds so much better than saying I slept it out'.

## Card Game

In 1983, twelve-man Dublin beat fourteen-man Galway in the All-Ireland final. After the match one wag remarked, 'The referee went ape. He pulled out more cards than Steve McQueen did in *The Cincinnati Kid.'*

## Mighty Meath

In the 1970s, Dublin's great rivals were Kerry, but in the late 1980s and early 1990s, their most intense rivalry was with Meath. In 1983 after Dublin won the All-Ireland, they travelled to Navan for the opening round of the National League. The All-Ireland champions were welcomed onto the field by the Meath team lined either side of the dugout. While the team applauded the Dubs, one photographer caught a Meath player giving the champs the two fingers!

### Barred

The rivalry between fans can be nasty or it can be witty. When Dublin played Meath in the 1996 Leinster final, Meath's Tommy Dowd was in a clash of heads with Dublin's Keith Barr. Some time later Barr's brother, Johnny, was also in the wars with Dowd. After the match, Dowd was going up for an interview when he banged his head against a bar in one of the barriers, an injury which subsequently necessitated four stitches. As he held his head in agony, a passing Dublin fan said to him, 'I see you made the hat trick'.

'What do you mean?' Tommy asked.

'Johnny Barr, Keith Barr and iron bar!' the fan replied.

### Generosity

During a Dublin–Meath game in the 1990s, the Dubs fans were giving Meath goalie, Mickey McQuillan, a bit of stick. A few started throwing coins at him. McQuillan collected the coins and discovered he had a 50 pence piece. He then went over to one of the umpires, presented him with the money and said, 'There you are now. Any square ball that comes in, you know what to do! Put the money towards a pint.'

### Immediate Impact

Meath football has always been a place where the weak don't survive. Hence a club secretary's report which stated, 'Frankie Kelly [the name has been changed to protect the guilty] made his championship debut in such a way that he will never be asked to make it again!'

*Revealing Slip*

In 1996 after the All-Ireland semifinal, two irate Tyrone fans were loud in their condemnation of the Meath team, particularly of their alleged ill-treatment of Peter Canavan. A Meath fan made an interesting and revealing slip of the tongue in response: 'You can't make an omelette without breaking legs.'

***The Road to Hell***

The face of Meath football was changed forever with the appointment of the great Seán Boylan as Meath manager in 1982. By profession, Boylan is a herbalist. In 1991, after Meath finally beat Dublin in the epic tussle which needed four games to decide the outcome, Boylan was walking off the pitch when some Dublin fans poked fun at his vocation by saying, 'Get away, ya bleedin' witchdoctor'.

After their clashes with Cork, in 1987 and 1988 in particular, Meath got the reputation for being hard men. Attending a funeral in 1989, Seán Boylan met a young recruit to the Meath panel who took the wind out of the manager's sails by claiming, 'When I die I want to go to hell'.

A bemused Boylan asked, 'Why do you want to go down there?'

'Well, now that I'm on the panel I want to be one of the lads in every way. If all the things that are said about them are true, the only possible place they could end up is roasting in the fires of the hell!'

## Westmeath Bachelors

Mick Carley was one of the few stars to emerge from the Westmeath team in the 1960s. The most memorable incident of his career came when he was marking Seán Heavin, whom he played with for Westmeath, in a club match. Carley was playing centre forward, but as he was at the end of his career his legs were going. At one stage, the ball came in to Carley and Heavin and was about 10 feet in the air. Heavin was younger and much quicker than Carley, so there was no way Carley was going to beat him. Just as Heavin was about to jump and claim the ball, Carley let a roar, 'Let it go, Seán'. Heavin stopped and let down his hands and the ball fell straight into Carley's arms. The whole field opened up for Carley, and he just ran through and tapped it over the bar.

### *Rough Stuff*

Carley once played a club match in Offaly against Walsh Island. After the game was over, he togged in and was about to go home when a fella called him over and told him he should stay for a junior match between Clonbullogue and Bracknagh. Carley didn't really want to but the man was adamant that he should stay. Carley agreed to stay for five minutes. There was nothing special for the first couple of minutes, but suddenly a fracas developed and all hell broke loose. Everyone was swinging and punching.

Carley found out later that all the players were inter-married and there was a lot of bad blood between them. It took about five minutes for the referee to sort things out. The ref sent one of the lads off, but the player in question didn't do the usual thing and go back to the dressing-room and take a shower. Instead, he stood on the sideline waiting for things to boil over again, so he could get back into the thick of the fighting.

He didn't have long to wait. Another mêlée broke out and they went at it again only twice as hard. The referee finally restored order. But almost as soon as he threw the ball back in another scrap broke out. There was no more than five minutes of football played in the first half. In fact, things were so bad that at half-time the priests from the two parishes went in to try and calm things down. Things then got really bad in the second half!

## Glorious Glen

Glen Ryan was a central player in Kildare's great triumphs in the late 1990s. Two Kildare fans were settling down to a match in Newbridge, when one realised that he had left his wallet in his friend's Mercedes. He returned from the car park ten minutes later, pale and shaken.

'I've got bad news, Jim. A lorry has crashed into your Merc and the impact set it on fire. It's totally destroyed.'

'And I have some bad news for you,' said Jim. 'Glen Ryan is out injured.'

Ryan has a share in a pub in Newbridge. In the late 1990s when Kildare had a very keen rivalry with Meath, it was rumoured that there was a sign in the pub which read, 'No Meath supporters served in this pub'. One day a man draped in the Meath colours came into the bar, 'I know you don't serve Meath supporters, but I'm desperate for a drink and I'll pay £5 for a pint'.

The barman thought this over, then decided to serve the pint. It was gulped down in one go. 'Same again,' said the Meath fan. 'In fact, I'll have two.' With this, he slapped a tenner on the bar. After a few minutes he asked for another. The barman said tentatively, 'That's another fiver'.

'That's okay,' he said, pushing a £50 note across the bar. 'I'll have a couple for the road. Keep the change.'

When the drinker had gone the barman put up a new sign: 'Only Meath fans served here.'

## The Wicklow Way

Club football in Wicklow is not for the faint-hearted, especially for faint-hearted referees. One of the most famous incidents in Wicklow's history was when a group of disaffected fans, after losing a club match, locked a referee in the boot of his car. In the return fixture, the nervous referee brought the two teams together and pointed to his whistle and said, 'Do ye see this yoke, lads? I'm going to blow it now, and blow it again at the finish and whatever happens in between ye can sort out yerselves.'

It has been said that there have been so many injuries in junior club football in Wicklow that it has generated more breaks than Kit Kat.

A referee's lot in such an environment is not a happy one. Their's is the only occupation where a man has to be perfect on the first day on the job and then improve over the years. One spectator at a club match in Wicklow was complaining bitterly all through the game about the referee's poor eyesight. At one stage, though, the fan was responsible for a enormous gaffe when he shouted, 'Ah, ref, where are your testicles?'

Sometimes, though, referees are their own worst enemies. Two midfielders were embroiled in a serious entanglement in a club match in Wicklow. When the ref finally blew his whistle, the captain of the home team asked, 'Who's the free for, ref?'

'It's for us,' he replied.

### The Road Less Travelled

A prospective young bank official was being interviewed for a job in Wicklow. The bank manager was chairman of the local club and said, 'We need a centre-half forward with courage and a strong set of hands like yours'.

'Sorry, sir,' said the lad. 'I don't know a thing about football.'

'No worries; we need referees, too.'

### Meeting His Maker

A man approached the Pearly Gates and was asked by St Peter whether he had ever done anything wrong. 'I was a referee in Wicklow,' said the man. 'I was refereeing a club game and I wrongly awarded a penalty against the home team when one of their players had committed an infringement.'

'That doesn't sound too bad,' said St Peter, 'if that is all you have done. How long ago did this happen?'

'About 30 seconds ago,' said the man.

At one point, God challenged the Devil to a football match. The Devil agreed, provided the match was played in Wicklow. 'Remember,' said God, 'we have all the good footballers up here.' 'Yes,' said the Devil, 'but we've got all the referees down here.'

### Get Your Man

A club team in Wicklow was facing defeat. At half-time the coach roared some fight into them. 'And you, John, it's about time you got ferocious.'

'What's his number?' said John.

### A Nose for the Action

Wicklow have always produced great footballers, though never enough of them at the one time. Among their greatest was Gerry O'Reilly in the 1950s. O'Reilly attributes the failure of the Wicklow team in the 1950s to the inadequacies of the county board. He claims that the men on the board were so incompetent they couldn't even pick their own noses!

# Clearly Cleary Spoken

John Cleary was one of the Cork stars, when the county regained the All-Ireland in 1989. Cleary was a very accurate forward, though not the biggest man in the world. Before one of Cork's clashes with Kerry, Jack O'Shea came up to him, and, in an effort to faze him, said, 'You're too small and too young for a game like this'.

Cleary said nothing until after the game when Cork emerged triumphant. As he walked past Jacko off the pitch, Cleary softly said, 'You're too old for a game like this'.

# On the Banks of My Own Lovely Lee

In January 2003, Paidí Ó Sé became embroiled in a major controversy, when he described the Kerry fans as 'f****** animals'. One Cork fan suggested immediately that Kerry's nickname should no longer be 'the kingdom' but 'the animal kingdom'. Another suggested that in future Cork should play all their home games against Kerry in Fota Wild Life Park to make the Kerry fans feel at home.

### Not Forgiven but Forgotten

Despite Ó Sé's iconic status as a player, there are some Kerry people who will never forgive him for his treatment of Maurice Fitzgerald. It was suggested that Paidí nicknamed Maurice 'the Judge' because he kept him on the bench for so long.

A young autograph hunter was chuffed to bits when he got Paidí's autograph after a match. The following week, he accosted Paidí again and got his autograph, and after the very next game he tried to get it again.

'Look,' said Paidí, 'this is the third time you've asked me for my autograph. What's going on?'

'Well,' said the youngster, 'if I can get eight more of yours I can swap them for one of Maurice Fitzgerald's.'

Paidí was a bit nervous one day when he had to make the journey into Fitzgerald's parish. His nerves were calmed immediately when an old man came to greet him and gave him a big smile and a most enthusiastic handshake. The old man then said, 'It's a great, great pleasure to finally meet you in the flesh. You are a true icon of the game... what's this your name is again?'

# Thy Kingdom Come

Success in Gaelic football comes in cycles. Kerry are the undisputed kings of Gaelic football. In 2002 Kerry and Cork figured in an historic all Munster All-Ireland semifinal. The Kerry manager Paidí Ó Sé asked for a home match for Kerry. Cork did not object, so the match was played in Croke Park.

## *Marital Affairs*

Jimmy Denihan was one of Kerry's stars in the 1970s. A bad injury caused Denihan to retire prematurely, but he went on to forge a new career in politics. It was a bit of a cultural shock for him, particularly as he got some weird requests from his constituents. The most strange was the woman who asked him to see if he could arrange 'infidelity benefit' for herself and her husband.

## *A Grave Matter*

Even the mighty Kerry have had their barren years. Jack Boothman was president of the GAA, at a time when Kerry football was in the doldrums. Boothman went to the funeral of the legendary Paddy Bawn Brosnan. Because of the pressures of time he was unable to make it to the church and went to meet the funeral at the graveyard. As he waited for the cortège to arrive, Boothman chatted with a few gravediggers. One of them gave a guided tour of the graveyard and pointed to the graves of all the famous footballers. It seemed that every second grave belonged to a former Kerry great. The gravedigger turned to Boothman and said, 'It's a very impressive collection, isn't it?'

Boothman replied, ''Tis indeed, but the way things are going you'll have to dig them up if Kerry are ever to win anything again!'

## *In the Name of the Father*

Kerry's Jackie Lyne was a great player himself and produced three fine sons who all played for the local club team: Dinny, Jackie and one who was just ordained to the priesthood, whom Jackie Snr always referred to as 'his Reverence'.

Jackie Snr always, always wore his hat. The only time the hat came off his head was during the consecration at Mass. After a club match, Jackie Snr was holding court in the pub reliving the crucial moments.

'Dinny kicked the ball out. Jackie caught it and kicked it in to his Reverence.' He paused his dramatic narrative to lift his hat at the mention of 'his Reverence'. However, the religious aura was quickly dissipated as he came to the climax:

'And he kicked it into the f****** goal.'

## Getting Your Priorities Right

Kerry legend Paddy Bawn Brosnan's commitment to football was evident at an early age. Attending the local Christian Brothers school, he was asked to conjugate the Latin verb 'venio'. Paddy Bawn simply shrugged his shoulders and said, 'Ah sure, Brother, I'm only here for the football'.

### *A Hard Man*

Paddy Bawn had the reputation for being a 'fear crua', but there were occasional moments in his glittering career when the macho mask slipped. One wet Sunday, Kerry were playing Clare in a league fixture on a waterlogged pitch. A high ball came in and hit a pool of water as Paddy Bawn went for the ball, creating a big splash which temporarily blinded him. He called for a towel but Jackie Lyne took it from the baggage man and stuck it in the mud before passing it on. When Bawn rubbed his face with the towel, he ended up making it ten times worse. As the players collapsed with laughter, nobody enjoyed the pantomime more than Paddy.

On another occasion, Paddy Bawn suffered a nose injury in a club championship match. To stop the blood, which was flowing with the ferocity of Niagara Falls, a piece of paper from *The Kerryman* was stuck up his nose. True to form, Paddy played on. A week later, he felt a stinging pain and went to the doctor. The poor medic had much more difficulty in extracting the paper than healing the fractured nose.

## Poetic Injustice

Mind games have long been part and parcel of football in Kerry, as the county's best-known poet, Brendan Kennelly, discovered to his cost. As a boy in one of his first matches, Kennelly found himself marking Pata Spring. Kennelly knew his opponent was good. As he lined up at the halfway line to mark Pata, he was really psyched up. Just before the ref threw in the ball, Pata said, 'Do you know anything about sex?'

Brendan replied, 'I don't Pata'.

'Well, I'll tell you about it now. It's like Kelly's bull and Sullivan's cow, and that's how it happens and that's how you were born. Would you ever think about that now?'

The ball was thrown in. Pata was gone up the field with the ball, while Kennelly was rooted to the spot burdened with the big questions of life.

## The Field and Other Venues

As a child, John B. Keane was enthralled at the idea of lifting the Sam Maguire Cup and dreamed of captaining the Kerry team to win the All-Ireland. So much was he exercised by this dream, that when his mother brought him to Mass one Sunday, as the priest lifted the chalice during the consecration, John B. turned to her and whispered, 'Why does he get to win the cup every Sunday?'

As a young man, John B. was very serious about football, so much so that he decided to give up the drink for Lent as a sign of his commitment to the game. One Ash Wednesday, John B. met his neighbour Micky Joe, or 'The Quack'. In local parlance, John B. was 'fond of a sup'. Micky Joe was shocked to hear that John B. was giving up drink for Lent. However, John B. then qualified his commitment by saying 'except in emergencies'.

'What does that mean, exactly?' asked Micky Joe.

With a twinkle in his eye, Master Keane replied, 'Well, someone might say, "What are you having, John B.?"'

### The Manager

In his later years, John B. ventured briefly into coaching. At half-time, his charges were losing and were being physically intimidated. John B.'s talk confirmed John O'Mahony's adage, 'Whenever a team loses, there's always a row at half-time but when they win it's an inspirational speech'.

John B. berated his side, 'Now listen, lads, I'm not happy with our tackling. We're hurting them, but they keep getting up.' In the second half the team showed more bite and ran out easy winners.

### First Impressions

In his later years, John B. went to the local hospital to visit the sick. He saw a man proudly taping his wife and new baby on a camcorder. 'Is this your first child?' John B. asked politely.

'No,' replied the father. 'First camcorder.'

### Declining Years

One of John B.'s favourite stories was about the two former Kerry footballers who had been friends for many decades. In their declining years, their activities had been limited to meeting a few times a week to play cards. They were playing one day when one looked at the other and said, 'Now, don't get mad at me... I know we've been friends for a long time, but I just can't think of your name. I've thought and thought but I just can't remember it. Put me out of my misery and tell me what it is.'

His former midfield colleague glared at him for what seemed like ten minutes, before he finally asked, 'How soon do you need to know?'

In John B.'s stories, the clergy always featured prominently. One night, he had an animated conversation about the shortcomings of the Kerry team with the local parish priest, a sprightly 85-year-old. After a few glasses of whiskey, the conversation took a more intimate turn. John B. asked, 'Father, at what age do men no longer find women attractive?' The priest pensively took a few puffs from his pipe before replying, 'Well, my son, if want to know the answer to that question, I'm afraid you'll have to ask a much older man than me'.

### No Objection

John B. was a great admirer of the pride people took in playing club football in Kerry. He used the following story as a prime example: Within hours of the tragic death of a Kerry corner-forward in a traffic accident, an ambitious young hopeful rang the local club chairman. 'I hope you don't mind me ringing at this time,' he said. 'But I was wondering whether I might take the place of the deceased...'

'I hadn't really thought about it,' replied the chairman, 'but if the undertaker doesn't mind, then neither will I.'

## The Greatest

At the top of the footballing hierarchy in Kerry was Mick O'Connell, the man from Valentia. O'Connell is reputed to have left the dressing-room immediately after captaining Kerry to win the All-Ireland and headed straight home for Kerry. Asked why he had to forgo the celebrations, he replied, 'I had to go home to milk the cows'.

In emphasising O'Connell's ability to strike a ball, John B. told a story which showed that he was as drawn to the sacred as the profane. O'Connell was rowing from Valentia to the mainland and decided to practise his striking by taking a free from the boat. He hit it so hard that the ball burst on its journey. The cover of the ball landed outside the presbytery in Lisdoonvarna. The bladder landed outside 'a hoor house in Buenos Aires'.

## Micko

One of O'Connell's team-mates was Kerry's most famous manager, Mick O'Dwyer. After Kerry won their eighth All-Ireland title under his management in 1986, O'Dwyer recognised that some surgery was needed on the team and one or two of the team's legends needed to be put out to grass. O'Dwyer approached one of the player's in question, 'You are one of the giants of the game. You have played a huge part in making Kerry the greatest team of all time. A hundred years from now people will still be talking about you.' The player's chest puffed up with pride, but his expression changed, as O'Dwyer continued, 'I just don't know how we'd get on without you. But we're going to give it a try.'

In 2002, Micko attended a social function with Dublin manager Tommy Lyons, while O'Dwyer was still Kildare manager. Lyons said to him, 'Micko, you and I will fill Croke Park this year'. O'Dwyer's reply was, 'Tommy, you and I wouldn't fill a bathroom'.

# The Lyons Den

After Dublin lost to Laois and Armagh in 2003, Lyons was subjected to severe criticism. His fall from grace is encapsulated in the comment of one former Dublin player: 'The only way Tommy Lyons can get up again is with Viagra.'

Dublin's demise also gave rise to two new jokes:

Q: What do Dublin footballers have in common with a wonderbra?

A: Lots of support but no cup.

Q: What do you say to a Dub in Croke Park on All-Ireland final day?

A: Two packets of crisps, please.

## *The Garden of Eden*

In fairness to Tommy Lyons, losing to Armagh was not the disaster some of his critics claimed, given the form Armagh showed in subsequent games. Armagh's focus and obsessive will to win was reflected in Colm O'Rourke's incisive observation: 'If Adam had been an Armagh footballer, Eve would have had no chance. Instead of an apple, he would have looked for a banana, as it was on the diet sheet.'

Nonetheless, the decline in Dublin's fortunes after the defeat to Armagh is reflected in the following story: Two bricklayers were chatting at work. 'Are you going to the match on Sunday?' said one. 'Dublin are playing Kildare.'

'No,' said the other. 'My wife won't let me.'

'What?' said the first. 'It's easy to get out of that. About an hour before the game, what you do is pick her up, take her to the bedroom, rip off her clothes and make mad, passionate love to her. Then she'll let you do anything you want.'

'I'll try that,' said the other man.

The following Monday the two men met on the building site. 'How come you didn't make it to the game?' asked the first man.

'Well, I'll tell you what happened,' said the second man. 'About an hour before I was planning to leave, I did as you said. I picked her up, took her to the bedroom and ripped off her clothes, and then I thought, Dublin haven't been playing that well lately.'

# Chapter Five
# Hurlers on and off the Ditch

## Rock DJ

In the beginning, God and DJ Carey were seen as quite separate individuals. It was only later confusion crept in.

One story illustrates DJ's status in the game. The All-Heaven hurling final was taking place between Kilkenny and Tipperary. The Tipperary team were powered by some of the giants of deceased hurlers. Captained by Ollie Walsh, the Kilkenny team also had the pick of players from their county who had gone on to their eternal reward. With just three minutes to go, Tipperary were leading by three goals and two points. Suddenly there was a gasp from the crowd as a sub appeared for the Kilkenny team, wearing the No. 14 jersey. In the final three minutes, four balls were pumped into the square. The supersub caught the four balls and stuck each of them in the net. The Cats won by a point.

After the game was over, Saint Peter went over to commiserate with the Tipperary stars. The Tipp players were stunned by the appearance of the sub and asked, 'I never knew DJ Carey died. When did it happen?'

St Peter replied, 'Oh that's not DJ. That's God. He just thinks he's DJ Carey.'

### With Friends Like You...

Mind you, a prophet is not always appreciated in his own land. In 1997, before Clare played Kilkenny in the All-Ireland semifinal, Ger Loughnane was asked in an interview what he thought of DJ. Carey had been absolutely brilliant in the All-Ireland quarter-final, a thrilling game against Galway in Thurles. He practically beat the Westerners all on his own. Loughnane mused, 'DJ will prove himself to be an outstanding player when he plays really well against one of the best players in the country in a big match. Next Sunday, he will be playing in a really big match against Brian Lohan, and if he plays really well against Brian Lohan, he will prove himself to be a really great player, but I won't regard him as great player until he does it against somebody like Brian on the big day.'

Nicky Brennan was Kilkenny manager at the time, and he taped the interview and played it on the bus on the way to the match. According to folklore, Brennan said, 'Listen to what that c*** Loughnane said about one of our best players'. Legend has it that Eddie O'Connor piped up, 'He's f****** right!'

## The Real Taoiseach

Hurling heroes have to be truly exceptional to be recognised in Cork. One hurler who gained iconic status on Leeside was the late Jack Lynch. It is said that rugby is a sport for ruffians played by gentlemen; Gaelic football is a sport for gentlemen played by ruffians; but hurling is a sport for gentlemen played by gentlemen. Lynch personified that gentlemanly quality.

Lynch performed great feats on the field, but went on to achieve even bigger things on the political stage. He once joked, 'A good speech isn't one that proves that the Minister is telling the truth, but one in which it cannot be proved he's lying'. He also enjoyed Oscar Levant's comment that, 'A politician will double-cross that bridge when he comes to it'.

During the 1977 general election campaign, Lynch went to visit an old folks' home to canvas for votes. One woman had a bad-tempered face and her voice seemed remarkably similar to a dog growling. She insisted on telling the prospective Taoiseach her life story: She had gone to the dentist to have her false teeth adjusted for the fourth time and they still didn't fit.

'Well,' said the dentist, 'I'll do it again this time, but no more. There's no reason why these shouldn't fit your mouth easily.'

'Who said anything about my mouth?' she answered. 'They don't fit in the glass.'

In later years, Lynch was occasionally asked to reflect on the ageing process. He loved George Burns's comment on turning eighty: 'I can do all the things today I did at eighteen which tells you how pathetic I was at eighteen.'

### Parting Shot

In terms of hurlers Lynch said, 'You know a player is great coming to the end of his career. A great player when he is gone will never be forgotten. A bad player is one who is not yet gone but is already forgotten!'

### Don't Forget to Remember Me

Asked how he would like to be remembered, Lynch once joked that he was afraid that he would suffer the same fate of John Arason and be remembered inappropriately. Arason was the last Catholic bishop of Iceland and was executed at Skalholt in 1550. The Icelanders, rejoicing in their complete religious freedom, felt that a monument should be erected on the site to commemorate his memory. They built a Lutheran church!

### Rivals

Another favourite Lynch story was about the man who went to an auction to buy a valuable parrot. He wanted the parrot badly and thought of bidding up to £40. The bidding went up to £120 before it was knocked down to him. Afterwards, he asked the auctioneer who the other man was who kept bidding against him. 'That wasn't another man; that was the parrot you bought,' replied the auctioneer.

### A Tidy Sum

As a pupil at the famous North Mon, Lynch had a keen appreciation for the role of the Christian Brothers in Irish life in general, and in the promotion of hurling in particular. He especially admired their commitment and the commitment they inspired in others. Lynch once told the story of a clever little boy at an expensive and liberal private school, who was underachieving badly, particularly in maths. The parents, devout atheists, sent him to a very strict Christian Brothers' establishment. He returned after the first day, tiny schoolbag brimming with books, and locked himself in his room for three hours with his homework. This went on for a few weeks and at the end of his first month he returned with his interim report card, which showed that he was first in his class in maths. His delighted parents asked what had awakened his drive and he said, a bit grimly, 'I knew that it was a serious subject when they showed me the guy nailed to the plus sign'.

### A Role in History

Jack Lynch was well able to tell stories against himself. One went back to his schooldays. His father said to him one day, 'Tell me, Jack, how did your test go today?'

'Well, I did just what Napoleon did.'

'And what's that?'

'I went down in history.'

## Lord of the Rings

Christy Ring is the prince of hurlers but he was a hard taskmaster. In the 1950s, a Cork hurler was greeted at the end of a disappointing performance in a Munster Championship match, with the frank appraisal of one Cork fan, 'That was the worst display I ever saw by a Cork player. You were complete rubbish. In fact you were even worse.'

The hurler, quite disturbed, informed Christy Ring what the man had said. Ring replied, 'That poor chap is not really responsible for what he says. He never has an original thought. He just goes around repeating what everybody else is saying!'

Ring was asked his opinion of an up-and-coming star in Cork hurling, who regularly boasted about his sporting prowess. Ring said, 'On his day Charlie is the best hurler in the world. Unfortunately, his day is always a Monday!'

Another time, Ring was asked what he thought about an up-and-coming Cork defender. Ring furrowed his brow and said, 'Oh he's got a bit of skill. The only problem is that he thinks "tackle" is something you take fishing with you. A good defender should be so mean that, if he owned the Atlantic Ocean, he wouldn't give you a wave.'

Ring was famous for his commitment to training. Ring's wife gave birth to their first son. A few hours later, he was said to have been on his way to training when he was greeted and warmly congratulated by a neighbour. When she saw his gear and hurley, the neighbour said, 'I'm surprised to see you training just after your wife gave birth to your son'.

Ring coolly replied, 'I don't care if 'twas a young bonham she had. I'm not going to miss training.'

Ring was very single-minded and once instructed a debutante on the Cork team to, 'always keep your eye on the ball – even when it's in the referee's pocket'.

### Media Management

Ring once met a young journalist on his way into an All-Ireland final. The journalist was trying to get information from him, but Christy was more impenetrable than the Dead Sea scrolls. Eventually, the journalist lost patience and decided to quit while he still retained a shred of dignity. He asked Ring one final question. 'Can you tell me where to go for the press box?'

'To hell and back,' Ring replied.

### Cheap Seats

Ring once attended a match at Croke Park as a spectator. It was explained to him at the turnstiles that there were seats for £5, £10 and £20 and that programmes were half-a-crown.

'Okay,' said Ring, 'I'll sit on a programme'.

### No Passengers, Please

One man does not make a hurling team, though Ring had his doubts. One Sunday, he was jumping over the stile instead of displaying his pass as he went into a match. A furious county board official, a former team-mate of Ring's, caustically inquired where the wizard of Cloyne's pass was.

'I don't have it.'

'But, Christy, you ought to have. You won no less than eight All-Ireland medals,' the official replied.

'And if I hadn't been carrying passengers like you, I'd have won at least eight more!' came the retort.

### *Eager to Help*

Christy and a friend attended a seminar on coaching in a church hall in Cork one evening. The priest approached the great man apologetically and said, 'There are very bad acoustics in here'.

Christy's friend replied reassuringly, 'Don't worry, Father. I'm not sure who these acoustics are, but if they start any trouble we'll throw them out.'

## Solidarity

Hurling in Cork normally creates a special collegiality. There's a story told about a famous Cork hurler of yesteryear – a guard who got into a heated 'altercation' with a member of the public. Some hard words were uttered and allegedly blows were exchanged. The affronted civilian went straight to complain about the guard to his superiors. As he made his complaint, copious notes were taken and when the guard's name was identified the officer in charge mentioned casually 'the hurler'.

The complainee went a whiter shade of pale and asked in a whisper, 'Is that who he is? God I don't want to get him in trouble. I'm dropping all charges.'

The man was out the door with a sprint that Sonia O'Sullivan would have marvelled at.

## The Three Wise Men

Another story relates to the three Macs: Charlie, Justin and Gerald McCarthy. The night before an All-Ireland final, they were supposed to be tucked up in their beds. The three young men decided to take a trip in to the city centre to sample the atmosphere. The problem was that it was much harder for them to get a taxi back to the team hotel. Two of the team mentors, Jim 'Tough' Barry and Donie Keane, were patrolling the corridor. The three lads knew that, if they were caught, they would be read the riot act. They hid until the coast was clear and then raced up the stairs and into their beds. Within moments, there was a rap on the door. The three amigos pretended to be fast asleep. Then came a louder rap that they could not possibly ignore, followed by the question, 'What were ye lads up to?'

'We're in bed.'

'Open the door.'

Charlie McCarthy nonchalantly walked to the door, pretending to rub the sleep from his eyes as he let the two mentors in, 'What's the problem, Jim? We were fast asleep.'

Jim looked at him with steely eyes, 'Is that so? Jaysus, Charlie, you're the only man I know to wear a collar and tie in bed.'

## Tipp Top

Tipperary star Mick 'Rattler' Byrne was a small man, but pound for pound he was the toughest player you could ever meet. Rattler could mark guys from Wexford three or four stone heavier than him and never be beaten. He was a great cornerback for Tipp but also a wonderful storyteller. He didn't have much time for modern players' talk about their injuries, especially about their 'hamstrings'. Rattler always said that the only time in his playing days he heard anybody talking about hamstrings was when they were hanging outside a butcher's shop.

Rattler's best story is about the day he went to New York with a very nervous Tommy Doyle, who was making his first airplane flight. Doyle sought comfort from the Rattler, who told him, 'Don't be worrying, Tommy. There are two parachutes under the seat; you put one on, jump out, count to ten, press the button and you jump to safety. What could be simpler?'

'But what happens if the parachute doesn't open? asked Doyle.

'That's easy,' answered the Rattler, 'you just jump back up and get the spare one.'

## Billy the Kid

In the 1950s, one of Tipperary's star forwards was a young Billy Quinn, whose three goals in the 1954 League final helped Tipp beat Kilkenny. Quinn is the father of Niall, who served Irish soccer with such distinction. Although soccer claimed Niall's career, his love of hurling remained unabated.

At a charity function in London, Niall paid a small fortune for a hurley signed by Jimmy Barry-Murphy, only to discover later that Jimmy hadn't signed it at all!

### Pride and Prejudice

Despite his pride at Niall's great success in soccer, Billy still feels the game is no match for hurling. He put his foot in it in 1990 when a journalist came to interview him after Niall scored the famous goal against Holland in the World Cup. When asked if he was proud of Niall, Billy replied without thinking, 'To tell you the truth, I'd rather if he had won a Munster medal!'

### A Shattering Experience

The family did play a price for Niall's devotion to hurling. As a boy, Niall always had a hurley in his hand. One famous day in Killarney, Babs Keating scored a last-minute goal from a free. Niall, who was about five at the time, was practicing frees in the back garden after the match. His mother, Mary, was doing the ironing, when the window was shattered to smithereens by Niall's sliotar. Mary nearly dropped dead with the shock of the shattering glass. All Niall said afterwards was, 'I was only doing Babs Keating!'

The one and only Babs is a man who knows all there is to know about the vagaries of hurling fortunes. He once said about management, 'It's a very short distance between a slap on the back and a kick in the arse!'

## Time Check

With time running out and Galway's victory apparently secure in the 1988 All-Ireland hurling final, Nicky English asked the referee how much time was left. The ever-helpful Slyvie Linnane butted in immediately to say, 'In your case, a year and five minutes!'

Injuries can wreak havoc on a player. Given the extent of English's injuries, Babs Keating once said to him, 'Nicky, if I had legs like yours, I'd be wearing nylons'.

## Shamateurism

In recent years, the GAA's relationship with amateurism has been riddled with hypocrisy. Despite the spate of rumours that have bedevilled the GAA about payments to managers, the Association has been powerless to act because of absence of proof. Former president Peter Quinn famously observed that while there were many claims that managers were being paid under the table, the GAA couldn't even find the tables!

## A Man's Game

Hurling is a man's game. Tourin took on Ballyduff in Lismore in a junior hurling match. Tourin's full-forward 'manhandled' Ballyduff's goalie. As a result, a mêlée developed around the goal. Everyone got involved. What made it unusual was that all thirty players ended up against the railing of the pitch and then things got so intense that they all ended up in the next field. As the faction-fighting was at its height, one wag was heard to remark, 'Come here for a laugh and you'll go home in stitches'.

Minister for Defence Michael Smith tells a story which reveals that hurling is no place for the faint-hearted: 'The toughest match I ever heard of was the 1935 All-Ireland semifinal. After six minutes, the ball ricocheted off the post and went into the stand. The pulling continued relentlessly and it was twenty-two minutes before any of the players noticed the ball was missing!'

## The Marble City

One incident which certainly illustrates the passion which hurling generates in the Marble City occurred in the 1970s. The great Dublin football team travelled down to Kilkenny for what they expected to be a meaningless feature against the county side. When they got to the ground they were very gratified to see a huge crowd was in attendance, obviously there to watch what were spoken of as the greatest team of all time.

The warm-up match was a club minor hurling championship fixture. When Dublin took the to field, their pride took a mighty dent. The ground was virtually empty; the majority of the crowd had gone home as soon as the hurling match was over.

### Knock, Knock, Knocking on Heaven's Doors

Two Kilkenny fans, sitting at a bar counter, were reliving the latest game they had seen. After a brief lull in the conversation, one said to the other, 'I wonder if there is hurling in heaven'. His friend said that nobody knew for sure, but suggested that they should make a pact there and then: whichever of them died first would come back and tell the other. They both agreed and the pact was soon sealed with another round of drinks.

In due course, one of the men died and the day after being buried he turned up at the foot of his friend's bed as arranged. The man in the bed almost died himself with fright, but soon remembered the purpose of the visit. He sat up immediately, eager to hear the news.

'Tell me quick,' he said, 'is there hurling in heaven?'

The dead man replied, 'Well, I have good news and I have bad news. The good news is that, yes, there's hurling in heaven alright. But the bad news is that there's a game next Sunday and you're playing full back.'

## RIP

Two stalwarts of a club in Kilkenny were distraught. One said, 'Have you heard the bad news? Old Frankin is dead. And to think he was going to play left-corner-forward for the Junior B team tomorrow.'

'My God, that's awful.'

'It's tragic! But wait a minute… Maybe we can get Micky Joe to fill in for him.'

### Not Tough at the Top

In the 1980s and early 1990s, Kilkenny's dominance of hurling ensured a bleak time for Wexford. This hopeless situation was most obvious on the Wexford side of the New Ross bridge, which separates counties Kilkenny and Wexford. A sign on the bridge read, 'You are now entering a Nuclear Free Zone'. A Kilkenny fan added a message of his own, 'You've now entered a trophy free zone'.

## The Boys from Wexford

All this was to change for a year or so, with the arrival of one of hurling's great evangelists, Liam Griffin, as Wexford manager. Griffin brought a new professionalism to the job and a lot of new practices. At one of his first meetings with the panel, Griffin gave the team a questionnaire to fill in. It had a number of questions such as 'Where would you prefer to train?'

At the bottom was an additional query: 'What is your favourite position?' Most players answered in the obvious way: full back, centre half-back, full-forward, etc. The exception was the joker from Faythe Harriers, Larry O'Gorman, who gave Griffin more information than he needed. His reply was simply, 'On top!'

### Medical Mistake

Griffin exuded charisma and enjoyed a laugh with the squad. One evening, he approached a sad-looking fringe member of his panel and asked, 'Why are you looking so down-hearted?'

'The doctor says I can't play hurling.'

'When did he see you play?'

### Minus One

Griffin attended a reunion of old hurlers. All the giants of the ash – such as Eddie Keher, Tony Doran, Joe Cooney, Jimmy Barry-Murphy, Anthony Daly and John Connolly – were there. An old hurler, who had the reputation of being an utter bore and whose opinion of his own extraordinary abilities was shared only by himself, approached Griffin, looked around the room and said, 'How many great hurlers do you think there are in this room?'

'One less than you think,' Griffin replied.

### Christmas Shopping

In 1996, Griffin led Wexford to the All-Ireland. Some Kilkenny fans couldn't handle the new hurling order, as the following story illustrates: That Christmas a Kilkenny family went into Callan to do some Christmas shopping. In the sports shop, the son picked up a Wexford hurling shirt and said to his twin sister, 'I've decided to be a Wexford supporter and I would like this jersey for Christmas'. His sister, outraged by the suggestion, slapped him on the face and said, 'Go talk to your mother'.

The boy walked with the Wexford shirt in hand and found his mother, 'Mummy dearest?'

'Yes, pet?'

'I've decided I'm going to be a Wexford supporter and I'd like this shirt for Christmas.'

The mother could barely speak with anger but eventually said, 'Go talk to your father'.

Off he went with shirt in hand and found his father. 'Dad?'
'Yes, son.'

'I've decided to become a Wexford supporter and I would like this shirt for Christmas.'

The father hit the son a thump on the head and said, 'No son of mine will be seen in a yoke like that'.

As they went home, the father asked the son if he had learned any lesson that day. The son thought for a moment before replying, 'Yes, I have. I've only been a Wexford fan for just over an hour and already I hate you Kilkenny f******!'

## The Hurler Strikes Back

Kilkenny fans are well able to get their revenge. One story they narrate is of the doctor who told his patient to avoid any excitement. The doctor encouraged him to start watching Wexford.

Another story is of the Wexford hurling fan who got so depressed that he dressed up in his full Wexford kit and threw himself in a river. When the police retrieved his body, they removed the strip and replaced it with stockings and suspenders. They told the coroner that they did this 'in order to avoid embarrassing the family'.

Kilkenny fans have also rewritten the Snow White story. In their version, Snow White arrived home one evening to find her house destroyed by fire. She was doubly worried because she'd left all seven dwarfs asleep inside. As she scrambled among the wreckage, frantically calling their names, she suddenly heard the cry: 'Wexford for the Liam McCarthy Cup.'

'Thank goodness,' sobbed Snow White, 'at least Dopey's still alive.'

## Hurlers on the Ditch

A great champion of hurling was the late Mick Dunne. In 1949, Dunne joined the *Irish Press* as junior librarian, before quickly graduating to a Gaelic games correspondent and later Gaelic Games editor of the Sports Department.

Dunne was well able to tell stories about his time on the paper. He once sat in a hotel having his breakfast the morning after a

Munster final. Two tables away, he could hear two men dissecting his report on the match. Their remarks weren't very complimentary.

Later that morning, Dunne stopped for petrol at a small shop outside Thurles. As Tipperary had lost heavily the previous day, the shopkeeper was in foul humour. He asked Dunne if he had been at the match. When Dunne replied in the affirmative, the shopkeeper went into a lengthy analysis of why Tipperary lost. He then proceeded to ask Dunne whether he had seen 'what that f****** b****** Mick Dunne had written in the *Irish Press*'.

When Dunne politely replied that he was aware of the contents of the article, the shopkeeper launched into a vicious tirade about Dunne's knowledge of hurling, casting a number of doubts on the journalist's parentage in the process. Dunne made no response until the very end, when the shopkeeper said, 'I bet that fella's getting a fortune for writing that rubbish. Tell you what, although I hate him I wish I had his money.'

Dunne calmly paid him for the petrol and said, 'Well, you've just got £5 of it'.

## No Ordinary Fan

In 1979, after Kilkenny beat Galway in the All-Ireland hurling final, Fan Larkin rushed off the field into the dressing-room to tog in. A clearly startled Mick Dunne went into the Kilkenny room just minutes after the match to prepare for a live interview, only to see Fan already fully clothed. Clearly Fan had missed the presentation. Dunne asked him why he was in the dressing-room so quickly.

'I have to go to Mass, Mick,' replied Fan in a matter-of-fact voice.

## First Things First

Dunne was one of the journalists involved in selecting the team that would travel to New York to play in the Cardinal Cushing games. It was almost the precursor of the All-Stars. They decided to pick some good players from the weaker counties. This, in turn, led them to speak about the terms of reference in selection decisions. One of their number blurted out, 'Let's pick the team first and we'll sort out the terms of reference later!'

## Get It Right

A fee-paying rugby school on the southside of Dublin challenged a northside Christian Brothers school to a game of hurling. The date was arranged and the Christian Brothers boys decided to adopt a gentlemanly stance and send the college a telegram, which read: 'May the best team win.'

The pedantic southsiders sent a grammatically correct telegram in reply: 'May the better team win.'

## Surfing USA

On the All-Star trips, romance often flourished. Irish GAA stars were highly pursued by misty-eyed Irish-Americans hoping their 'cailín' would get married to one of the sports heroes from the auld sod. However, two of the less-worldly All-Stars, who on a quest for a holiday romance, got one hell of a shock when they discovered that they had arranged a double date with two transvestites!

To compound their embarrassment, the two lads had been heard using very suggestive chat-up lines to the 'girls'. The first had said, 'You know what, I'd look good on you'. The second was even more expansive, 'Your eyes are like spanners. Every time you look at me, my nuts tighten.'

Perhaps these tactics were a response to their failure the previous night doing the rounds of a nightclub. They had struck a blank using the line, 'Tog out. You're selected.'

### *There Go the Boston Burglars*

On the All-Star trip to America in 1978, the All-Stars were hammered by fourteen points by Cork in the opening match in Boston. The Cork half-back line was absolutely outstanding. After the match, the All-Stars were told by the management that they were a 'disgrace' and that unless they upped their performance in the next match in San Francisco there would be 'severe repercussions'.

The great Pat Hartigan, who was team captain, gave a speech in the dressing-room before the second game. He threw his jersey on the middle of the dressing-room floor and said, 'Anyone not prepared to die for the jersey throw it in there and get out of here now'.

Pat Delaney from Offaly was the All-Star's wing-forward. Delaney was marking Denis Coughlan. With the first ball that came into him, Delaney let fly and struck Coughlan on the side of the head, splitting it open. Delaney then moved into the centre and the next ball that came his way, he again let fly, aiming for Johnny Crowley. He missed Crowley and struck his own man, Tony Doran. The game was only five minutes old and he had sent two men to hospital!

There was an immediate cry, 'Get that so and so off'. Delaney was substituted. He was very disappointed afterwards but not in the way that might be expected. He said, 'What harm, but if they had just left me on another minute or two it would have been great. I was just going to move on Dermot McCurtin.' He had taken it on himself to wipe out the entire Cork half-back line!

### Called to the Bar

In 1971, Mick Bermingham was selected at right corner-forward in the inaugural All-Stars series. Bermingham's career with Dublin spanned four decades. He first played senior inter-county hurling with Dublin as a sixteen-year-old in 1959; his last game for Dublin in 1982 was at intermediate level.

One of the impediments to Bermingham's hurling career was his work in the pub business, which caused him to work anti-social hours. There was one memorable moment when his job came back to haunt him on the hurling field. Bermingham played in the 1963 Leinster Final against Kilkenny. It was a lovely, sunny day and he was the free taker. Micheal O'Hehir had been praising him in his commentary. Then Dublin got a free into the Canal End goal and O'Hehir said, 'The diminutive Mick Bermingham is about to take a free for Dublin and this will surely be a point'.

When Bermingham was lifting the ball, it tilted away from him and he put it wide. When he ran back into the corner after the free, he heard a Dublin voice ringing out clearly among the 40,000 crowd saying, 'Ah sure, Bermingham, you can't score a point and what's worse you can't f***** even pull a pint!'

# Quirke-y

Carlow dual star Paddy Quirke played senior football and hurling for his county in the 1970s and 1980s. The highlight of Quirke's career came when he was chosen as the dual All-Star replacement. He also played hurling in San Francisco and found it really tough and physical. At one stage, he put in his hurley, angled with the bos to the ground, to block an opponent; however, he got a severe belt across the face and was rushed to hospital. Quirke had no social security cover, but his friends who were with him decided to re-christen him Patrick Foley (a genuine holder of social security). The only problem was when Paddy heard the name Patrick Foley being called out in the hospital, he forgot that that was supposed to be him.

At that stage he was not in very good shape and was expecting some sympathy from the doctor. Instead all he said was, 'Were you playing that crazy Irish game?'

### No Real Damage

In 1985, Quirke played for his club Naomh Eoin against the Westmeath champions Brownstown in the first round of the Leinster club hurling championship. A few days later, one of his team-mates was asked how bad the pitch was. He replied, 'Well the grass was so long a hare rose at half-time!'

Carlow have been waiting for any silverware for a long time. In the middle of the night, the Carlow county chairman was woken up by a call from his local garda station. 'I'm afraid the trophy room has been broken into, sir.'

Horrified, the county chairman asked, 'Did they get the cups?'

'No, sir,' replied the guard, 'they didn't go into the kitchen.'

# Tales of the Unexpected

Antrim's Dessie Donnelly has a special place in his heart for his team-mates, whose words are every bit as entertaining as their achievements. In 1989, after sensationally beating Offaly in the All-Ireland semifinal, Antrim were training hard coming up to the All-Ireland final. To get a bit of a break, Paul McKillen and Donnelly went to see the All-Ireland football semifinal between Cork and Dublin. They were having a great chat before the game and, as the players were coming on to the field, McKillen noticed the big screen for the first time. Donnelly said to him, 'This should be a great game today'.

McKillen looked up at the big screen and then he turned around and asked Donnelly, 'Is this game live?' Donnelly nearly died laughing.

However, McKillen is not the Antrim hurler who bought a JCB and set up his own business with the slogan, 'With us you're guaranteed your hole'.

## The Great Escape

The 1994 All-Ireland hurling final was one of the most dramatic matches in the history of the game. Although Offaly's Johnny Pilkington was making victory speeches before the game – and he wasn't even the captain – Limerick had outplayed Offaly throughout the match. Limerick held an apparently unassailable five points lead with just minutes remaining. Then Johnny Dooley scored a goal from a free. Within a minute, Pat O'Connor had a second goal. Limerick seemed to flounder into impotence, whereas Offaly had a new kick in their step. It seemed that they could score points at will. A new joke was born:

Q: Why are Limerick magic?

A: Because they can disappear for five minutes.

## An Awfully Offaly Mess

Offaly made the breakthrough to win the All-Ireland hurling title in 1981, defeating Galway. The Westerners fully expected to retain their title, as one of their banners in the crowd indicated: It read, 'We're Offaly sorry'.

### Daylight Robbery

One of Offaly's stars was the late, great Pat Carroll. After his death, a story was told to illustrate Carroll's commitment to the game. One day, he said to his friend, 'My hurley was stolen this morning'.

**Friend:** That's terrible; where did you lose it?

**Pat:** In the car park.

**Friend:** Did the thieves damage your car much?

**Pat:** I don't know; they stole that too!

### Driven to Destruction

Another Offaly hurler's dedication wasn't quiet as intense. The night of the presentation of the All-Ireland medals he had a few glasses of lemonade too many and as he drove home he was unable to take a corner and drove his car through a farmer's wall, absolutely wrecking his car in the process. A passer-by was soon on hand and recognised the famous driver, even though the blood was pumping out of his forehead. The Offaly hurler instructed the passer-by to shine his flashlamp into the car. 'Are you looking for your All-Ireland medal?' inquired the Good Samaritan.

'Ah, no, sure I'll find that sometime but I've got a five naggin bottle of whiskey in here somewhere and I want to be certain it didn't break in the crash.'

A few months later the same player travelled to a remote small town in Offaly to play in a club tournament game. After he parked his newish car, he was approached by a tourist who asked him, 'Scuse me, where's the nearest boozer?'

The Offaly hurler calmly replied, 'You're talking to him'.

His team took a hammering in the match and afterwards he was asked, 'Are your team members good losers?'

'Good? They're perfect!'

## The Limerick Leader

Ironically, when Offaly beat Limerick to win their All-Ireland title in 1994, they were trained by a Limerick man, Eamon Cregan. Cregan never managed to achieve the same thing with Limerick. In 2002, his stewardship of the Limerick team was famously marred by great rancour and all kinds of machinations within the county board.

One day, Cregan was walking along a beach when he came across a bottle. When he unscrewed the top, a genie appeared and said, 'I'm so grateful to get out of that bottle that I will grant you one wish'. Cregan thought for a moment and said, 'I have always dreamed that there could be a motorway from outside my front door all the way to Croke Park'.

The genie thought for a moment and then said, 'I'm sorry; I can't do that. Just think of all the bureaucracy and red tape involved and all the local authorities who would have to be involved in putting that together. I'm sorry, but could you ask for an easier wish?'

Cregan said, 'Well there is one other thing. I'd like to train Limerick to win the All-Ireland, with a fully united panel, management team and county board behind me'.

The genie thought about it for a few minutes, and then said, 'So do you want two lanes or four on that motorway?'

### *Polished Performance*

In 1999, Cregan listed former Clare hurler Jimmy Smyth as one of the top-five hurlers of the twentieth century. The same year, Smyth was presented with an award as Clare Person of the Year. In his acceptance speech, Smyth remembered a story his uncle used to relate regarding a fella who couldn't get out of bed in the morning. The man made a firm resolution that this would be rectified. He employed the services of his landlady, who assured him that in the future he would be called at 8 am sharp.

However, the man's friends heard of this arrangement and blackened his face with shoe polish when he was asleep. The landlady, true to her word, called him promptly at 8 am. He got up immediately, looked at his face in the mirror and said, 'Good God, 'twas the wrong man she called'. With that, he jumped back into bed.

The 'polish' was flowing so liberally the night he got his award, Smyth didn't recognise himself either.

## From Clare To Here

Christy Jones, the goalkeeper on Smyth's club team, had a great puck out. Back then, the sliotar was much heavier than it is today. Smyth and Jones grew up in Ruan, which is about eight miles from Doora. Doora might as well have been South Africa, because it was too great a distance for them to travel at a time when no one had a car. Smyth once asked Jones what was the greatest puck out he had ever struck. Jones answered, 'If I had the ball they had today, I'd drive it to f****** Doora.'

## A Real Fan

There was a man in Ruan who was a great admirer of Smyth's. One day, Smyth was bearing down on goal in a very tense match and the harder he ran the more the Ruan crowd was getting excited. Everyone was shouting out advice and he could hear all kinds of suggestions about what he should do. Then, just as he was trying to concentrate, he heard his No. 1 fan roaring out over the din, 'Take no notice of them, Jimmy, make your own arrangements'.

## Confessions

Smyth had not always such a happy relationship with priests on the hurling field. He was playing a club match one day, when a fracas developed and most of the crowd invaded the pitch. A priest came and abused Smyth, who responded, 'Father, you should be on the sideline giving a good example to the young'. The next day the priest's mother came to visit Smyth and thanked him for the good advice he'd given her son.

## Last Will and Testament

Bishop Willie Walsh has got to know many great characters through his love of hurling, particularly Paddy, 'the Duggie', Duggan. Duggie, whose whole life was hurling, was a mentor to a host of teams in Clare. When he became ill, Bishop Walsh went to see him in hospital. Duggie had received the news that day that he only had a short time to live. He said to the bishop, 'I'd like you to do the funeral Mass and make all the arrangements'.

The bishop agreed. Then the Duggie said, 'That's fine, Willie. I still believe that we'd have won the county final last year if they'd listened to me at half-time.' As soon as the funeral was arranged, he was straight back to the most important thing in life – hurling!

## The Man from Clare

As a Clare minor Ger Loughnane's first introduction to inter-county hurling was under the 'Duggie'. Duggan gave an amazing speech in the dressing-room in Limerick. While whacking a hurley off a table, and as his false teeth did three laps of his mouth, he called on the team to kill and maim the opposition before saying an 'Our Father' and three 'Hail Marys'.

## Going Dutch

As a player, Loughnane won two All-Star awards and two National League medals. As a result of their success in the late 1970s, the Clare team were invited by a hockey team called 'the hurling club' to play an exhibition game against Wexford in Holland, to mark the Dutch club's centenary. The hosts took the hurlers to the Heineken factory in Amsterdam and were amazed at the gusto with which the Irish delegation attacked the free samples.

The match itself took place on a manicured lawn in Amsterdam. After the game, the Clare team somehow ended up in a bar in a seedy back lane in Amsterdam's red light district. Much later on in the night, Loughnane noticed one of his team-mates leaving the bar, very much the worse for wear. Loughnane left to see his friend stumbling into a dark alley, which was obviously very dangerous. As Loughnane went to escort him to safety, he was greeted by the question, 'Is this f***** O'Connell street?' The other player thought he was in Ennis!

## The Bushman

Loughnane had a stormy relationship with officials, including those in Clare. Among their number was Brendan Vaughan, the former chairman of the county board. Both Loughnane and Vaughan were teachers; they nearly came to blows at a schoolboy match between their two schools. There were two coats down as goalposts. There was no crossbar. Vaughan was umpire at one side; Loughnane was umpire at the other. A head-high ball came in. Vaughan said it was a goal; Loughnane said it was a point. After a full and frank exchange of views, Vaughan looked at Loughnane disdainfully and uttered the immortal words, 'Get away, you bushman from Feakle!'

## Start as You Mean to Continue

Clare started training for the 1995 Munster Championship the previous September. Clare trained all the way through the League. Luxurious conditions were not conducive to good winter training, so they trained in Crusheen. Mike McNamara was excellent for putting the players through that hard physical slog. The players will never forget their introduction to McNamara's training methods and personality. On his very first night standing on the pitch in Crusheen he said, 'Okay ladies, let's go for a jog'.

After eighty-one years in the hurling wilderness, Clare finally won the All-Ireland in 1995. The county went into a dizzy state and tickets for the final were chased with a passion. An advertisement appeared in a parish magazine a few days before the final. 'Young hurling supporter of good appearance and sound health offers hand in marriage to any young lady with two tickets to the final next Sunday. Please send photograph of the tickets.'

### Lynch Mob

In 1998, the Colin Lynch saga dominated. Lynch was controversially given a long suspension for an incident, which the referee had not deemed punishable in the match. To Clare fans, the evidence appeared very flimsy. As a result, Lynch missed all three of Clare's All-Ireland semifinal games against Offaly.

Even more controversy erupted when Ger Loughnane gave a sensational interview on Clare FM lambasting the Munster Council. Only the Mick McCarthy–Roy Keane saga has warranted more column inches. One wag suggested that Irish industry lost £25 million because workers were talking about Ger Loughnane when they should have been doing their jobs!

Loughnane claimed that the role of manager was the second oldest profession and mused, 'I have come to realise that it bears a very close resemblance to the first'.

### Technological Advances

Loughnane's most explosive relationship was with the Munster Council. In 1998, to get away from all the hassle, Loughnane went for a holiday in America. He went into a hi-tech electrical store to buy a car radio. The salesman launched into the hard sell: 'This is the very latest model. It's voice-activated. You just tell it what you want to listen to and the station changes automatically. There's no need to take your hands off the wheel.'

When Loughnane returned to Ireland, he had the radio installed. Driving to training from Shannon to Crusheen, he decided to test it. He said, 'Classical' and the sound of the James Last orchestra filled the car. He said, 'Country' and instantly he was listening to Garth

Brooks. Then suddenly two pedestrians stepped off the pavement in front of him, causing him to swerve violently. He shouted at them, 'F****** idiots!' Then the radio changed to a documentary on the Munster Council.

## Greetings

During his time as Clare manager, Loughnane was not always very popular with Tipperary fans. After Clare beat Tipperary in the replay in the 1999 Munster Championship, Tony Considine and Loughnane decided they would walk into Cork city from Pairc Uí Chaoimh. It was about three quarters of an hour after the game, so the crowd had dispersed. They were walking along, when they saw this van up ahead of them with a Tipperary registration. When they were about 20 yards away, the driver spotted them and jumped out of the van. Loughnane said to Considine, 'Here's trouble'.

The driver greeted him with, 'Howya, Ger! Any chance of the autograph?'

Loughnane was relieved that he wasn't going to attack him! He told him it was no problem. The driver handed Loughnane the programme to sign, and told him it was for his wife. Loughnane wrote, 'To Marion, Best wishes, Ger Loughnane'. The driver never looked up at him, but turned to his friend and said, 'Jesus, Johnny, she'll get some surprise when she gets home this evening. Christ, wait till she sees this.'

Then he turned to Loughnane and said, 'You have no idea how much she hates you!'

## A Howler

Despite Loughnane's happy capacity for weathering hostility, the strains that had been mounting mercilessly over the years as manager, strains whose ravages the obsessive in him deflected, took their toll. The biggest casualty was his hairline. At the peak of the Clare team's success, there was a table quiz in Shannon. For one of the rounds, they showed pictures of well-known people when they were younger. A photo of Loughnane was included from back in the days when he had long hair. When one of the teams was asked to identify his photo, they answered, 'Princess Diana'!

## Power to the People

After Loughnane stepped down as manager of the Clare team, there were strong rumours that he would get involved in politics. He was subsequently courted by two political parties. Loughnane's mischievous streak may have been a contributory factor to this round of speculation.

In 1999, he agreed to a request from Clare FM to take part in an April Fool's Day joke. The local elections were coming up at the time, so he announced on Clare FM that he was going to stand for the county council. Loughnane stated that there were things more important than hurling and that he was going to stand as an independent, and that a lot of the Clare team were going to campaign for him. He then launched into a passionate tirade about the need to improve the roads in east Clare. So convincing was he, that many people swallowed the story hook, line and sinker and the station was inundated with phone calls. Such was the reaction that the station had to issue a statement that evening to admit that it was all a joke.

## In the Public Eye

Loughnane was called a lot of things, but one person he was never compared with was Mother Teresa. Yet they had one thing in common: Mother Teresa famously said, 'Facing the press is more difficult than bathing a leper'. During his tenure as Clare manager, Loughnane had a stormy relationship with the media. Before the 1995 All-Ireland, he said of his media interviews, 'I say nothing but I never stop talking'.

In 2002, Loughnane was having a quiet meal with his wife, Mary, in a restaurant in Ennis. Out of the corner of his eye, he noticed the *Sunday Tribune*'s hurling correspondent, Enda McEvoy, entering the restaurant. A natural-born mischief-maker, Loughnane dispatched Mary to make contact. McEvoy was hardly seated when Mary approached him and said, with Nicole Kidman-esque acting skills, 'I'm very sorry, sir; I'm going to have to ask you to leave'.

McEvoy was gobsmacked. 'What do you mean?'

'Well, Sir, the last time you were here, you were caught on video camera leaving without paying your bill.'

McEvoy was stunned, 'But... but... but I've never been here before'.

A pantomime developed, with an exchange of the lines, 'Oh yes you did'; 'Oh no I didn't'. The journalist could not believe he was being accused of such an offence and was getting increasingly bewildered and distressed. Eventually, he heard the loud laughter coming from another table and turned around to see Loughnane splitting his sides laughing.

## Celestial Protocol

There are many strange stories about Loughnane, though few are printable. One deals with the day Loughnane, Christy Ring and Mick Mackey faced God at the throne of Heaven. God said to them, 'Before granting you a place at my side, I must ask for your beliefs'.

Ring stared God directly in the eye and said, 'I believe hurling is the meaning of life. Nothing else has brought so much joy to so many. I have devoted my life to spreading the gospel of hurling.'

God was moved by his passion and eloquence and said, 'You are a man of true faith. Sit by me at my right hand.'

He then turned to Limerick's most famous hurling son, 'Now, my child, tell me what you believe'.

'I believe courage, bravery, loyalty, team-work, dedication and commitment are the soul of life and I dedicated my career to living up to those ideals.'

God replied, 'You have spoken well, my child. Sit by me at my left hand.'

Then he turned to Loughnane, 'And you, Mr Loughnane, what is it that you believe?'

Loughnane gave him the withering look, which he usually reserved for referees and members of the Munster Council, and replied, 'I believe that you are sitting in my chair'.

# Chapter Six
# Easy Riders

TED WALSH has re-written the lexicon of horse racing commentary, popularising such phrases not found in the BBC manual of proper English usage: 'a great lepper'; 'bits of chances'; 'gutsy buggers'; 'arse over tip'; and most famously 'I rode her mother' – a reference to a horse whose mother he had ridden, lest there be any confusion.

Racing seems to lend itself to possible misinterpretations. The *Sporting Life* left itself open to similar misconception in 1977, with its report that, 'John Higgins fractured a bone in his left leg in a fall from Mrs Higgins at Edinburgh on Monday, and will be out of action for a month'.

Peter Bromley once said on BBC, 'The Game Spirit Chase, named after Game Spirit, a lovely horse owned by Her Majesty the Queen Mother, who dropped dead here after a long and distinguished career'.

## Father Ted

Ted Walsh is one of the great storytellers of Irish sport. Enthusiasm is stamped emphatically on every facet of his personality. He tells the story of the three Irishmen at the World Cup finals in 1990. They were travelling outside Rome, when they came upon the Popemobile overturned on the side of the road. They recognised it instantly, having seen the Pope driving in it when he said a special Mass at Galway racecourse in 1979. The Pope lay dead at the wheel. The Pope had seriously breached protocol and slipped out of the Vatican for a quiet drive in the country.

At this precise moment, Vatican officials arrived on the scene and were anxious to cover up this indiscretion. They made the Irishmen swear a solemn vow never to reveal what they had seen. The Pope's death was not to be announced until the following Monday. The official line was to be that he had died quietly in his sleep after a few days of illness. As the men from the Emerald Isle were all former altar boys, they readily agreed to this request. After bidding goodbye to their new-found friends, the threesome quickly came up with a plot to make a killing. They would get great odds from the bookies on the Pope dying by Monday.

The following week, the three men met up again. Two were deliriously happy, having made a fortune; the other was crestfallen. When asked why he looked so gloomy, he replied that he had made no money: 'I doubled my bet on the Pope dying with one on the death of the Queen Mother.'

### Genetic Transmission

It is difficult to know whether it is harder to breed a jockey or a horse. There are already signs that Ted's son Ruby has inherited his father's legendary wit. When asked how he performed in his Leaving Cert exams, Walsh the younger quipped, 'I rode three winners!'

### What's Seldom Isn't Wonderful

Leopardstown is a great place for atmosphere, but it can be a bad place for punters. It is a great way of getting nothing from something. At a Christmas meeting, Ted had bad luck with a few favourites. One fan screamed at him, 'Well, you wouldn't get a ride in a whorehouse'.

One of his friends, who was an amateur jockey, defended Ted but the crowd turned on him and said, 'Look at him, he's only a pancake jockey. He only gets a ride every Shrove Tuesday.'

### Unfair Rules

Ted started a race at Leopardstown as an odds-on favourite, but by the home turn the horse had run out of puff and was going backwards through the field. After the race, the despondent owner approached him: 'What the hell was going on?'

'The horse simply wasn't good enough,' explained Ted sadly.

'Rubbish,' roared the trainer. 'You could have done much better.'

'Maybe I could,' said Ted, 'but you know as well as I do the rules state I must stay on the horse's back.'

## Make Haste Slowly

When another horse with Ted in the saddle trailed in hopelessly last at the Leopardstown Christmas meeting, the owner was furious. Ted was not entertaining any blame for the fiasco and said, 'The horse was so slow, I kept a diary of the trip. If I ever ride him at an evening meeting, I'll be wearing my pyjamas.'

## Turning Defence into Attack

As a jockey, one of Ted's biggest disappointments occurred at Cheltenham. Years after his 'mishap', Ted was forcefully reminded of his embarrassment on live television by his Channel 4 colleague, John McCririck. 'Ted, you fell off the Irish favourite in the Champion Hurdle,' said the sartorially challenged one.

Quick as a flash Ted responded, 'Yeah, I got a fortune for it!'

# Little John

John McCririck always has a nightmare trying to pronounce Ted Walsh's Rince Ri. His most usual pronunciation is 'Rinky Ray'. (Naming horses is a curious business. Isidore Kerman named his most famous horse Kybo after the initials of the advice his mother had once given him, 'Keep Your Bowels Open'!)

On another occasion, McCririck said a horse would walk it in at a big race in Haydock Park. It did, but all the others galloped.

## A Lesson in Reincarnation

McCririck is a racing institution. In fact, a few cruel people have suggested that he should be put in an institution. When God gave out the racing brain, McCririck was close to the head of the queue. Unfortunately, when God was giving out the good looks, he was at the very back of the queue.

One day, the sartorially challenged one met a female racing fan, who was not overly impressed by his physical appearance. The conversation diverged from racing to the bigger questions in life, and the woman mentioned her interest in reincarnation. McCririck asked her to explain reincarnation. She said, 'It's when you die and go to heaven and come back as something else'.

The racing broadcaster replied, 'So, it's like if I died and came back as a pig'. The woman gave him a withering look and scanned him from head to toe, not making much effort to conceal her revulsion as she said, 'You weren't listening carefully to my explanation, were you?'

## The Price of Progress

There could not be a greater contrast to McCririck than the BBC's Julian Wilson. The old Etonian, with his top hat, unflappable manner and beautifully spoken delivery, is the voice of racing on television. Wilson was filming a piece for television in the run up to the Epsom Derby near a quiet country road. He was in full flow: '300 years ago the king of England, Charles II, would hack up on this very hill and watch in fascination as the horses passed by. Nothing's changed in the last 300 years....'

At that point a motorbike roared by. Wilson's response was out of character, 'Of course, what has changed is f***** motorbikes'.

## Getting His Teeth into It

An Irish jockey, who shall remain nameless, was once invited to ride for the Queen Mother. It was very unusual for an Irish jockey to be granted this honour. The only snag was that he had false teeth, which he couldn't wear while racing. The jockey knew he would be introduced to the Queen Mother just before the race. Normally, he would have left his teeth in a safe, clean place well before the race, but there was no way he was going to meet the Queen Mum toothless.

He met Her Majesty and did all the courtesies and everything beautifully. The problem was that the race was then about to start. He couldn't possibly compete with his false teeth, so he gave them to some fella, who put them in his back pocket without really looking at them. The jockey went on to win the race, but then his problems were only starting. He knew he would have to meet the Queen Mother again. He had a mad rush to track down his teeth. When he finally found his man, he popped in the teeth, not realising that the man's pocket was full of horse hair, cigarette ash and God knows what else. When the jockey met the Queen Mother, he almost puked on her!

## First Among Equals

Arkle and Pat Taaffe were Ireland's racing royalty. However, it was not a case of love at first sight. Taaffe said of his famous partner, 'You could have driven a wheelbarrow between his hind legs'.

Taaffe had a gentle sense of humour. He once rode an unpromising horse at Fairyhouse. Later that day a friend asked, 'How did he do, Pat?'

'Second.'

'Wow. That's great.'

'Not really. He was second last!'

## Traffic Stopper

It was only after Arkle had won his second Gold Cup that his trainer Tom Dreaper admitted he might possibly be a better horse than Prince Regent, his last ride, whom he also trained. Were it not for the acquisitive tendencies of Adolf Hitler, Prince Regent would certainly have a more prominent place in the racing canon. Had there been a Cheltenham Festival in 1942, when he won the Irish Grand National, or in the following three years, it is speculated that Prince Regent could have won five consecutive Gold Cups, emulating Golden Miller's achievement.

In 1939, Prince Regent was on the brink of greatness but by 1945 his star was waning. The following story highlights his popularity: One day, Dreaper was leading a string of his horses on foot, because of the absence of transport during 'the Emergency', to a major crossroads. He asked a guard to stop the traffic. The guard is reputed to have asked if Prince Regent was present. When told he was, he said: 'I'll stop all the traffic on both sides for you so!'

## True to Form

One story told about Dreaper is that he was asked to the morgue to identify an old hack jockey who had been killed in a car crash. The trainer lifted the sheet off one body and shook his head. It wasn't his jockey. He lifted the second sheet and shook his head again. He lifted the third sheet and sadly announced, 'Again, he hasn't run a place'.

# Performance-enhancing Drugs

A less honest trainer, who was a contemporary of Dreaper's, was giving last minute instructions to his jockey and appeared to slip something in the horse's mouth just as a steward passed by.

'What was that?' inquired the steward.

'Oh, nothing,' said the trainer, 'just a Mintie'.

He offered one to the steward. 'Here, have one. And I'll have one myself.' After the suspicious steward departed, the trainer continued with his riding instructions. 'Just keep the horse on the rails. You are on a certainty. The only thing that could possibly pass you down the straight now is either the steward or me.'

# The Master

In the pantheon of racing greats, a special place is reserved for Vincent O'Brien. No less a diplomat than a wonder trainer, O'Brien had a stock reply for owners who demanded unmerited praise of their less-than-talented horses. 'Master,' an owner would enquire, 'do you think I have a great horse?'

'Ah, my good man,' O'Brien would reply with the utmost sincerity, '"great" is not the word to describe it!'

# The Price is Wrong

O'Brien struck up an unrivalled partnership with Lester Piggott. It was said of Piggott, 'If he is only riding a donkey, bet on him'.

Piggott had a reputation for being tight with money. According to legend, Piggott was given an eye test and presented with a pair of glasses. The optician said they would cost £300.

'Too much,' said Piggott.

'They're bi-focal,' said the optician.

'I don't care if they're by Arkle. It's too much.'

### Nearly Right

One day, Lester went into a shop to buy an ice-cream. The excited girl at the counter asked, 'Are you Wilson Pickett?'

# Trade Secrets

The O'Brien racing tradition lives on in Balydoyle in the person of
Aidan O'Brien. In 1996, the dynamic duo of O'Brien and Charlie
Swan delivered Ireland's second winner at the Cheltenham Festival,
Urubande – O'Brien's first victory at the equine promised land.

Former jockey and Channel 4's racing front man, Brough Scott,
advanced with his microphone and asked the winning trainer: 'We
have seen your statistics; well over 200 winners in one year. What is
your secret?' Immediately, a small Irishman stuck his head through a
tiny gap in the circle of people and said, 'Don't tell him'.

# Cheeky Charlie

In 1993, Charlie Swan became the first jump jockey in Irish racing
history to ride 100 domestic winners in a calendar year. Swan left a
lasting impression on racing enthusiasts at the Curragh in 1984,
when he briefly became Cheeky Charlie. He was riding a filly in a
one-and-a-half mile handicap. The valet had given him breeches
that were too small for him. As Swan burst out the stalls, the poppers
that his trousers were done up with burst open. After half a furlong,
the breeches were down to his knees. He kept trying to pull them up.
Christy Roche yelled at him, 'Leave them alone. You'll fall.'

Nonetheless, Swan kept trying because he didn't want people in
the stands looking at him in his underpants. It was completely
impossible to pull them up, and he eventually gave up. He rode for
the line with his breeches hanging loose below his knees, feeling a
right fool. He finished a close third, and were it not for the breeches
he could have won. Since then many people have told Swan that they
saw him that day – not the memory he wants people to have of him.

Swan won the Ritz Club Trophy at the Cheltenham Festival
meeting as leading rider in both 1993 and 1994. One of his most
notable victories came in the 1994 meeting on Time For A Run,
when the trainer, Edward O'Grady, famously told him to go out and
ride 'with balls of steel'.

# The Gallant Jonjo

Riding is the art of keeping a horse between yourself and the ground.
Few people understood this better than another Cheltenham

superhero, Jonjo O'Neill. Jonjo had a number of bad injuries in his career. At one point, an extensive metal plate and screws had to be inserted to help bind the bones in his right leg. In his own words, it was 'like a sack of gravel'. Years later, Jonjo would joke, 'When I was struggling with cancer and not earning, the metal out of my legs got me a few bob as scrap'.

Jonjo was a very focused competitor. He was the last person anybody in the weighing-room would have imagined likely to play a practical joke – unlike his celebrated rival John Francome. One day, as Francome walked into the weighing-room, Jonjo approached him and told him to give one of their colleagues, Alan Brown, a ribbing about his mother's musical talents because she had been featured in the local paper playing the piano. True to character, as soon as Francome walked in, he began slagging Mrs Brown about her piano playing. A tense silence fell on the room. Brown looked as if he was going to burst into tears, as he said in a muffled voice, 'My mother has no hands'.

Francome wished the ground would open up and swallow him. When he regained his composure, he rushed in rage over to Jonjo and was about to thump him, when all the other jockeys present burst into laughter. There was absolutely nothing wrong with Mrs Brown's hands and she was alive and well!

Francome was not used to being the butt of such a joke. He decided he would have to take revenge on his colleagues by setting up another jockey in the same way. His target was Bob Champion, famous for coming back from cancer to win the Grand National on Aldaniti in 1981. Francome set up Bob beautifully and was brimming with pleasure at the thought of the look of horror on his colleague's face when they reached the punchline. The problem was that the joke went completely over Champion's head. Far from showing embarrassment, Bob asked in all earnestness, 'Does she want to sell her piano then?'

Jockeys can be cruel. At the 2003 Cheltenham Festival, champion jockey Tony McCoy had four falls, breaking his collarbone at the final one. At the appearance of the Real McCoy, his colleagues in the waiting room said in unison, 'Here comes the man who's been on the grass more often than Prince Harry'.

# Shakin' All Over

One of Ireland's leading writers, Joe O'Connor once posed the question: Is football better than sex? Joe's witty argument could readily be transposed onto the world of National Hunt Racing. At first glance, this might be considered a highly contentious statement, as the two activities are so remarkably different. One involves the complete engagement of the senses, wild abandonment, heart-stopping elation and above all orgasmic bliss.

The other is sex.

Few know the sheer toe-curling ecstasy of winning a race at Cheltenham better than Florida Pearl's owner Archie O'Leary. Spectating is no sport for the unfit. At best, it leaves you shattered, at worst it could kill you. When Florida Pearl won his first race in Cheltenham in 1997, O'Leary didn't enjoy it. He normally doesn't get overexcited before a race once he sees the horse has settled down, but that day he was so nervous his glasses were shaking. Ted Walsh said after the race that having a winner at Cheltenham is like losing your virginity to Kim Basinger. It's all downhill from there. Mind you, when O'Leary heard that, he had to ask his wife who Kim Basinger was!

# Dual Star

O'Leary is a thrice-capped Irish second row forward, who toured Argentina and Chile with Ireland in 1952. O'Leary claims that rugby was more fun then than now, although it was pretty tough on the pitch. In fact, one of his clearest memories from his Ireland career is going down on a ball, getting kicked and breaking two ribs. Despite his injuries, O'Leary had to play on because Mick Lane had already gone off. On the Monday afterwards, O'Leary had an X-ray done, which cost £1 11s 6d. He sent the bill to the IRFU; in return he got a snotty reply which stated that rugby was an amateur game and that there was no way in hell they were going to pay for it.

### Silence Is Not Golden

Professionally, O'Leary is an insurance mogul, employing over 100 people in his insurance business. Apart from his headquarters in South Mall in Cork, he also has offices in Mallow, Galway and

Dublin. He is proud of his achievements, 'I started off on my own in 1961 with one fella and a girl. As if that wasn't scary enough, the fella wouldn't even talk to me!'

### Revealing

O'Leary's father was a doctor in Cork. He was the first to scale the flagpole at UCC, then called Queen's College, to haul down the flag that was there, and replace it with the tricolour. He was wearing an Irish kilt at the time!

## Jack's Back

The late Jack Doyle was a Renaissance man of Irish sport. He was a champion sprinter in his youth, a show-jumper of distinction, a rugby protégé in Bray who went on to play for his country, a jockey, a trainer of an Irish Grand National winner and a finder of new horsing racing talent, notably Mill House who won the Gold Cup in 1963 and Bruni who won the English St Leger in 1975.

Doyle had the distinction of first introducing Robert Sangster to John Magnier in the early 1970s, and thereby was indirectly responsible for a revolution in the international bloodstock arena. That meeting spawned 'the syndicate' with Vincent O'Brien that ultimately led to the establishment of the Coolmore Stud. The Sangster–O'Brien–Magnier triumvirate benefited enormously from a decision taken by then Minister for Finance Charlie Haughey, which decreed that all income generated by stallions should be exempt from tax. This led to a steady stream of top thoroughbreds crossing the Atlantic from America to Ireland. When it was subsequently suggested that Magnier might have been the real brains behind the tax decision, Magnier replied with typical self-deprecation, 'Sure, I was only milking cows at that stage'.

Jack Doyle died in October 1998. A few months before he died, a function was held in his honour. One of the guest speakers was Tony O'Hehir, who told a story about his father, the legendary Micheal O'Hehir. One day, Michael called with the racing correspondent Louis Gunning to collect Doyle from his house in Shankill. They were waiting a long time for Doyle. Like all of us, Doyle had his ups and downs and periods when he owed money to a lot of people. So eventually the two boys were sent a message that whatever door Jack was coming out it wouldn't be the front door!

Another story told recalled Jack's experiences as a jockey at a race meeting in Navan. There was a terrible pile up at the third-last fence; horses and jockeys were sprawled everywhere. Despite two broken ribs, Jack managed to remount and in agonising pain but with great applause from the crowd, he rode on and was the only one to finish the course. The trainer greeted him with a kick in the bum and said, 'You big dope. You remounted the wrong horse!'

## Trainers

The legendary Mick O'Toole claimed that you should never train winners for owners until the owners have been with you for ten years and until you put manners on them.

Tom Foley trained the people's champion, Danoli. Foley is a long way from what Brendan Behan memorably described in a typical phrase as the 'horse-arse Anglo-Irish' from Kildare and Meath. He was not in the least fazed when the *Times* said of him, 'He has an accent that causes cultivated Home Counties voices to ask if they are listening to Urdu'.

## Fast Sex

Cork-born jockey Mick Fitzgerald is as famous for his euphoric sound bites as he is for his victory on Rough Quest in the Martell Grand National in 1996. 'Sex will be an anti-climax after that,' was his description of the experience. He described the National as the best twelve minutes of his life. His fiancée, Jane Brackenbury, responded by saying, 'He's never lasted twelve minutes in his life!'

## Speechmakers

Top jockeys are developing the corporate aspect of their livelihood. Each day of a big meeting like Cheltenham, leading jockeys act as corporate speakers for guests, by providing pre-race analysis. As such, a jockey's agent's most important job during the festival is to synchronise his jockeys' timetables. They have to show up for the sponsors when they are expected, but have to be back with their horses for the race.

Inevitably in this high-pressure environment, there can be the odd faux pas. Before racing in Windsor, Mick Fitzgerald was due to address some clients in the corporate box. Through no fault of his own, he arrived at the course a bit late and had to go directly to the race. Fitzgerald had rides in the first two races and came in first and second, respectively. As he was free until the last race, he rushed up to the sponsor's box and apologised most profusely for having missed the pre-race analysis. For forty minutes, he launched into a masterly incisive and entertaining analysis of the day's racing. As Fitzgerald finished, he went around to everybody and again apologised profusely for missing the pre-race analysis.

Later an agent asked the sponsor what he thought of Mick Fitzgerald. The sponsor said he had never turned up. Mick had been given the wrong directions and had gone to the wrong box!

## Yes, Minister

One of Irish racing's most devout patrons is Minister of Finance Charlie McCreevy. However, McCreevy has not gone so far as to compare himself to a horse, unlike a former Chancellor of the Exchequer Norman Lamont who once commented: 'Desert Orchid and I have a lot in common. We are both greys; vast sums of money are riding on our performance; the Opposition hopes we will fall at the first fence; and we are both carrying too much weight.'

One of McCreevy's constituents is the 'racing priest', Fr Sean Breen. Every other priest in the country counts Pentecost Sunday in terms of Sundays after Easter, but Fr Sean counts it in terms of Easter and the Punchestown Festival!

Charlie Haughey remains a keen horseman, though he did have a few famous falls during his career. Haughey was once alleged to have said that he chose black and blue as his colours, because he was black and blue so often from his hunting mishaps. He laughs when quizzed about the veracity of that remark. 'I think you'd have to take that as apocryphal!'

CJH is very knowledgeable about horses and very affable when attending race meetings. He was once asked for a tip. He replied, 'Life is too short to be drinking bad wine!'

# With God on Our Side

In 1994, Father Donal Bambury launched Doncaster's trial Sunday meeting with a service. Almost immediately, he was promoted to Monsignor. His cousin, Irish bookie Pat Bambury, responded to this development by saying, 'We had him at 10,000–1 to be the next Pope. I suppose we will have to adjust the odds now.'

# Roscommon Rejoices

In 1993, Montelado became the first horse to win consecutive races at Cheltenham. He closed the 1992 festival by winning the bumper, the National Hunt Flat Race, and he won the opening race, the Trafalgar House Supreme Novice Hurdle, in 1993. It was a dream come true for the Roscommon-based syndicate that owned him. The syndicate was led by Ollie Hannon, whose poultry company is one of the biggest employers in the area.

The race was on 16 March. That evening at the vigil Mass in Roscommon the priest said, 'I'm not going to keep you this evening, because we're all out to celebrate the Cheltenham victory'.

# Urgent Requirement

Historically, the festival has attracted a large number of Irish clerics, who come with a reputation for other habits. A man stuck his head into the compartment of a train heading for the Cheltenham Festival and asked, 'Is there a Catholic priest on board?' A concerned passenger replied, 'Does somebody need the last rites?'

'No. I just need a bottle opener.'

# Baptism of Fire

Catholic priests are sometimes seen sprinkling holy water over horses at Cheltenham. One punter noticed a priest sprinkling holy water over one horse, which duly went out and won the opening race of the festival by ten lengths. The punter decided to follow the priest and witnessed another horse getting the holy water treatment. This time, the horse won by twenty lengths. Next time, the punter had £1,000 ready, and as soon as the priest blessed another horse, a skinny nag, he was off to the bookies and got odds of 500–1. After the horse dropped dead coming up the Cheltenham hill, the punter tackled the priest for an explanation.

'If you were a Catholic,' said the priest, 'you would have known the difference between a blessing and the last rites.'

## Beware the Ides of March

Cheltenham is a Mecca for Irish racing fans, although there are more horse's asses at the festival than there are horses. Hence, one punter's whine, 'I backed a horse at ten to one. He came in at ten past two.'

Another was more philosophical: 'The only way to follow a horse at Cheltenham is with a shovel and brush and sell it to the people that grow roses'.

Many Irish punters were to re-learn that lesson the hard way at the Millennium Cheltenham Festival. A forlorn Irish punter of high intelligence, mature wisdom and sophisticated social sense, was slowly making his way through customs at Birmingham airport. The customs officer asked, 'Anything to declare?' After a dramatic pause the Irish man replied in a voice as miserable as a flooded meadow, 'Nothing but empty pockets'.

## Superstitious Minds

Another punter was luckier and cleaned out a bookie with a huge bet on a horse at 200–1. His friends were curious and asked him about the secret of his success. 'I'm superstitious and I watch for omens,' he replied. 'On my way to the races I tool a number 6 bus. It made six stops on the way and it cost me £6 to get into Prestbury Park. It was three sixes telling me something. So I added them up, three sixes are 21 so I backed number 21 and it won by a mile.'

Another day, he misread the signals and had to explain a massive loss to his wife. 'As I walked into the racecourse a sudden gust of wind blew my hat off. It was a sure sign,' he said. 'So I put it all on a horse called Gone with the Wind.'

'And it didn't win?'

'No. Some foreign horse called Mon Chapeau won by a mile.'

# Always Look on the Bright Side of Life

Top racing journalist Hugh McIlvanney has written about a previously unidentified condition known as GOS, 'Groundless Optimism Syndrome'. This affliction is a delusional condition which strikes for the three days of the festival. The condition causes people who have lost the family silver on previous visits to Cheltenham to become convinced that they have new mystical powers of prophecy which will enable them to bet with certainty. Inevitably, when they leave Prestbury Park three days later their wallets are anaemic.

J P McManus is not afflicted by GOS, but bets huge sums at the festival nonetheless. This is music to the ears of Victor Chandler, with whom J P has put his money on the line many times during the festival. McManus is famously reported to have said of Chandler, 'He has the face of Mother Teresa and the mind of Al Capone'.

# The Sundance Kid

J P's interest in gambling was evident at an early age. His punting was a handicap to his academic advancement. He tells a story from his schooldays about a history exam which was due to start at 2.30 pm. The problem was that he knew that after forty-five or fifty minutes a Brother would come to stand at the door to ensure that no one slipped out early. McManus fancied a horse running at Limerick. He managed to get out of the room before the Brother took up duty and cycled like mad to the racecourse, only to arrive at Greenpark just as his fancy was passing the post – a winner!

# Sense and Sensibility

Horse sense is something a horse has that keeps him from betting on men. One year, an Irish punter, who had lost heavily, put his last few quid on a fancied Irish horse to win the last race. He was so nervous he couldn't bear to listen to the race, so he went into the toilet and kept flushing it until the race was over. He stopped just as the result was announced. The horse he had backed came fifth!

Not everyone at Cheltenham is an expert. When the Polish-bred Galileo won on the Wednesday of the 2002 festival, a woman was heard to remark with conviction, 'That's his first victory since the Derby last year'. Her husband sighed with the resignation of a man who had suffered a lot and said, 'No, my precious. That's a different Galileo.'

## The Piano Man

A crucial difference between the English and Irish at Cheltenham is the way they react to victory. The English tend to temper their reaction with some of their hallowed reserve and aloofness. The Irish let their emotions run wild and have no inhibitions. Who could ever forget the exuberance of Dawn Run's famous victory?

For years, scrum-half Danno Heaslip was the heart of the Galwegians rugby team. Clashes between Danno and Liam Hall, the great Garryowen scrum-half, were a real battle of wits, in every sense of the term. Danno and his brother, Mick, provided Ireland with another Cheltenham win, when their horse For Auction won the Champion Hurdle at 40–1 in 1982 under the stewardship of Colin Magnier. According to racing folklore, Danno and Mick placed a special bet for champagne money, netting £2,000 in the process. On arrival back to their hotel, Danno is said to have instructed the manager to open 100 bottles of champagne. His second instruction was to the manager to get a piano.

'But we don't have a piano in this area,' the manager replied.

'Then buy one,' said Danno.

## Book Him, Danno

Probably the only Irishman with mixed feelings about the victory was Danno Heaslip's friend, former government minister Des O'Malley. He had been all geared up to attend the festival, but then a general election had intervened and he found himself back in office at the start of March, and at the last minute had to cancel his trip to Cheltenham. He instructed Danno to put £25 each way on the horse for him. Danno went to Cheltenham on the Sunday but before leaving posted a letter to O'Malley's home in Limerick, saying that so many people had asked him to back the horse that he couldn't possibly get it all on, particularly as he was backing the horse himself. The only problem was that O'Malley had left for Dublin before the post arrived on the Monday morning and didn't get the letter until after the race – having calculated that he had just won £1,250 on his investment!

## Paradise Lost

Racing is the best fun you can have with your clothes on, but sometimes you can lose your shirt. Most punters are dismissive of the story of a rich bookie, a poor bookie and the tooth fairy who were in a room with a £100 on the table. All of a sudden the lights went out. When the lights came back on the money was gone. So who took it? It has to have been the rich bookie because the other two are figments of the imagination.

## Punters

Punters don't always get the facilities they deserve. Navan has long been recognised as one of the best racing surfaces in the country, but its facilities have always been below standard (as thieves discovered when they broke in, in 2002, under the erroneous impression that they might find something worth pinching. Rumour had it the burglars sued the racecourse for wasting their time.)

A punter in the Curragh bet £1,000 on the winner of the first race, at 15–1. When he went to collect, the bookie told him he didn't have £15,000 in the bag and asked whether he could drop back a few races later. The punter did, and the bookie, who was losing all round, still didn't have enough cash.

'Will you take a cheque?'

'No, I bet cash and I want to be paid in cash,' the punter snapped. 'And if you're going to be running me around like this, I'd just as soon call the bet off!'

Punters are notoriously partisan. Patrick Kavanagh once backed a horse at the Phoenix Park which led all the way and was fifteen lengths clear at the end. He declared it the most thrilling finish he had ever witnessed.

Occasionally punters strike back. A man went into Sean Graham's bookies in Belfast and asked, 'Can you back a horse in here?'

'Of course you can. Sure, that's what we're here for.'

The man went out and started backing a horse in through the door!

## Money Talks

A famous English horse owner phoned a psychiatrist. 'Doctor, my wife needs help. She thinks she's a horse.' The doctor heard a few more details and said, 'Mmm, it sounds serious. The treatment could take a long time, so it could be very expensive.'

The owner replied, 'Money's no object. She's won her last three starts.'

Two wealthy horse owners ran into each other at the door of the psychiatrist's office.

'Hello,' said one. 'Are you coming or going?'

'If I knew that,' replied the other, 'I wouldn't be here.'

## The Sun Falls

In the late 1970s, as part of a competition for the paper, the *Sun* editor Kelvin Mackenzie instructed his racing correspondent Claude Duval, 'the punter's pal', to buy a horse to run in the Grand National. Duval went to Ireland and purchased a horse called Blackwater Bridge. Everything went hunky-dory. Duval got Red Rum's trainer Ginger McCain to train the horse; Blackwater Bridge even took up residence in the stable behind Red Rum. The horse was even brought to Aintree with 'Rummy' to see Beechers, the race's most famous fence.

A lot of photos were taken of Blackwater Bridge with the winner of the *Sun*'s competition, who would get to keep the horse after the National. As the hype built up, the bookies cut Blackwater Bridge's odds from 66–1 to 50–1 in one day! A few weeks before the race, Ginger McCain rang Duval to say the stable lad couldn't stop the horse on his morning runs. It was essential that the horse would have a run in advance of the Grand National. A race at Haydock with just four other runners was found for him the week before the world's most famous race. As the warm-up race progressed, it suddenly became apparent that there were only four runners left. Blackwater Bridge had fallen spectacularly.

Ginger and Duval raced across to check on their horse. They discovered that not much of the fence was left and that twigs were still flying in the air. The hapless jockey was groaning in pain and covered in blood. After his initial shock had subsided, Duval tentatively asked, 'Will he be all right to run in the Grand National next Saturday, Ginger?'

Through gritted teeth Ginger snapped back at him, 'He's bloody dead, Claude!'

Duval went a whiter shade of pale. The most frightening prospect was having to break the news to his editor. Mackenzie had a fearsome reputation and was not the sort of man to whom any sane person wanted to break bad news.

Duval started to breathe more easily when he discovered that Blackwater Bridge was not in fact dead and Ginger was eventually able to take the horse back to the yard. On the Sunday, Duval rang Ginger to see if the horse would be okay. His heart sank as Ginger told him that the horse's injuries were so severe that he would have to be put down.

Duval again faced the terrifying prospect of having to tell Mackenzie. He rang Mackenzie's Kent mansion, desperately hoping that he could get one of his staff to pass on the bad tidings. No one was willing, and Duval was put through to his boss. The conversation was brief but the message was forcefully conveyed nonetheless.

'How's Blackie?' began Mackenzie.

'Things aren't good, I'm afraid; in fact things are bad. Things are very bad.'

'Spit it out, man. What's wrong with him?'

'Ginger McCain says he has to be put down.'

'While he's at it, tell him to spare a bullet for you,' barked Mackenzie angrily, before slamming down the phone.

## Say Little but Say It Well

The late Duke of Norfolk used to have a trainer called Sid Fidell. Whenever the Duke had a runner and couldn't be at the meeting, Fidell always sent him a detailed telegram with all the facts of the race. This was despite the fact that they met every Friday to discuss the week's racing. The Duke got tired of the long telegrams and told Fidell to send him short telegrams in future and they would discuss the races in more detail on the Friday sessions.

Soon afterwards the Duke had a horse running. That evening, he received the following telegram: 'S.F.S.F.S.F.S.F.' At the Friday meeting, the Duke asked Fidell to explain what it meant. 'Oh, your grace, it's quite simple really: "Started, farted, slipped and fell. See you Friday. Sid Fidell."'

# Chapter Seven
# Amongst Women

WOMEN DON'T have it easy in sport. Try getting into most golf clubs in Ireland if you are not male. That is why many women think golf is really an acronym: Gentlemen Only Ladies Forbidden.

Women also get a hard time from male sportswriters. Hence Brian Glanville's comment, 'A woman playing football is like a dog walking on its hind legs. It is not done well but you are surprised to find it done at all.'

Women often suffer at the hands of sports-mad husbands. Elsie Revie, wife of Don, the legendary manager of Leeds United, often told her two children, 'See that man walking past the window. That man's your father.'

It may be for these reasons that there are relatively few apocryphal stories about the great female sporting personalities. Irish sport has produced phenomenal female talents, like Sonia O'Sullivan, Catherina McKiernan, Jessica Chesney, Mary McKenna and Angela Downey. Yet, for whatever reason, they have never spawned the same lore and legend as their male counterparts. Sadly, this limits the selection of stories for this chapter.

## When a Woman Loves a Fan

In American football, the quarterback is the glamour boy of the team, as he has the pivotal position. As a result, he is invariably the subject of a lot of female attention. Joe Namath, New York Jets quarterback, spilled the beans, 'When we won the league championship, all the married guys on the club had to thank their wives for putting up with the stress and strain all season. I had to thank all the single broads in New York.'

Asked why he got married at 11 am, Paul Hornung of the Green Bay Packers said, 'Because if it didn't work out, I didn't want to waste the whole day'. Henny Youngman famously said, 'The first part of our marriage was very happy. The problem was the second part of the marriage. That began on the way home from the ceremony.'

Dorothy Shula, wife of Miami Dolphins football coach, Don, said, 'I'm fairly confident that if I died tomorrow, Don would find a way to preserve me until the season was over and he had time for a nice funeral'.

## Men Only

Cricket is often considered to be a bastion of male chauvinist pigs. Hence the notice on many cricket clubs, 'No Dogs or Women'. For over 200 years, the Marylebone Cricket Club (MCC) adhered to a No Women policy. This meant no women members, no women in the Pavilion on match days and no women guests allowed. In 1988, a poll was taken on the revolutionary suggestion to allow women into the Pavilion as guests. Not surprisingly, the motion was overwhelmingly defeated. Three years later, another motion was put to members: should women be allowed to join the twenty-year waiting list. Again this innovative proposal was roundly rejected.

Many people might have misgivings about these chauvinistic tendencies. The MCC though rejoice in it. The move to give women a greater role in cricket came at a time when Will Carling had got into serious trouble by saying that rugby in England was run by 'fifty-seven old farts'. MCC President Sir Oliver Popplewell responded immediately, 'Well, you won't find fifty-seven old farts here. There are 18,000 of us.'

## One Woman and Her Horses

The Honourable Dorothy Wyndham Paget, with her imposing physical presence and old-fashioned clothes, is a legend in horse racing. Paget certainly came from good stock. Born in 1905, she was a great-granddaughter of Henry Paget, First Marquess of Anglesey, who commanded the cavalry at Waterloo. Her father was Lord Queenborough, owner of St Louis, winner of the 2,000 Guineas in 1922.

An early indication of Paget's temperament came when she was expelled in quick succession from six of the most expensive girls' schools in England. A quirk of fortune led her to racing. One day, she was out riding, when her horse, which was called Bridget, bolted with her on board. Afterwards Bridget was sent into training and won a race.

Having been bitten by the bug of gambling on a horse, Paget decided to become a serial owner. She normally had a very torrid relationship with her trainers. In this case statistics don't lie: in thirty years her horses moved to at least seventeen different stables in England. She had trainers in Ireland also.

Paget was shy and usually spoke only to her immediate entourage and her trainers – though in the case of the latter it was usually via the telephone or one of her secretaries. She once said that the proximity of strange men made her vomit! As if to illustrate the point, Paget once wrote to the Minister of Transport, to enquire if the war-time ban on the reservation of railway carriages might be waived in her case. The minister politely replied that, while he regretted any inconvenience she might be subjected to, he was unable to comply with her wishes in the interests of the war effort.

After the war, Paget was on her way to a race meeting when her car broke down. The only transport around was a butcher's van. She instructed her secretary to purchase it. The butcher sought and received £300. According to legend, Paget arrived at the race meeting sitting between two carcasses. After that she refused to travel by a car again, no matter how short the distance, without at least one car in tow.

Paget's passion for horses was almost matched by her passion for food – or vice versa. Once she ordered four steaks in a restaurant. When they were ready, the waiter asked if she would like them served immediately, or would she like to wait for her guests.

'Who said anything about guests?' replied Paget.

Her initial choice of Basil Briscoe as her trainer was hugely influenced by the fact that he was training Insurance and Golden Miller, the most promising hurdler and steeplechaser seen in Britain in living memory, respectively.

Briscoe himself held brief tenure of Golden Miller in 1930. That March he got a telegram from Ireland from Captain Farmer, best known for his partnership with prominent Northamptonshire trainer John Drage, offering him an unbroken three-year-old 'out of' Miller's Pride for the tidy sum of £500. Briscoe was impressed by the heritage, having trained two successful horses out of the mare, so he responded: 'Yes, sending cheque.'

The following week, the three-year-old horse arrived but, when he saw the state of his latest acquisition, Briscoe cursed himself for buying a horse he had never seen. The horse had been running in a field all his life and his former owner had not bothered to scrape the mud off him when he sent him across the Irish Sea. Briscoe's fading hopes for his horse could not have been boosted when he told his head lad that he had named the beast Golden Miller, only to be told, 'That's too good a name for a bad horse'.

Briscoe countered, 'Well, he'll improve a lot'.

He was told in reply, 'He's f*** all good now and even if he improves 1,000 per cent, he'll still be f*** all good'.

It is estimated that Paget spent almost £3 million on racing up to her death, at the age of fifty-four. In the final years of her life, most of her horses were with Sir Gordon Richards. Paget's relationship with Richards dated back to Royal Ascot in 1939, when he pulled off a feat almost as great as any of his illustrious achievements in the saddle – he succeeded in making her laugh! Paget had just lost a small fortune, even by her opulent standards, on her colt Colonel Payne, whom Richards had ridden for Fred Darling's stable in the Cork and Orrery Stakes. The trainer had informed her she should put her maximum bet on. As Richards unsaddled, Paget marched up to him forcefully demanding to know where Darling was. The jockey coolly replied, 'I wouldn't be quite sure, Miss Paget, but I've a pretty shrewd idea he's on the top of the stand, cutting his throat.'

## Little Women

In Japan, many of the caddies are women, many of whom are very attractive. It is not unusual for a pro to kiss his caddie. According to legend, one golfer started out playing alone with his caddie. By the ninth hole, they were engaged and when they finished on the eighteenth they had a foursome.

## Ladylike

Mrs Elspeth Mustard, secretary to the Secretary at Muirfield, Edinburgh, told an American woman visitor, 'I am sorry we don't allow ladies in the clubhouse'.

The American woman replied, 'Then, what are you?'

## Appearances Can Be Deceptive

During Harold Macmillan's time as prime minister of England, he received a grave message about a diplomatic disaster during a parliamentary recess. BBC radio reported the event as follows: 'These dismal tidings were delivered to the PM on the golf course, where he was playing a round with Lady Dorothy.' The words read fine in print but when spoken the sentence took on a very different connotation!

## A Royal Performance

At Epsom in 2000, two men decided to streak in front of the Queen Mother. The official line was, 'We are not amused'. However, the next day the tabloids published photos of the Queen Mother gazing intently at the two men through her binoculars.

## To the Russian with Love

Mark Roberts is heading towards his 200th appearance as a streaker. The most prominent was at Wimbledon 2000, when he put on a show for Anna Kournikova. Roberts hurdled the net and leapt around as Kournikova giggled. Roberts had scribbled across his chest, 'Only the balls should bounce', a blatant reference to the slogan used for Kournikova's sports bra adverts.

Kournikova has won precious few tennis tournaments; some say she wins few enough matches. However, because of her looks she makes a fortune in endorsements. In December 2002, Kournikova came to Dublin to display her talents as both a tennis player and a fashion model. One wag was heard to ask: which of the two is her part-time job?

Kournikova first sent men's pulses racing at the 1996 French Open. Although she didn't make it to the final, for two weeks most of the media comment was about her. The final pairing was Monica Seles and Arantxa Sanchez Vicario. Former English tennis player Chris Bailey was commentating on the match for BBC and at the end the producer asked him to give a snappy sound bite to sum up the tournament. Bailey said, 'A great Vicario win. All the talk may be of the young glamour babes coming through, but just look at the podium, there is life in the old dogs yet.'

# Gorgeous Gabby

Before Kournikova, the beauty queen of tennis was 'Gorgeous Gabby', Gabriela Sabatini. Indeed one year at Wimbledon, the acclaimed journalist, John Feinstein, formerly of the *Washington Post*, was told to stop 'panting in print' about her by his exasperated editor. Gabby was not as well known for her brains as for her beauty. When asked for her favourite restaurant in Rome, she replied, 'There are a few. There's one with my name. I mean I just love the food, the Italian food.'

# Situation Vacant

There's an old saying in tennis circles: 'Pro tennis is a game where you have to be smart enough to do it and dumb enough to think it matters.' As Gorgeous Gabby's star waned in the mid-1990s, her mantle as the unofficial tour 'looker' passed on to Mary Pierce. Pierce is proud of her body. She once publicly stated, 'I'm not ashamed of my body. I like to walk naked around my house and garden.' When she subsequently sought applications for a part-time gardener, thousands of men applied. A number offered to do to the work for free.

# Lifestyle Choices

Nine-times Wimbledon champion Martina Navratilova did not have an easy time with the fans. She had the honesty and courage to live openly as a lesbian. In terms of sponsorship deals, she would have been better served by denial. Hence the voices in the Wimbledon crowd shouting, 'Come on Chrissie, I want a real woman to win'. Another claimed that: 'The real problem with Martina is that she never dated Burt Reynolds.'

Navratilova took it in her stride and was even funny with it.

'Martina, are you still a lesbian?' inquired a male sportswriter.

'Are you still the alternative?' she replied.

Navratilova used the analogy of bacon and egg to describe the difference between involvement and commitment in sport: the hen is involved in the process through laying the egg but the pig is totally committed!

## The Sisterhood

Collegiality does not always reign supreme amongst tennis stars. Pam Shriver never really fulfilled the potential she showed when reaching the final of the US Open at the age of sixteen in 1978. The main successes of the woman from Baltimore, Maryland, were achieved as Martina Navratilova's doubles partner.

However, Shriver is the queen of the after-dinner speeches. During the latter stages of Chris Evert's difficult pregnancy, Shriver told her peers: 'I've just spoken to Chris and she wants you to know that she will not be appearing nude à la Demi Moore on the cover of *Vanity Fair* magazine. But she said she would be would be willing to appear on the cover of *Inside Women's Tennis*, if it would improve circulation – the magazine's and hers.'

Her humour often had such an edge to it. In her book, *Passing Shots*, Shriver remarked that all three Maleeva sisters reminded her of basset hounds because of their doleful expressions. Accordingly, she called them Boo, Hoo and Boo-Hoo. Maybe it is for the cutting remarks like this that the queen of the grunters, Monica Seles, was compelled to say: 'I definitely have some friends who are not my friends.'

## Run for Home

America is a country where the Olympics and divorce lawyers have the same slogan: go for gold. Before the 1984 Olympic Games, everybody was worried about the traffic in Los Angeles. However, the only real traffic jam was when Zola Budd sensationally tripped Mary Decker as she had gold in her sights.

## Pin-up Girls

An Irish hockey club coach, who shall remain nameless, was bemused when all her players burst out laughing when she came into the dressing-room and announced, 'All the girls playing in the Saturday friendly match will be pinned to the notice-board'.

## Dedicated Followers of Fashion

Fashion sense is an issue of major concern in horse racing. In 1971, the authorities decreed that ladies in hot pants would only be allowed to enter the Royal Enclosure at Ascot if the 'general effect' was satisfactory.

## Eva

Eva Shain was one of the most influential figures in boxing in the last generation. The Jewish grandmother, who lives in New Jersey in the United States, made history in 1977 when she became the only woman to judge a Muhammad Ali world title fight. Ali was defending against Earnie Shavers at Madison Square Garden. At the press conference after the fight, Ali was asked if he had been aware that one of the judges was a woman.

'No,' he replied.

'What did you think of this lady judge?' a journalist asked.

'How did she score the fight?' Ali inquired.

'She scored it 9–6 in your favour.'

'She's a mighty fine judge.'

In 1985, Eva was inducted into New Jersey's Boxing Hall of Fame. Ali was the star guest at the function. Turning to Shain, he asked in confidential tones: 'Doesn't all that blood bother you?'

'No,' Shain replied.

'Why not?' Ali wondered.

'Because it's not mine.'

# Chapter Eight
# A Sporting Stew

## A Fan for All Seasons

All sports produce great characters. In 1992 Trinity College justifiably celebrated 400 years of existence with a fanfare. Past students such as President Mary Robinson were celebrated. One famous student who was not mentioned at all was Jonah Barrington. Barrington's great rivalry with Geoff Hunt helped create the squash boom, bringing the game from the elite to the masses. His victory in the British Open in 1973 – squash's equivalent of Wimbledon – was his sixth title in seven years and firmly established him as the world's greatest squash player.

However, Barrington's omission from the Trinity Hall of Fame is perhaps not all that surprising. After an unhappy time during his teenage years in secondary school, Barrington followed family tradition and went to Trinity in 1958. Ireland's oldest university came as a culture shock to the Englishman. No time was this more evident than when Barrington turned up late for a nine o'clock lecture, one of the rare occasions when the fun-loving teenager struggled in for an early morning class. Thirty-two students should have been present but there were only four. However, when the lecturer called the roll, all thirty-two names were answered without any puzzlement. Then half an hour later when Barrington arrived, the lecturer was struck dumb in amazement: 'Glory be to God. Is it yourself or your ghost that I'm seeing at the door?'

### Cross-dressing

Barrington's escapades did not endear him to the college authorities. He had precious little respect for the college rules, as he proved when he brought one of his girlfriends for dinner into the all-male bastion of Commons. Women were absolutely forbidden but he tried to get around the problem by dressing her up to look like a man. The fact that she was generously proportioned made this task rather difficult.

## *The Final Straw*

That indiscretion was relatively minor by comparison with the incident which led to his expulsion. Barrington attended the end-of-term celebrations with a bag of flour hidden on his person. The target for this missile was to be a Nigerian friend as he went up to receive his degree. Tragically, Barrington's aim was askew and the flour landed on a distinguished visiting Hungarian academic, who had travelled over especially to receive an honorary doctorate. Just at that moment, the heavens opened and the flour became a dense white paste. To temporarily escape the college porters, Barrington was forced to seek refuge in the college chapel.

## *Searching for Love*

Although he played rugby for Trinity's second team and was the college's number two squash player, Barrington is best remembered for his extra-curricular activities. One of his biggest problems was holding down a residence for longer than a week because of his love of 'wine, women and song'. Incidents like tripping over the lavatory seat in a drunken stupor and falling straight through a window naturally did not endear him to his landlords.

Barrington's most spectacular fall came in Trinity itself. In the middle of the night, he was clambering around on the roof of the women's hall of residence, with a view to serenading some attractive ladies. However, thanks to Mr Arthur Guinness, Barrington's footing was not so sure and he slid rapidly down the steep roof and disappeared over the edge of the building. Incredibly, he escaped without serious injury.

## *Nursing a Grievance*

The combination of heavy drinking and the search for romance was once more to the fore when Barrington and his friends heard a rumour that there were a number of nurses shored up in a local hostelry. After closing time, they climbed over the college's walled gate and crept stealthily up to the windows. Just when they reached their vantage point, a large matron came to the window and they bade a hasty retreat. They decided to wait outside until she went to bed, only to discover that she had rung the guards. Barrington was introduced to the Kerry accent in all its glory when a big guard said, or appeared to say: 'Well, young fella, what do you think you are doing here at this hour of the night?'

'I'm sorry, sir; we got lost.'

'Listen, son, we all know 'tis the nurses ye're after, but let me tell you one thing. Ye're making a fierce mistake. They're the ugliest lot you ever saw!'

## Cricket

To outsiders cricket is simply a strange social ritual, with the most bizarre and incomprehensible rules, many lengthy tea breaks and an obsessive desire to ruin countless pairs of white trousers. This may be why the Duke of Edinburgh, when asked in 1987 if he had any complaints about modern cricket, declared, 'I only wish some of the players' trousers fitted better'.

However, to its devotees cricket is an abiding passion. This was probably most graphically revealed in the 1970s when England were playing a test series in Australia. A man and his wife were making love. Suddenly, she noticed something sticking in his ear. Not surprisingly, she enquired what it was. He replied, 'Be quiet; I'm listening to the cricket'.

## Beefy

The old adage 'He burned the candle at both ends' applies to few sportsmen more directly than Ian Terence Botham, or 'Beefy'. Indeed, it might be suggested that Beefy frequently set fire to it in the middle!

In the post–George Best era, only Gazza has inspired the same number of column inches as Beefy, particularly in the tabloid newspapers. Often it was difficult to separate fact from fiction. Some of Beefy's problems were of his own making, given his habit of putting his foot in his mouth.

Beefy was a thorn in the side of the cricket establishment; he once colourfully described the English selectors as a curious hybrid of alcoholics and senile geriatrics. He was banned for confessing to having played cricket on grass (the type you smoke) and was expelled from the Queensland team following an 'incident' on a plane. Beefy was often depicted as the male equivalent of Madonna – before she found marital bliss – in the chastity stakes.

Botham went to the West Indies and was met at the airport by his great friend, Viv Richards. The boys then went for a few rum punches. The jet-lagged Botham could only taste the orange juice, so he kept knocking them back, even though they were about 150 per cent proof. Assuring Richards that he felt fine, Beefy went back to his hotel and they arranged to meet later. When Beefy didn't show up at the appointed time, Richards went to his hotel room. He got very worried when Botham didn't respond to his knocks. Richards persuaded the chambermaid to let him in. He found Beefy out for the count. Richards and a few of his team-mates borrowed some women's make-up and turned him into a drag queen. When Beefy finally woke up and looked at himself in the mirror, it was said that the mirror cracked at the sight of such a monstrosity.

### When Beefy Met Gazza

Beefy was well able to help other sports personalities to take a drink. He was also very competitive. When he was captain of one of the teams on the popular BBC series *A Question of Sport*, he was always trying to pull one over on his opposing captain, Bill Beaumont. During his time as a Spurs player, Paul Gascoigne was scheduled to appear on Bill's team. His manager, Terry Venables, gave strict instructions that the studio should be an alcohol-free zone.

Beefy decided to help an unsuspecting Gazza beat the ban, without the Geordie's knowledge. He convinced Gazza that advocaat was non-alcoholic. Gazza put a fair few away before he realised what a kick it had. The problem was that just before the programme was recorded, Beefy discovered that Gazza was on his own team. Needless to say, Beefy's team got hammered in the quiz as well as in the bar.

### Does My Bum Look Big in This?

Like 'fat boy spin' Shane Warne, Botham is a people's champion. Once while he was on tour in India, a fan ran up to Botham, grabbed him by the family jewels and tried to plant a kiss on him. The fan started screaming, 'Iron Bottom, Iron Bottom, I love you, I love you'.

Botham was happy to be called 'Iron Bottom', but his team-mates decided to amend it to 'Tin Arse' instead.

Beefy always carried a little more weight than he would have liked. Years ago, his five-year-old son was showing a playschool friend the bathroom scales his dad had bought. 'What's it for?' asked the guest.

'I don't know. All I know is when Dad stands on it, he gets really mad.'

### These Boots Were Made for Walking

Beefy is England's answer to Donnacha O'Dualing and is famous for his many walks to raise money for leukaemia research. One of his walks was all along the east coast of Britain. When Beefy told Jimmy Greaves about his plans, Greavsie said, 'Christ, Beef. This is going to be the longest pub crawl of all time.'

According to the tabloids Beefy would occasionally stray from the marital bed. A journalist once asked, 'Did you have a hard time trying to explain the test match to your wife?'

Beefy replied, 'Yes, especially when she found out I wasn't there.'

## Confidence Booster?

Former English cricket captain David Gower was going through a slump in form. When playing in a test match at the Oval, Gower was just walking down the steps of the pavilion going in to bat when the secretary told him he was wanted on the telephone. As he got near the phone, he heard the secretary say, 'He's just going in to bat, will you hold on?'

### Put on Your Dancing Shoes

At his club's social dance, Gower had troubling dancing with his new partner.

'Sorry,' he said, 'I'm a little stiff from bowling.'

'I don't care where you come from,' she said, 'just keep off my feet.'

## Old Boys' Network

The cricketing powers that be are often out of touch, not only with society but with the players they are in charge of. Before he became a cricket correspondent with Sky television, Bob Willis was one of the finest bowlers in world cricket. During his prime with England, Willis was once approached by one of the selectors who asked him, 'Who was the man I have had just seen you talking to?' Willis looked at the selector in total disbelief. He had been talking to spin bowler Phil Edmonds, one of the biggest stars on the English team. Incredibly, the selector didn't recognise him.

In 1973, Alec Bedser, chairman of the England selectors, was hosting test trials. In all earnestness, Bedser greeted two of his star players with the words, 'Good morning, Roy; good morning Peter'. He was talking to Ray East and John Lever.

In the interest of fairness, it has to be acknowledged that the cricket establishment has its share of thoughtful, considerate people. One Marylebone Cricket Club member died peacefully in his seat during a match at Lord's. Fortunately, his remains were discovered early in the morning. In order to spare fellow members any discomposure, two members of staff were assigned to sit on either side of him, propping him up until the end of the day's play when he could be removed discreetly.

The bureaucrats are not the most despised group in cricket, however, that honour is reserved for the umpires. Sometimes the criticism is misplaced. Two village cricket teams were playing their annual match when, on an appeal for 'leg before wicket', the umpire gave the batsman 'out'. Walking off the pitch in a bad temper, the dismissed batsman went up to the man in the white coat and panama hat and protested that he was not 'out', adding 'you need glasses'. 'So do you,' said the man, 'I'm selling ice-cream.'

## The Bare Facts

Unlike the fans, sportsmen generally dislike streakers. Former Australian cricket captain Greg Chappell had a particular disdain for them. Chappell was in full flow at the crease during a test match, when a student, wearing only headphones, ran towards the stumps. Chappell said, 'I had my bat in my left hand and gave him a couple of sharp cracks across the buttocks just to try and get him to stand still'. The incident did seem to have an effect on Chappell. He was run out the next ball.

Chappell is not the only sports star to lose his cool in this way. In 1996, just before the Wimbledon men's singles final started, Melissa Johnson, a catering assistant with the figure of a model, appeared on centre court, wearing a miniature apron, 'a big smile and not much else'. MaliVai Washington appeared to have been badly affected by her appearance because he capitulated easily to Richard Krajicek. He said, 'She lifted the apron and was smiling at me. I got flustered and three sets later I was gone.'

Happily, sports administrators seem less prone to having their concentration thrown by streakers. In 2000, twenty-two-year-old Tracy Sargent streaked at an indoor bowls event. One could not but be impressed by the diligence of the officials and their commitment to the cause of duty. They later issued a statement: 'Having studied the incident on forty-three occasions, including slow-motion replays, we have decided against implementing a rule that spectators should remain clothed at all times.'

## The Ruth Will Prevail

Baseball and booze have often gone hand in hand. One of the most colourful illustrations of this was when the Yankee stars Mickey Mantle, Whitey Ford, Yogi Berra, Hank Bauer and Johnny Kucks went to New York City's Copacabana to toast their flamboyant team-mate Billy Martin. At the same time, a Bronx man named Edward Jones was celebrating with a group of friends. Hostilities broke out between the two camps, leading Bauer to break Jones' nose. Considering his .203 batting average for the season, the outfielder came up with a classic alibi: 'Hit him? Why, I haven't hit anybody or anything all year.'

The Yankee players were handed down a $1,000 fine a few days later in Cleveland, but it was Martin who paid the highest price, finding himself traded to Kansas City.

Three years later, Martin was in hot water again when he socked Cubs pitcher Jim Brewster with sufficient force to provoke a $1 million lawsuit. Martin's reaction was typical of the man: 'How does he want it? Cash or green stamps?'

Ryne Duren, the Yankee reliever of the early 1960s, confessed, 'I never really knew what it was like to pitch a sober inning'.

However, no one personified the association between baseball and alcohol more than the legendary Babe Ruth. One of the many stories told about Babe was that when he left the train for the ball park, he would remind the porter to have the bathtub full of beer by the time he returned.

Babe wasn't always as romantic as his ladyfriends would have liked. One girlfriend asked him, 'You did mean those three little words you whispered to me in the cinema, didn't you?'

Babe replied, 'Course I did... I had seen it.'

Two of the pall-bearers at Babe's funeral in August 1948 were two of his team-mates, pitcher Waite Hoyt (himself an alcoholic) and third baseman Joe Dugan. As they carried out their duties, Dugan whispered, 'I'd give $100 for a cold beer'. Hoyt replied, 'So would the Babe'.

## Potty Training

Snooker players have always enjoyed a great 'rapport' with women. Alex Higgins had the reputation of being a womaniser, a fact the Hurricane acknowledged. 'I know I've got a reputation like George Best. I've found that it helps being world champion, especially at snooker. I always tell them [women] I'm a great potter. They know what I mean.'

The ever-chivalrous Tony Knowles saw himself in the tradition of Alex Higgins when it came to women: 'I never buy them a drink. I never buy them a meal. I never dance with them. The only thing I offer them – apart from myself – is a lift home. And it works – every night of the week and sometimes several times a night.'

When asked if there was anything he wouldn't do, Knowles quoted the advice of a former leader of the Conservative Party who told his male cabinet members: 'Never get caught in bed with a live man or a dead woman.'

Dennis Taylor gave snooker a more wholesome image. Most of Taylor's stories are about his uncle Seamus, rather than sex. When Seamus went up in a two-seater plane with his best friend Pat he shouted, 'If we fly this plane upside down, will we fall out?'

Pat replied, 'Don't be stupid, we'll still be friends.'

Uncle Seamus' big problem in life is that he can't understand why he has only one brother while his sister has two.

## The Fairer Sex

Snooker players are not the only sports personalities who have a reputation for their interest in the fairer sex. The manager of the San Francisco Giants baseball team, James Craig, sliced his fingers as he tried to remove the strap of his girlfriend's bra. Undaunted, he continued his lovemaking without regard for his personal discomfort. Many men might have been embarrassed about such an incident. Not so Craig. He leaked the story to the media.

## Chess Nuts

A large number of chess enthusiasts had checked into a hotel, and were standing in the lobby discussing their recent tournament victories. After a few hours, the manager asked them to disperse. 'But why?' they asked.

'Because,' he said, 'I can't stand chess nuts boasting in an open foyer.'

## Pistol Pete

Obsession defines the top achievers in sport. The statistics, in terms of Grand Slam wins, indicates that Pete Sampras is the greatest tennis player of all time. It is said of Sampras that, 'he would rather drop his wife than drop his serve'.

Sampras is largely responsible for thwarting the Wimbledon ambitions of the perpetual British hope, Tim Henman. Every year, Henmania inevitably ends with a whimper. Henman's failure to cope on big occasions has led to the joke:

Q: What's the difference between George Graham and Tim Henman?

A: When Tim Henman returns a backhander he's considered a hero.

## New York, New York

Sampras is much more sedate than his famous countryman Jimmy Connors. Connors contrasted the difference between American and British audiences, 'New Yorkers love it when you spill your guts out there. Spill your guts at Wimbledon and they make you stop and clean it up.'

## The Chalk Dust King

John McEnroe's generally blamed the umpire for any of his tennis failures. As a boy, McEnroe wasn't an enthusiastic student. One day he announced to his mother, 'I've decided to stop studying'.

'Why's that, John?'

'I heard on the news that someone was shot here in New York by the mafia because he knew too much. I don't want them to do that to me.'

## It's a Miracle

Miracles do happen in sport. Claude Stevens won the silver medal at the discus at the Montreal Disabled Athletes Olympics. Stevens was a merchant seaman for twenty years until he fell off the hold of a ship and was paralysed from the waist down. He was renowned for his sense of humour. One of his favourite stories was of the wheelchair athlete who flew to Lourdes for a cure. The man was so exhausted when he got there that they were afraid to take him out of the wheelchair to immerse him in the pool, as is the traditional practice for pilgrims, for fear he might collapse. Instead, they put him, wheelchair and all, into the sacred pool. Then another of the great Lourdes miracles took place. The man was not cured, but when he came out the wheelchair had a new set of tyres!

## The Golden Mile

The greatest moment in the history of the Irish athletics came in 1956 when Ronnie Delaney won the gold medal in the Melbourne Olympics. In the millennium year, Delaney was honoured at a special function in Dublin. He was feeling chuffed until he was approached by a man from the audience, who said, 'Mr Delaney, you've sure got a lot of mileage out of that one mile you ran'.

## The Strong, Silent Type

Before becoming famous for his acting talents (?), Arnold Schwarzenegger had great success in the competitive world of bodybuilding. On the subject of Arnold Schwarzenegger, JFK Jr once said, 'When my cousin Maria introduced her fiancé, Arnold, to Uncle Ted, she said: "Don't think of him as a Republican, think of him as the man I love. And if you can't do that, think of him as the man who could break you in two."'

## 007

Despite his great success as an actor, Sean Connery had a lean period in the 1970s when work nearly dried up. One day Connery was thrilled when he finally got a call from his agent. The agent said, 'Sean, I've got a job for you. Starts tomorrow, but you've got to get there early, for 10-ish.'

Sean frowned and replied, 'Tennish? But I haven't even got a racket.'

## Radio Daze

In the course of a court case, Michael Jackson was asked whether he had memory lapses. 'Not that I recall,' was his reply.

That is not an experience Jimmy Magee would ever share. One of Jimmy's most embarrassing moments was presenting *Junior Sport Magazine* on RTÉ radio in the 1960s. Commentating on the 100 yards in the NACA championships, Jimmy momentarily became lost for words, as he sought to describe an official hammering down the starting-block. Jimmy said, 'And he's taking out his tool now...'. As radio listeners conjured a particular image in their heads, Jimmy compounded the situation by saying, '... to hammer down his block of course'.

Jimmy was the face of the popular *Superstars* programme, which ran on RTÉ television in the late 1970s. At one stage, he journeyed to the international superstars competition in Tel Aviv. The BBC were also there in force and Jimmy watched their presenter combing his hair and brushing his impeccable clothes to introduce the programme. His opening words were, 'Hello. Good afternoon and welcome to the Holy Land, a Mecca for tourists.'

## Mistaken Signals

Confusion is not something which only afflicts commentators. A man found himself partnering a woman at a bridge game – a woman he had never met before, let alone teamed up with at cards. She was an experienced player, whereas he was almost a beginner, so he was rather nervous. The game progressed without incident until he reached a point when he was undecided as to what card to play. Looking at his partner for inspiration, he noticed her hand move towards her left breast. Taking this as a signal he opted to 'pass'. They lost the game. Afterwards she was furious. 'Why did you pass? Hadn't you understood my signal?'

The man replied, 'But I thought I did.'

'I put my hand on my heart and you should have lead a heart.'

'Oh, I'm so sorry. I saw you touch your left nipple, so I left it.'

## Water, Water Everywhere

The Irish swimming fraternity had long been waiting for an Olympic-size swimming pool, before the situation was finally rectified. In 2002, the IRFU began construction of the first phase of its new pitch at Lansdowne Road. Ireland played autumn internationals against both Australia and Argentina during downpours. The pitch was covered in water in many places and was barely playable. One swimming fan watching the Argentina match from the stands remarked, 'Congratulations to the IRFU in giving us our first ever 100-metre swimming pool'.

## King of the Road

The late, great Joey Dunlop was taking part in the North West race. On the day before the race, Joey decided to practice by racing on open roads near his Ulster home. It wasn't long before he attracted the attention of the police and they paid a visit to his home. Joey's wife, Linda, answered the door.

'Where is he?' the policeman asked her.

'He's out,' she replied.

'Yes, we know that,' said the policeman. 'He's just passed us at 150mph!'

'What are you going to do?' enquired Linda, trying to disguise the panic in her voice.

'We just wanted to wish him good luck for tomorrow!'

# Fast Eddie

McLaren chief Ron Dennis once memorably described Formula One as the 'Piranha Club'. Jenson Button said that driving a Formula One car was like the 'best-ever sex mixed with winning the lottery'.

Eddie Irvine was sceptical of Button's talent, or lack of talent as he would see it, and described him as 'the weakest link'. Irvine is one of Ireland's greatest-ever racing drivers, but he has a reputation for being a little disorganised and untidy. This trait was evident from an early age. While the Irvine family were away when Eddie was a child, a friend was looking after the family home. He went in to check on the house and all was fine until he got to Eddie's room. It was in such a mess, he thought the family had been burgled. He rang up Eddie's dad immediately:

'I think you've been burgled.'

Mr Irvine was horrified, until the friend told him all the damage was in Eddie's room. Mr Irvine reassured him that no burglary had taken place, 'No, no, no. Edmund's room's always like that.'

Fast Eddie also has a reputation for being a ladies' man. Irvine may be largely responsible for his notoriety. When asked in an interview whether he had any role models, Irvine replied, 'No, but I've had loads of models'.

One of Irvine's most serious relationships was one with a young Dutch model, called Anouk. Yet the relationship almost never got the chance to flourish. A mutual friend had arranged a first date for them in Milan. She told Anouk, 'His name is Eddie, he's Irish, he's in Formula One; he is young and handsome and great fun'. Anouk had agreed to the date on that basis. However, before the date happened, she had a dramatic change of heart. When Damon Hill announced his retirement, Eddie Jordan, whom Hill drove for, was interviewed on countless channels about it. Anouk saw one of the interviews and was crestfallen. She rang her friend, 'You told me this guy Eddie was thirty years old. Jesus, what are you thinking of?'

The friend was completely baffled until Anouk protested that there was no way she was going to spend the weekend with Eddie Jordan. The friend patiently explained that Eddie Jordan and Eddie Irvine were both Irish and both in Formula One but were different men!

In fact, both Eddies are very good friends but Jordan has one reservation about Irvine. A few years ago, Jordan's daughter had bumped into this 'vaguely familiar-looking guy' while jet skiing. The man had started to chat her up and invited her for a drink on his boat. Ms Jordan rang her father and told him that she really fancied this guy. He was delighted at her new romantic interest – until he discovered that her new amour was Eddie Irvine. Jordan got over to her like a shot to prevent the rendezvous from taking place. He subsequently said, 'The last person I want any of my daughters to have anything to do with is Eddie Irvine. Great driver, great guy, but just stay away from my daughters!'

## We're All Going on a Summer Holiday

Sport is a universal language. In the late 1970s, an English tourist was on holiday with his wife and children in a remote, mountainous part of Spain, when his car came to a dead halt. After detailed scrutiny on the part of the owner, it emerged that serious repairs was called for. A mechanic was going to be needed. Apart from a few mountain goats, there was no sign of life. The man left his family and walked a number of miles in the scorching heat in search of help. Finally, he came across a rundown farmhouse. The man knocked on the door and an enormous farmer appeared, who had obviously just finished a lavish meal of some form of garlic dish. The farmer expansively gestured for the Englishman to enter. Hygiene was obviously not a prime concern. In fact, the house was so untidy that it was the sort of place that you had to wipe your shoes after leaving. The tourist politely and respectfully enquired, 'Do you speak Inglais?'

'Si.'

Breathing a huge sigh of relief, the Englishman launched into a full-scale explanation of his predicament. After he had patiently explained all the details, he started to get worried by the continued blank look on the farmer's face. The show of sympathy he was hoping for was not forthcoming. Again he asked the farmer, 'Do you speak Inglais?'

'Si. Bobby Charlton.'

The tourist once again told his story, but this time with less detail and more extensive sign language. Again there was no flicker of recognition.

'Do you speak Englais?'

'Si. Bobby Charlton.'

'Do you speak any Inglais other than Bobby Charlton?'

'Si. Jackie Charlton.'

'Help me, please, and I will take you down to the bank and get you some money. Comprende bank?'

'Si. Gordon Banks.'

'Please, help me fix my car. Automobilia. Comprende?'

'Si.'

'Automobilia?'

'Ah, si, si. Automobilia. James Hunt.'

## A Brush with the Law

Hunt was once stopped by a policeman for speeding. The policeman didn't recognise the former world champion.

'Give me a name,' he said.

'Weren't your parents supposed to that?' Hunt replied.

After his retirement, Hunt carved out a new career as a commentator, where he struck up an unlikely partnership with Murray Walker. Walker has redefined the world of sporting commentary with lines like, 'Proust can see Mansell in his earphones'.

## Eaten Food Is Not So Soon Forgotten

The late Jack Morris was only a little taller than a dwarf and was as thin as a goose with anorexia. His grey hair stuck out in little wisps round his forehead and ears. Two pale, green oval eyes stared down over permanently freckled cheeks. In many ways, he was a child who had never grown up. He loved a good yarn but was never unduly bothered about trifles like veracity.

Morris was a greyhound trainer and had a few wins at venues like Shelbourne Park and Harold's Cross. At least once a year, a photographer would come to take pictures with Jack and his dogs for some publication or other. But what really clinched his fame for the locals was that he knew Micheal O'Hehir.

Any wife or child would have been delighted to receive the type of attention Morris lavished on his dogs. It was difficult to understand how Morris could have sired a son like Mick. Mick was a giant of a man, with an astonishing appetite. He had bright blue eyes, sun-blonde hair and muscles that left women gasping. His young eyes had an apparently indestructible vitality and he had a face in which even the bones looked determined. His lips were so thin, they hardly existed.

One day, Mick picked potatoes using old socks for gloves. It was a bitterly raw autumn afternoon, and although he was wearing a heavy overcoat, scarf and balaclava, the frost penetrated into his every bone.

When his task was completed, Mick came to the gap in the hedge, which served as his gate. He crunched his way up the tangled garden, glanced round at the trees, which were now quite naked and thin, and blew into his hands and stamped his feet into some semblance of life. Mick's eyes lit up when he walked into the house. A huge plate of meat lay on the kitchen table. The steam rose tantalisingly. Five minutes later, Mick patted his tummy contentedly having literally licked the plate clean.

A short while later, Jack entered the room. Despite his whispering voice, there was an undercurrent of menace in his tone as he asked, 'In the name of God, what happened to my plate of dog food?'

Jack was once interviewed by a reporter from the *Evening Press* and was asked to explain what a short head meant in racing parlance. His reply was not as illuminating as might have been expected: 'It's when the dog's nose is just in front of its eyes.'

## Fishy Stories

A fisherman was taken to court for catching ten more salmon than his licence allowed. 'Guilty or not guilty?' asked the magistrate.

'Guilty,' said the sportsman.

'€100 plus costs,' stated the judge.

After cheerfully paying the fine, the fisherman made an unusual request, 'And now I'd respectfully like to ask for several copies of the court record to show my friends'.

A woman, seeing an old villager fishing on the banks of a stream, asked, 'How many fish have you caught?'

Well, ma'am,' replied the old fisherman thoughtfully. 'If I catch this one I'm after, and then two more, I'll have three.'

## Recruitment Policies

Many sports clubs adopt unusual recruiting strategies to attract new members. A school fencing club didn't perhaps think through their invitation adequately: 'New blood always welcome.'

A rifle club hoped to attract newcomers to the sport and, with an eye to giving opportunities to people with disabilities, announced, 'We are now especially targeting the disabled'.

## Russian Roulette

Leonid Brezhnev, former General Secretary of the Communist Party and Russian premier, was a big shooting fan. Once he went to visit a remote part of the USSR to partake of some bear shooting. The local secretary of the Communist Party was notified to provide a bear for Brezhnev to shoot. There were no bears in the area, but the secretary was anxious to secure promotion so he knew he had no option but to find a bear. Eventually, he found a bear in the local circus. The bear was duly taken to the middle of the forest and placed on a track a mile and a half from where Brezhnev would be hiding with his rifle. The bear was then pushed off in the direction of Brezhnev. Two minutes later, a woodman was cycling home when he was stunned to be met by a bear. He fell off his bike with surprise and ran off into the forest. The bear was not fazed. Being a performing bear, he picked up the bike and rode off along the path towards Brezhnev. Ten minutes later, Brezhnev, with his rifle cocked, was astounded to see the bear cycling along the path. He was so surprised that his rifle went off and he shot himself in the foot.

Some shooting accidents can be even more serious. Camille Jenatzy, 'the Red Devil', was a prominent Belgian racing driver who went on a hunting group with friends in 1913. The problem was that there were no wild boars about so the gang went for a few drinks. Later that night while the others were sleeping, Jenatzy got a great idea for a practical joke. He sneaked outside their cabin and started grunting and snorting like a boar. He was so convincing that one of his party rushed out and shot at the spot the noise came from. Jenatzy died within minutes.

# A Tall Tale

One of the most bizarre monuments in Irish sport is the shrivelled and blackened right arm of Dan Donnelly, Ireland's greatest bare-knuckle fighter. The arm rests in a glass case in The Hideout pub in Kilcullen, County Kildare. Donnelly was said to have had the longest arms in the history of boxing. He was reputed to be able to button his knee britches without stooping!

# Thank You Very Much, Mr Eastwood

In more modern times, Barney Eastwood has been one of Irish boxing's most famous personalities. Eastwood was always very reticent about certain topics in media interviews. Asked by a journalist if it were true that he was a millionaire he replied, 'If you had what I owe, you'd be a wealthy man'.

Training facilities have improved immeasurably since Eastwood began in boxing. It has gone from blood, sweat and tears to blood, sweat and Perrier.

# Beware the Bell

Tommy Farr fought Joe Louis for the world title in 1936. Louis trounced him, but Farr was such a hero in Wales that the Welsh all claimed he was robbed. When Farr died, his funeral service was almost exclusively attended by former boxers. Most had severely disfigured noses and cauliflower ears; a lot of them were in a pretty bad mental state.

The minister was afraid of a riot and before the service started he called over the altar boy and said: 'Brown, whatever I say and whatever I do, don't ring that bell or they'll start the mother of all fights!'

# Frankly Speaking

Frank Bruno was one of Britain's most popular sportsmen in the 1990s, even though he seemed to lose all his really important fights. Organisers of a debate were disappointed when he failed to show to speak on a motion that boxing is unethical and unsporting. They explained to the disappointed audience, 'Frank Bruno would have been here tonight but for a conflict of interest. He didn't want to come.'

Bruno carved out a successful career in pantomime, but his one venture into serious acting was a disaster. The show closed after one night. A foul play was suspected.

## More Than Words

For years, Joe Frazier held a deep hostility toward Muhammad Ali. It was all the product of a simple misunderstanding. Long before Eamon Dunphy took to referring to Johnny Giles as an 'Uncle Tom', Ali constantly used that term in interviews to describe Frazier. Frazier took grave exception to the term because he always thought an 'Uncle Tom' was the same as a 'peeping Tom'!

George Foreman regularly fought against both Frazier and Ali. Foreman is the father of ten children. His five boys are all called George. Asked why he had taken such a route, Foreman explained, 'When you've been hit as hard on the head as often I have by the likes of Ali and Frazier, it's too much trouble to remember five different names'.

After losing to Ali, Foreman had a crisis of confidence. The day after the fight, a dog appeared before George the great. He patted the dog on the head and said, 'At least I still have one friend'. Then, the dog bit him.

## The Greatest

Muhammad Ali went about the job of becoming world heavyweight champion with 'a real zeal to turn himself into the real deal'. Years later, a young man asked him what he should do with his life. Ali replied, 'Stay in college, get the knowledge. And stay there until you're through. If they can make penicillin out of mouldy bread, they can sure make something out of you!'

On a trip to Africa to promote 'the rumble in the jungle', Ali was forced to take a seat on a small airplane. When meal time came, the flight attendant asked her famous passenger whether he would like dinner. 'What are my choices?' Ali asked. The flight attendant replied, 'Yes or no'.

Ali had a number of marital problems. He was once asked his opinion on marriage: 'Boxing is like marriage. The preliminaries are often better than the main event.'

Ali was told that a young boxer was getting married the following day. 'Congratulations, my boy,' said Ali. 'I'm sure you will look back on today as the happiest day of your life.'

'But I'm not getting married until tomorrow,' protested the young boxer.

'I know,' said Ali.

· · · · ·

As I sit here at the crossroads of the global interface, my publisher rings. He thinks my writing is all over... It is now.